MARTIN BREUM is a journalist and renowned Arctic expert. His first book *When the Ice Disappears* was awarded the Danish Authors Association's award for the best non-fiction work of 2014. It was followed by *The Greenland Dilemma*, now available in English. In 2016 he produced (with documentarist Jacob Gottschau) a series of TV documentaries on the common history of Denmark, Greenland and the Faroe Islands. He corresponds on the Arctic for the media in Denmark, Norway and Greenland, and for the *EUobserver*. His writing on the polar region has been published in the *New York Times*, *National Geographic* and many other international media outlets.

'This is an important and refreshing addition to the literature on Arctic politics, seen through the journalistic eyes of Martin Breum. It is also one of the few contributions that has a particular focus on Denmark and Greenland, which deserves attention in its own right. This is a highly readable book that I can recommend to anyone interested in Arctic affairs.'

Geir Hønneland, Director of the Fridtjof Nansen Institute and author of *Russia and the Arctic* (I.B.Tauris, 2016)

COLD RUSH

THE ASTONISHING TRUE STORY OF THE NEW QUEST FOR THE POLAR NORTH

MARTIN BREUM

I.B. TAURIS

LONDON · NEW YORK

Published in 2018 by
I.B.Tauris & Co. Ltd
London • New York
www.ibtauris.com

Copyright © 2018 Martin Breum

Translation from Danish:
Sara Hollænder Schousboe, cand.ling.merc, translator, project manager
Stina Flecks Gottschalck, cand.ling.merc, translator
Mette Nørgaard Thomsen, cand.ling.merc, translator
Initial translation by Kevin McGwin appeared in *The Greenland
Dilemma* by Martin Breum, 2015
http://www.fak.dk/publikationer/Pages/TheGreenland-Dilemma.aspx

This book is based on selected, widely re-written chapters from two books
in Danish: *Når isen forsvinder* and *Balladen om Grønland*, both published
by Gyldendal.

Every attempt has been made to gain permission for the use of the images
in this book. Any omissions will be rectified in future editions.

References to websites were correct at the time of writing.

ISBN: 978 1 78831 242 4
eISBN: 978 1 78672 413 7
ePDF: 978 1 78673 413 6

A full CIP record for this book is available from the British Library
A full CIP record is available from the Library of Congress

Typeset by Riverside Publishing Solutions, Salisbury, Wiltshire
Printed and bound in Great Britain by T.J. International, Padstow, Cornwall

MIX
Paper from
responsible sources
FSC
www.fsc.org   FSC® C013056

CONTENTS

PREFACE

For centuries, the fate of Greenland, the world's largest island, has been intertwined with that of the greatest powers on Earth. In early times, rumours of metals from meteors that had crashed in Greenland brought prospectors across from North America, seeking their fortunes. Much later, in 1814, as the unrivalled ruler of the North Atlantic, Great Britain wielded decisive powers over Greenland's destiny after the Napoleonic wars. In 1946, on the brink of the Cold War, the United States offered to buy Greenland from Denmark, readying 100 million US dollars in gold in the belief that Greenland was of crucial importance as a buffer against the Soviet Union.

Today, Greenland lies on an Arctic trajectory – it is on the route for potential missiles between North America, Russia and North Korea. China and the European Community are mounting efforts to embrace Greenland and its vast mineral resources. They also acknowledge its potential as a hub on new Arctic cargo routes, formed by the melting of the sea ice, which are likely to cut up to one-third of the distance between markets in Asia and those in Europe and the United States. In the Arctic, the landmass and importance of Greenland makes the Danish Kingdom, to which Greenland still belongs, a crucial acquaintance to any state, scientist, tourist or business leader who wishes to engage in the Arctic. This book is an account of events in the Arctic and in the Kingdom of Denmark and Greenland in the ten years from 2007 to 2017. Throughout this decade Denmark and Greenland found themselves at the centre of a tremendous surge of global interest.

I am a journalist. The following is my personal account of what happened and how Arctic developments are changing behaviour in the modern Arctic. Ten years ago, for instance, no one imagined that Denmark and Greenland would dream of claiming the North Pole for themselves – but then it happened. The top of Greenland is the northern-most piece of land in the world and its bedrock continues far into the Arctic Ocean. As a result, in 2014, Denmark and Greenland suggested to the UN that the rights to 895,000 square kilometres of ocean floor all the way past the North Pole to Russia's territorial waters should belong to the Kingdom of Denmark. This was extraordinary. The claim was to an area larger than Sweden and Norway combined. Russia soon followed suit with its own demands and the two claims now overlap by about 500,000 square kilometres. Soon Canada will add its overlapping demands and the three countries will face a complex conflict of interests.

Does this all matter to people in the United Kingdom, the United States and the rest of the world? My claim is that it does. For a start, the Arctic Ocean is the first ocean in the history of man to change from a state of complete inaccessibility to one of openness and access for human exchange, culture, trade, fisheries and exploitation. An entire new ocean is availing itself to us and our worldview will have to transform in exchange. Imagine if the Mediterranean Ocean was only now allowing us to meet across its expanse, ships to pass, cultures to meet, fish to be caught and commerce to flourish. The Arctic is the world's most rapidly changing region, as a consequence of climate change. Arctic glaciers are melting, causing sea levels to rise across the world; the oceans have become more acid, making the life of crustaceans precarious. Arctic animals such as polar bears are threatened, suffering and moving. Ocean currents change while polar storms erode coastlines no longer protected by sea ice. Melting permafrost destroys railroads, power lines and housing in the entire Arctic, and these changes are likely to happen on the rest of the planet as climate change speeds up. This is why scientists from the entire global community are travelling to the Arctic. Climate change happens twice as fast in the Arctic as anywhere else, and the changes do not stay in the Arctic. As EU Commissioner Margrethe Vestager emphasized recently in Nuuk, Greenland's capital: 'When you come to Greenland, you can't help noticing how interconnected we all are. The ice sheet is thinning, not because of what Greenlanders are doing, but because of American aircraft, Chinese factories, European cars. And if the ice sheet melted, then much of New York, Shanghai and Copenhagen would be under water.' Other visitors in the last few years include UN Secretary-General Ban Ki-moon, German Chancellor Angela Merkel, US Secretaries of State Hillary Clinton and John Kerry, South Korean President Lee Myung-bak and other political luminaries.

In the midst of the global spotlight on Greenland, in 2008, the Danish government called a historic conference in Ilulissat in northern Greenland for the five states bordering the Arctic Ocean. The object: 'To preserve peace in the Arctic as climate change diminished the polar icecap.' In 2007, a Russian mini-submarine had planted the Russian flag on the ocean floor at a depth of 4,300 metres – exactly at the North Pole. In Copenhagen and other capitals around the world, fears developed that Russia would pursue this gesture with even more powerful moves. In May 2008, in Ilulissat in Greenland, at Denmark and Greenland's invitation, all invited states, including the United States and Russia, signed a treaty, which still stands as a milestone in the Arctic. The Ilulissat Declaration bolstered peace and Arctic co-operation and – so designed by Copenhagen – provided the Arctic states with wide powers over the future of the Arctic and the Arctic Ocean.

Denmark grew to understand itself – with Greenland and the Faroe Islands – as a key Arctic power. Denmark's idea is that the Kingdom, by constructively exploiting its Arctic opportunities, may contribute to Arctic peace and prosperity and increase its own international clout and attractiveness. Thule Air Base in the far north reminds us how significant Greenland already is to the United States and NATO. Greenland also holds some of the world's richest deposits of uranium, rare earth elements and other metals vital to modern industry, and its offshore regions offer dizzying promises of oil and natural gas – enticing to industry, worrying for those eager to curb carbon emissions. Fishing is flourishing, promising to meet some of the increasing global shortage of proteins, and there are visions of marine Arctic bio-tech, and exports of some of Greenland's unlimited supply of nourishing rock-dust that might help resuscitate depleted farmlands at the Equator. To Copenhagen's dismay, however, Greenland seems particularly occupied with pursuing its own, separate future. Eager to break with its colonial past under Danish rule, modern Greenland embraces foreign friends and investors, including China and other Asian states. The majority of the people in Greenland share a vision of independence, even if many realize it is not likely to happen soon. After 300 years of colonialism and then semi-autonomy, Greenland still relies on Danish subsidies for its economy and on Danish defence capacities for its sovereignty. Co-operation with Denmark works well on a day-to-day basis, but the prospect of formal independence is appealing to most who live in Greenland. Denmark, 4,000 kilometres away, is still working on the right answer to this challenge.

Developments in the Arctic cannot be left out when one tries to understand climate change, Brexit, political upheaval in the United States or China's and India's escalating needs for raw materials. In 2016 and 2017, at conferences in Iceland, I heard the First Minister of Scotland, the eloquent Nicola Sturgeon, reach out to her North Atlantic neighbours Greenland, Iceland and the Faroe Islands in ways that would have been unlikely before Brexit. Friends in the North Atlantic are important as Sturgeon considers Scotland's independence. The global significance of the Arctic increases rapidly: as I write these lines, media reports in Copenhagen tell us that Denmark's Prime Minister has blocked the sale of a derelict naval facility in Greenland to General Nice Group, a Chinese mining conglomerate. The Prime Minister is worried that a Chinese presence at these disused barracks would unsettle delicate relations with the United States.

Over the past years, I have turned such developments into books, television documentaries, news coverage and public lectures based on my work in the Arctic. This English volume is based on selected, updated chapters from my books in Danish. It is designed to provide readers who are not Danish or Greenlandic with an introduction to Denmark's and Greenland's ways in the New North. I hope you will share comments, queries and ideas. Please email me at mb@martinbreum.dk.

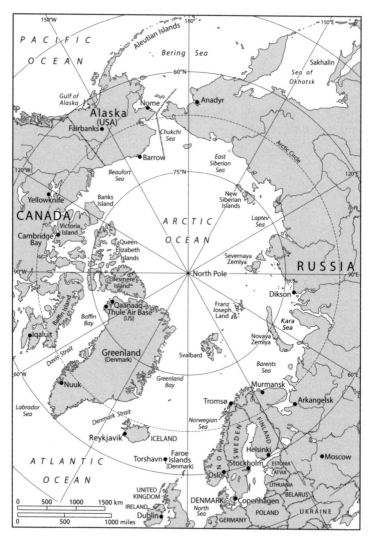

The Arctic: Climate change, disappearing polar ice, geopolitics and a quest for resources, influence and the maintenance of peace has turned the Arctic region into one of the most dynamic on Earth, but there is no fixed geographical definition of 'the Arctic'. As a popular reference, however, the Arctic Circle, seen as a dotted line on this map, is often used as a signifier of 'the Arctic'. North of this line the sun is visible for 24 hours at least once a year – and more often, the closer one gets to the North Pole.

PROLOGUE

The pilot turns his head, smiles and looks out the window. 'The North Pole is right down there, on the left.' In his C-168 Challenger jet from Defence Command Denmark, it has taken Michael Munkner and his co-pilot two and a half hours to fly the 930 miles from Thule Air Base, the United States' northern-most airbase, across the northern points of Greenland and in a straight line over the deserted polar icecap to the North Pole. In a gut-clenching dive, he forces the plane to only 980 feet above the ice, and then circles sharply around the North Pole. Through his Plexiglas window, he sees bright light and open sky over a vast and deserted sheet of polar ice, a view only hampered by the sharp glare from the sun. The speedometer indicates 125 mph. His small crew and the guests onboard may now enjoy the azure melt-water lakes on top of the ice, the blend of crystal clear and coloured sheets of ice, ice packs and ice ridges. In intricate patterns streaks of seawater stretch like green incisions in the ice, revealing the deep Arctic Ocean.

The year is 2012. The two pilots record that no man-made objects are visible on the ice. Nor does the plane's radar or its heat-seeking camera find any North Pole expeditioners in distress, Russian flags or anything else that requires action. All is peaceful at the North Pole this Friday afternoon. The jet trembles slightly on the sharp rolls. To save fuel, three crewmembers and all unnecessary luggage have been left at the US air base at Thule. The immense distances, unpredictable weather patterns and isolation pose great risks even for this modern jet. If the plane on its return to Thule Air Base should find the runway closed by fog or storms, the nearest emergency

landing field is two hours southbound at Greenland's international airport in Kangerlussuaq. If this should also be closed
by fog or other, Munkner's only other alternative would be
the world's northern-most military facility, Canada's military
base at Alert, several hours of flying to the west. An emergency
landing at this latitude is not an attractive option. As Munkner
jokingly put it: 'Remember, we *are* the rescue team.' His small
jet on this day is the northern-most spearhead of the Kingdom
of Denmark – or the Unity of the Danish Realm, as it is also
known. The jet demonstrates how the Kingdom is trying to
seize new opportunities, while acting as a responsible and
constructive partner in the Arctic.

In Copenhagen and Nuuk, the political decision makers are
keenly aware of the global surge of interest in the Arctic and
ever mindful of the history that goes with it. In 1814, after
the Napoleonic wars in northern Europe, the North Atlantic
islands of Greenland, Iceland and the Faroe Islands remained
part of an almost bankrupt Danish Kingdom. Denmark
was among the losers in the wars, but Great Britain honoured
a promise to Denmark and returned the islands to its care.
Through an Order in Council of 7 February 1810, the British
Government had used its naval powers in the Atlantic to shield
Greenland and the two other island communities from the
brutality of the wars. In 1814, when the post-war settlement
was negotiated in Kiel in what is now northern Germany,
the Danish Kingdom suffered the loss of all of Norway, but
got to keep Greenland, Iceland and the Faroe Islands. The
reasons for this arrangement and why Britain did not claim
the islands for itself remain a subject of research by historians.
Perhaps the British rulers simply wished to keep their promise.
Perhaps, also, they had no desire to take over cumbersome
responsibilities for deliveries of food, Bibles and other supplies
to the far-flung islands. They could have let the islands follow
Norway and drift into Sweden's domain, but then Britain might
have run the risk that Sweden, one of the victors of the wars,
would grow to be a competitor in the Atlantic. Whatever the
exact reasoning, the British navy remained firmly in control of

the North Atlantic, while Britain left the servicing of the three island communities to the troubled Danish king.

Danish sovereignty over Greenland was seldom uncontested. In 1931, the Norwegian government in Oslo, long free of Swedish influence, claimed a huge part of north eastern Greenland, arguing that this largely uninhabited stretch of icy territory was *terra nullius*, a no man's land, and therefore now rightfully Norway's. Trappers from Norway had been busy in tiny huts all along the coast for decades. Only after two years of arduous negotiations at the International Court in the Haag was Denmark's sovereignty over the entire island confirmed.

In the 1940s during World War II, German troops established weather stations in the same north eastern part of Greenland, and from 1941 US troops established landing strips at several places in Greenland as crucial pit-stops for thousands of fighter planes flying from Canada and the United States to the war against Nazi Germany. After the war, when Denmark tried to convince the United States to withdraw from Greenland, astonished Danish envoys to the United States were presented with an unexpected American offer. Washington suggested that the United States could buy the entire island, just as they had bought three Danish islands in the West Indies back in 1917, the islands we know today as the US Virgin Islands. In 1946, the United States was ready to buy Greenland for 100 million dollars in gold. The government in Denmark flatly refused, but the US troops never left Greenland. In 1951, an accord was brokered that provided the United States with broad permissions to run military bases in Greenland for as long as NATO, the new North Atlantic Treaty Organization, exists. Denmark – and Greenland, its colony – were incorporated into NATO, and the United States has continued to run defence facilities in Greenland ever since.

It is against this historical backdrop that Michael Munkner navigates close to the North Pole. The polar ice is setting its own record: Never before has the Arctic Ocean been free of ice to the same degree as in 2012. For the first time in the history of man, a new ocean is appearing, and Denmark and Greenland are on the front lines. Like Russia and Canada, Denmark and

Greenland are trying to expand their kingdom all the way to the North Pole and beyond. With icebreakers, aircrafts and camps on the pack ice, they are attempting to obtain the right to a vast piece of the floor of the Arctic Ocean.

The disappearance of the ice has spurred significant action in the Danish Realm. In the 1980s sea ice stretched all over the Arctic Ocean most parts of the year. Polar bears hunted on solid ocean ice north of Greenland and north of Ellesmere Island in Canada, and more ice was densely packed across the Beaufort Sea north of Alaska, across the Bering Strait to Siberia and onwards to Russia's Kola Peninsula and Murmansk. Ice blocked the Fram Strait along East Greenland and north of Peary Land at the top of Greenland.

The world does not look like that any more. In 2012, as Michael Munkner swerves across the North Pole, the summer ocean along Siberia is blue and navigable, as it is far out into the Beaufort Sea north of Canada and into the Chukchi Sea north of Alaska. The Arctic Ocean is opening, even if there is still plenty of ice remaining in its central parts. While Munkner prepares for his dive at the North Pole there is ice as far as he sees, but the polar ice is thinner than before and the perennial ice, that which remains all year round, has become an endangered species hiding only in a few areas north of Greenland. Much of the ice that Michael Munkner flies over has only been here for one winter, and it is only three to five feet deep. Next year, it will be even thinner.

Denmark and Greenland are key players in this New Arctic. As Greenland expert and French scientist Damien Degeorges puts it, 'If Greenland was a stock, its value would have increased by 500 per cent in two years.' Oil has yet to be found in the ocean off the coast of Greenland, but both here and in the rest of the Arctic large findings are possible, and the dream of fast money flourishes. Sofie Petersen, the bishop in Nuuk, the capital of Greenland, fears that the people of Greenland are selling their souls, and in 2012, a million people, including Paul McCartney, support Save-the-Arctic, a Greenpeace anti-oil campaign online.

In Nuuk Greenland's leaders are thinking of writing Greenland's own constitution. Most people in Greenland agree that independence is still at best several decades away. Some wish to remain in the Danish Kingdom, but an independent Greenland is no longer a completely inconceivable concept. Ever since Danish missionary and trade activities in Greenland began in the eighteenth century, the dialogue between Denmark and Greenland has been difficult. Today, the prospect of oil, uranium and other strategic minerals complicates the conversation even further.

On the way back from the North Pole, all is quiet onboard the C-168. On both sides of the jet, land is now visible. On the eastern horizon lies Cape Morris Jesup, the northern most point on Earth that is not a separate island. Only the tiny Kaffeklubben Ø (the Coffee Club Island) a bit further out in the Arctic Ocean is closer to the North Pole. Almost a hundred years ago, Danish Arctic explorer Lauge Koch mapped this coastline, and his fellow Dane, explorer and anthropologist Knud Rasmussen traversed the ice cap by dog sled.

Now, the C-168 soars over a cloudless north west Greenland. In the cabin, coffee and sandwiches are served. The sun dissolves any remains of clouds and fog; a flawless approach to Thule is expected. Shortly before Thule Air Base, the pilots eye the top of Mt Dundas on the edge of North Star Bay, which Knud Rasmussen used for orientation. It was he who named Thule, and it was here that he established his trading post in 1910 and made sure the region was secured for Denmark. Knud Rasmussen disappointed another great explorer, the famous Robert Edwin Peary, a rear admiral of the US Navy, who had already made his mark. Robert Peary, who was supported by President Theodore Roosevelt, travelled for years in northern Greenland before making his historic attempt to reach the North Pole in 1910. Robert Peary and his chief aide, Mathew Henson, an African-American, also fathered children in the region, but Robert Peary failed to convince Washington to make territorial claims before it was too late.

In the end, nature wins. As Michael Munkner prepares to descend, unexpected local fog over Thule Air Base appears.

It is so thick that a landing is impossible. After two attempts, and two aborted landings, he turns his jet upwards and heads for the first port of refuge in Kangerlussuaq. In the Arctic, the unexpected must be expected. So it is at Thule, in man's relation to the Arctic nature and between the Arctic and the rest of the world. We do not know how fast the ice will disappear or how climate change will transform this region. But we do know that change will remain the order of the day.

1

DENMARK AND GREENLAND EMERGE AS ARCTIC POWERS

In 2007, with short notice and spurred by a spectacular Russian flag-planting stunt at the North Pole, the Danish government conducts a major diplomatic drive to maintain international co-operation and peace in the Arctic and to pursue its own national interests. The Ilulissat initiative and its results emerge as a milestone in Arctic history, actively backed by Norway, Canada, the United States and Russia. More than ten years later, presidents and foreign ministers from Ottawa, Moscow and Washington will often allude to the Ilulissat Declaration as the agreement that binds them together in the Arctic and shields their favoured power-sharing arrangements in the Arctic from China, the EU or other non-Arctic parties. The following is the story of the Ilulissat Declaration, the peace initiative, and how a second agenda, tacitly introduced by the Danes, surreptitiously took on global significance.

* * *

Suddenly, the signals that were supposed to ensure their safe return to the surface disappear. Captain Anatoly Sagalevitch and his crew in *MIR-1*, a Russian mini-submarine, are carrying out a perilous deep-sea experiment. For nine years, they have prepared themselves, and now they are in *MIR-1*, nearly 10,000 feet under the ice at 90 degrees north. They are on their way to becoming the first humans in history to reach the seabed at the geographical North Pole, but in total darkness two-thirds from the bottom they encounter a problem. The signal from the three electronic transmitters at the ocean surface disappears from the computer screen. This signal is supposed to guide them back to the opening in the ice where they descended. Without the signal, finding their way back to the opening might be extremely difficult. The small submarine will not be able to break through and make a new opening in the thick ice of the Arctic Ocean.

When it comes to deep-water expeditions, Anatoly Sagalevitch is one of the world's leading submarine captains. He was expedition leader of the deep-sea recordings in the blockbuster movie *Titanic*, and before that he led difficult submarine dives to downed Japanese bombers and sunken German warships. None of this compares to the dive to the ocean floor of the North Pole, a dive to 2.7 miles depth in waters always covered by sea ice. Anatoly Sagalevitch manages the special deep-sea programme at the P.P. Shirshov Institute of Oceanology in Moscow, and this ultimate expedition to the ocean floor under the North Pole has been on his mind for more than ten years.

By now the dimensions of the project are remarkable. In the close quarters of Anatoly Sagalevitch's own submarine, *MIR-1*, in addition to Sagalevitch himself, we find Vladimir Gruzdev, a multi-millionaire and a member of the Duma, the Russian parliament, and the 67-year-old engineer Artur Nikolajevitch Tjilingarov, who is the leader of the diving expedition. Tjilingarov is one of Russia's leading Arctic explorers. He is vice-president of the Duma, and close with the President of Russia, Vladimir Putin.

The three men onboard *MIR-1* are not travelling alone. *MIR-1* is accompanied by *MIR-2*. *MIR-2*, which is being piloted by one of Anatoly Sagalevitch's colleagues from the institute, is also carrying two passengers. Here we find one of Sagalevitch's old acquaintances, the Australian Mike McDowell, who is running Deep Ocean Expeditions, a travel agency for eccentric deep-sea enthusiasts, and the Swede Frederik Paulsen. The latter of the two has paid a substantial share of the staggering expedition costs. Frederik Paulsen is passionately interested in polar research, and he has previously participated in expeditions to both the North and South Poles. He has funded these expeditions with the fortune he has made as owner of the pharmaceutical company Ferring Pharmaceuticals.

MIR-1 and *MIR-2* are descending, and the signals from the transmitters at sea level have disappeared. Now is the time to raise the alarm. Later, Frederik Paulsen tells Russian TV that the three men onboard *MIR-2* reckoned that there was about a 50 per cent chance of survival. Ordinary compasses hardly function at this proximity to the North Pole, and radio contact with the research ship, *Akademik Feydorov*, which has transported the submarines to the area at the North Pole, does not contribute to navigation. But Anatoly Sagalevitch and Artur Tjilingarov onboard *MIR-1* are not turning around; they continue their descent, and *MIR-2* follows them.

The stout-hearted Artur Tjilingarov represents the long Russian tradition of ambitious research expeditions in the Arctic. When a *National Geographic* reporter later visited him, the journalist noted that Tjilingarov's office in the Duma was not only decorated with a photo of Vladimir Putin but also with a poster depicting a Russian icebreaker with fangs on its stern, and with a large globe that had been turned 90 degrees so that the poles appeared as the centre of the earth and not as its periphery. According to the bearded Artur Tjilingarov and many other Russians, the mythical epicentre of the Arctic's ice landscape with all its history, symbolism and strength naturally belongs to the Russian Arctic sphere. Until 2007, they had – like everyone else – accepted that the North Pole was an inaccessibly situated *terra nullius*, a no man's land. But in a time when the climate changes alter everything in the Arctic, it is time for Russia to take action.

That is what Artur Tjilingarov thinks in 2007. His motives are clear. On the other hand, the question of what the Russian government wished to achieve with the diving expeditions remains difficult to answer. The submarine expedition led to numerous speculations and analysis in the rest of the world, but a final answer has never surfaced. On *MIR-1*, Tjilingarov only represented the Russian government indirectly, even though he was vice-president of the Duma and close to the President. Artur Tjilingarov was the expedition leader. He advised President Putin in Arctic matters, but the expedition was mainly funded by private means. The foreign participants had brought the flag of the Explorers Club in New York, and afterwards both Foreign Minister Sergej Lavrov and President Putin went to great lengths to explain that the diving expedition had not been Russia's attempt to conquer the North Pole. Time and again, they have made it clear that the expedition did not change Russia's intentions of a peaceful delineation of borders in the Arctic. However, to the other Arctic capitals, the signals Moscow was sending in 2007 seemed very alarming.

Later, when Arthur Tjilingarov and the others were on their way home on *Akademik Feydorov*, President Putin was already applauding the *MIR* expedition over the phone. In Moscow, the members of the expedition were received with full honours and a military orchestra. Tjilingarov and the two Russian submarine pilots were awarded the highest honorary title of Russia, 'Heroes of the Russian Federation'. Even the head of the Russian Orthodox Church, the Patriarch of Moscow and all of Russia, applauded the expedition. However, on the outside, the Russian government maintained that the *MIR* expedition was a private undertaking. Disarmingly, Russian Foreign Minister Lavrov explained to the world press that the small amount of mud *MIR-1* and *MIR-2* brought up from the ocean floor was to be used in a Russian attempt to prove that the Russian bedrock is connected to the ocean floor under great parts of the Arctic Ocean. In this complicated way, Sergej Lavrov tried to explain how Russia would still follow UN legislation on how new borders must be drawn in the Arctic, despite the submarine operation. Denmark, Canada, Norway and the United States follow the same legislation. Already in 2001, Russia had submitted demands to the UN about immense areas of the Arctic Ocean all the way to the geographical North Pole. However, UN experts returned the demand, requesting further documentation, which the Russian have worked on gathering since then.

Did Putin control the submarine operation from the Kremlin? Was the operation evidence that Russia is playing a game where politicians and smooth diplomats are talking about peace, while in reality, Russia is considering a more tangible use of force in the Arctic? In May 2011, the controversial private organization WikiLeaks published a series of previously undisclosed documents adding additional fuel to the flames. According to a report from the American embassy in Copenhagen to Washington, an anonymous Russian diplomat had informed the Americans that Artur Tjilingarov was following orders from Putin's party 'United Russia' when he carried out his dive.

Morten Larsen Nonboe, Danish political scientist and Russia researcher at the University of Oxford, analysed the Russian dive in 2010. He reached an even more complex explanation. His conclusion was that Russia actually wishes to respect the agreements they have made with the neighbouring states about peaceful delineation of borders in the Arctic Ocean. However, he also found that competing groups in Moscow are fighting internally for the Arctic policy of Russia. With another member of the diving team, Vladimir Gruzdev, Arthur Tjilingarov represented the vigorously nationalistic groups in Moscow. These groups are also known by the Russian military and intelligence community. In the eyes of these groups, the Arctic Ocean north of Siberia and all the way to the North Pole forms a natural extension of Russia. At the other end of the spectrum, Foreign Minister Lavrov leads a more pragmatic line, which continuously dominates Russian diplomacy.

Cape Morris Jesup, the rocks at the northern-most point of Greenland, rises farther towards the North Pole than any point in Russia. However, that clearly meant less in Tjilingarov's equation. He had hired the diver Gennadyi Kadachigov as an adviser on the diving project. In 1968, Kadachigov was the first person to dive underneath the ice near the North Pole. The flag at the bottom is also there to remind the Russians of how Russian pilots and scientists flew to the North Pole in 1948, most likely making them the first people on the actual Pole. In the eyes of Artur Tjilingarov and many other Russians, the case is clear. The North Pole and its vicinity were incorporated into the Russian nation a long time ago. But let us return to actual events.

It is 2 August 2007, and the two submarines have been heading for the bottom for four hours. At 08:00 that morning, two cranes onboard the *Akademik Feydorov* hoisted the submarines through a hole in the ice found by the assisting nuclear-powered icebreaker *Rossiya* close to the North Pole. The sea ice surrounding the hole spreads hundreds of kilometres in all directions. Despite the summer heat, the ice keeps a thickness of somewhere between one and two metres. In some places it is even thicker. Deep underwater, the two pilots are no longer aware of the exact position of the submarine, but they continue towards the bottom. The echo sounder on *MIR-1* is being used to guide them downwards. When the green blips on the onboard screen of the echo sounder show 200 metres to the bottom, Anatoly Sagalevitch turns on the external projectors as well as the pump, which blows ballast water from the tanks of the submarine, making it sink slower. A rough landing can mean an abrupt finish to the adventure. In his own account of the dive in the magazine *Sea Technology*, from where the details of this narrative originate, Anatoly Sagalevitch describes how he now, at exactly 12:11, for the first time in human history, glimpses the ocean floor.

The depth recorded shows 4,261 metres from sea level. Sagalevitch is suddenly aware that he is now the first person to see the bottom of the North Pole. However, strictly speaking, the sight is not particularly interesting. 'The bottom is flat and covered in muddy sediments', he writes. 'The deserted landscape is populated by an average of one to two small, white *actinaria* (sea anemones) per square meter.' After approximately one hour, *MIR-2* arrives and the two submarines start gathering samples of the ocean floor. In reality, the samples have limited scientific value, but along with water samples and other data collected by *Akademik Feydorov* along the way, the samples from the ocean floor ensure that Sergej Lavrov can subsequently call the expedition a part of the scientific contribution by Russia. Several metal casings from *MIR-1* are placed on the ocean floor. Future pole-divers will be informed of those aboard *MIR-1* and *MIR-2* by enclosed messages in the casings, exactly like the beacons left on the bedrocks by polar explorers on land with messages for their successors and to mark who was there first.

After approximately one and a half hours at the bottom, the expedition completes the deed, which subsequently will go down in history. Only a few hours later it will be broadcast on TV screens worldwide, including in numerous government mansions. Anatoly Sagalevitch, who refers to himself as the pilot, describes the course of events: 'Now there was only one task left: to plant the flag of the Russian Federation at the bottom. In order to plant the titanium flag, the pilot moved *MIR-1* from the mud and placed the flag in the manipulation arm. Carefully, the pilot placed the flag construction at the bottom, and the bottom part partly disappeared in the sediments. Thereafter, the flag was hoisted one metre above the bottom.'

That is all Anatoly Sagalevitch writes about the flag. He is busy thinking about the hole in the ice, four kilometres closer to the sun. However, a picture of the flag, which shortly afterwards paraded around the world, is taken. The picture is taken through the transparent front part of *MIR-1*. It shows the android arm with the prehensile claw, which has just loosened its grip on a metallic flagpole, as well as the bottom part partially buried in the fine layer of mud on the ocean floor. The projectors of *MIR-1* illuminate the flag in such a way that its top white stripe casts light back into the camera lens. At a depth of 4,300 metres, a titanium flag does not flicker. It is stock-still. Thus, the message cannot be misconstrued: Russia was here!

After the placement of the flag, the submarines are directed towards the surface, steered solely by Anatoly Sagalevitch's intuition. His best estimate is that the stream has led *MIR-1* and *MIR-2* approximately one and a half kilometres away from the positions of *Akademik Feydorov* and *Rossiya* at the surface. The first ten minutes of the ascent are hair-raisingly slow. The colossal water pressure holds firm on the submarine, but after a brief while, they rise approximately 30 metres per minute. At 14:35, the submarines pass the depth of 3,000 metres, and to the relief of the two crews, the signals from the surface are now back on the monitors. Anatoly Sagalevitch assumes that the signals have been disturbed by an underwater mirage. A false reflection of the ocean floor is not unknown at these depths. Sagalevitch determines that the submarines have moved approximately 1,300 metres from *Akademik Feydorov*. This is quite close to his estimate.

For yet another while, they rise through the column of water, and then they are up. The submarine dive to the North Pole has taken less than eight hours. On 2 August 2007, in the late afternoon, the whole thing is over. Not long after, Artur Tjilingarov speaks energetically to the awaiting TV cameras onboard. 'We are delighted to have been at the ocean floor, where no one has been before. No humans for millions and billions of years – I do not know how many. We reached the point by the North Pole, and there we planted the flag of Russia.' A new page had been turned in the history of the Arctic.

Several years later, the Russian flag at the bottom of the Arctic Ocean still stands as an irrefutable mark in the middle of the recent Arctic history. The flag became the beginning of profound considerations in the Pentagon, in the White House, in Ottawa, Oslo – and in the small Danish town of Kirkelte. This was the home of Denmark's former Foreign Minister, Per Stig Møller, from the Danish Conservative Party. According to him, this was where he woke up one morning, soaked in sweat, shortly after the dive to the North Pole seabed by Artur Tjilingarov. Subsequently, he initiated one of the most pronounced diplomatic moves in the Arctic since World War II.

From his office in the Danish Ministry of Foreign Affairs, he summoned the head of the ministry's legal service.

He explained to him that he felt convinced that there was an actual risk that the Arctic would develop into the next conflict area of the globe. In Washington, the spokesman for the American Ministry of Foreign Affairs disparaged the Russian dive by saying that he did not know whether the Russians had 'planted a metal flag, a rubber flag or a bed sheet on the ocean floor'. In Canada, Foreign Minister Peter MacKay reacted: 'This is not the fifteenth century. You can't go around the world and just plant flags and say: We're claiming this territory.' Behind these rejections was the exact same anxiety that Per Stig Møller felt. All over the world, newspapers and the electronic media followed closely. The components of the story, the North Pole, oil, aggressive Russians, created big headlines.

Canada's foreign minister Peter MacKay, a conservative, won lasting fame as he vented his frustration in an interview with the Canadian Broadcasting Corporation. 'This is posturing. This is the true north strong and free, and they're fooling themselves if they think dropping a flag on the ocean floor is going to change anything.'

In unison, the United States National Security Council and the State Department in Washington called for a series of consultations with participation of the White House. On 6 August 2007, the conservative American research think tank, the Heritage Foundation, published a condemnation of the Russian flag-planting on its website. 'This latest move by Moscow is also a chilling throwback to the attempts during the 1930s to conquer the Arctic during the years when the Soviet Union was seized by fear and hatred. Stalin and his henchmen executed "enemies of the people" by the hundreds of thousands, after mock trials … today's expedition is a chilling reminder of the brutal era when millions of Gulag prisoners were sent to the frozen expanses to build senseless mega-projects for the power-mad dictator.'

Few reactions were that shrill, but in Denmark the expedition was also presented within the frame of conflict, commotion and escalation. Even before the Russian submarines had entered the Arctic water, the Danish newspaper *Jyllands-Posten* wrote: 'The race for the North Pole has begun. Russia has initiated the race for obtaining the right to the enormous oil resources, which are said to be found below the ocean floor of the North Pole, and which will be recoverable concurrently with the melting of the ice.'

The Danish Ministry of Foreign Affairs was contacted by the Danish news agency Ritzau Bureau and one of Per Stig Møller's chief aides tried to pour oil on troubled waters: 'Planting a flag only has political meaning because it can make the media care. It is our assessment that it will not have any legal significance and it will not alter our possibilities of advancing our claims in the same area.'

Based on this, Per Stig Møller started an initiative, which instantly designated Denmark as a key and adept player in Arctic politics. Possibly, the minister also had an annotation from the intelligence agencies in mind. On 8 August 2007, for the first time since the Cold War and now with strategic bomber aircrafts, the Tuplov TU-95 Bear, Russia resumed routine flights over the Arctic and the northern part of the Atlantic Ocean. The planes returned to Russia, but even if no formal rules had been broken, the NATO countries noted the incident with attentiveness.

Per Stig Møller put two and two together – the Russian submarine expedition, Vladimir Putin's praise of the divers and the undetermined borders in the Arctic Ocean – and he worried. He did not trust the assurances of Russia. When I talked to him in 2010, he explained his thoughts immediately after the Russian dive: 'It could end up in a political conflict with many protracted negotiations. But it could also end up with the countries saying, "Here we take the law into our own hands." That was my biggest fear, the Arctic becoming a *fait accompli*. After all, in that context we are the weak nation. If someone would take the law into their own hands outside of Greenland and say, "We will take this" and then, for example, drill for oil without asking for permission, what could we do? That is why I, as the Danish Foreign Minister, decided on a joint initiative.

The needs of neither America nor Russia are similar to ours. It is not the strong one who needs the law. It is always the weak one.'

In the following months and years, this 2007 analysis hid under more conciliatory and diplomatic declarations from Denmark's representatives. Willingly, they underlined how peaceful the development in the relationship with Russia was, and not until November 2012 was it made clear that the fundamental distrust towards Russia was still thriving. At this time, the Danish Defence Intelligence Service published an analysis of all current threats against Denmark. Herein, the intelligence agents assessed that it was only realistic to assume that Russia would follow the UN rules for delineation of borders in the Arctic Ocean if the process led to the results wished by Russia.

In 2007, Per Stig Møller intervened. He called a high-profile conference for all five states immediately adjacent to the Arctic Ocean. Jointly, and with the attention of the international community, they would, once and for all, call off 'the fight about the Arctic'. They were to send out a joint, binding declaration, in which they would all explicitly promise that any disagreements concerning the borders in the Arctic Ocean would be resolved with peaceful means approved and sanctioned by the UN.

In a number of days, a small task force was working. The head of this taskforce was Per Stig Møller's chief aide, ambassador Peter Taksøe-Jensen, who came to lead a process of shuttle diplomacy with the head of the Danish ministry's international law department, Thomas Winkler, between the United States, Russia, Norway and Canada.

To begin with, Per Stig Møller's idea seemed simple, but it turned out differently. The Danish initiative was meant to ensure peace. However, it also provided a very tempting opportunity to ensure Denmark's own vital interests in the Arctic. During discussions with his aides, Per Stig Møller became convinced that his initiative to preserve the peace should not stand alone. He would also use the opportunity to fight a series of proposed alternatives to the Arctic states' key dominance and power in the Arctic. Governments, environmental movements, activists and scientists outside the Arctic Circle should, if possible, be brought to a deeper understanding of who had the primary right to influence and to exploit the riches in the Arctic now that the ice was disappearing. Coupled with the call for continued peace in the Arctic, Per Stig Møller's conference became the sledgehammer to pulverize all alternative conceptions and ideas of UN solutions for the Arctic, international Arctic treaties or other international measures that could undermine the true powers of the Arctic nations themselves.

Several proposals for expanded international governance of the Arctic had already been floated, some with a significant level of legal sophistication. These proposals were quickly gaining political traction. A British member of the European Parliament, Diana Wallis of the Liberal Democratic Party, proved particularly tenacious in promoting the concept of an Arctic Treaty or at least a legal regime for the Arctic that included more than the Arctic states themselves. In time she mustered backing from a significant number of other European MPs, including a number of Scandinavians. Diana Wallis, who later went on to become the director of the European Law Institute, illustrated through her example how the issue of Arctic governance was quickly moving up on the international agenda, and in Copenhagen the diplomats sharpened their intentions. Per Stig Møller's plan to preserve the peace in the Arctic quickly transformed into a strategic initiative to also quell any of these alternative models. With this, the case for the Ilulissat meeting became really controversial. The Danish initiative crashed directly into a difficult global discussion about the Arctic and the Arctic Ocean. Should it be the Arctic states alone who were in charge of the Arctic Ocean? Who should have access to the riches of the ocean? What influence would China, Japan, the EU and the rest of the world have? Would the Arctic states protect the unique Arctic environment, or would they prioritize oil, gas, minerals, fishing and maritime freight?

In 2007, this debate was not considered important in Denmark, even if it had been on the international society's agenda for some time. It was now being explosively fuelled by Tjilingarov's submarine dive in 2007. Never had so many journalists, politicians and scientists asked so many questions about the Arctic. Who was allowed to drill for oil? Who was authorized to use the new trade routes to China? A number of political assemblies, scientists and environmental organizations each had an opinion about the Arctic, and many suggested an Arctic treaty as well as more international control with the development in the region.

Then things started to take off in Denmark. Less than a month after Artur Tjilingarov surfaced on 2 August 2007, the Danish task force booked an entire luxury hotel, Hotel Arctic, in Ilulissat, Greenland to host a conference in May 2008. Per Stig Møller convinced the premier of Greenland's Home Rule, Hans Enoksen, to act as co-host, and he sent invites to Washington, Ottawa and Moscow. Norway's foreign minister at the time, Jonas Gahr Støre, arrived personally in Copenhagen to receive his invitation.

At first, all did not go well. Jonas Gahr Støre was anything but pleased with the Danish operation. In 2007, Jonas Gahr Støre was chairman for the eight nations in the Arctic Council and with the Council behind him, he protested. He argued that Per Stig Møller undermined the Arctic Council since Denmark had only invited the five countries who had a coastline to the Arctic Ocean. Sweden, Finland and Iceland were not invited despite the fact that they were all members of the Arctic Council. Per Stig Møller stuck to his guns.

Denmark's foreign minister was not in the mood to go through the Arctic Council, and he tried to convince Jonas Gahr Støre that the five Arctic coastal states had special issues and obligations, which they should discuss privately. The Norwegian foreign minister left Copenhagen before the two reached common ground.

Later, Per Stig Møller explained to me why he was in such a hurry. 'We were anxious that through long negotiations in the UN, we would get tangled up in a big muck. The risk was that special rules for Arctic would be put into effect which would undermine the Law of the Sea and international law more generally. We feared that we would not be able to control a treaty process. We feared that the development opportunities for the Inuit people in the Arctic would be undermined. We could end up with a bunch of restrictions, just like in Antarctica, which would shut down all activity.'

Denmark had consistently supported Greenland's wish for rapid production of oil, gas and minerals, and other Arctic states' focus on the economic options in the Arctic. Per Stig Møller used the 2007 peace conference in Ilulissat to secure this priority against interventions from the UN, just like his successors have since dismissed suggestions for increased international control of developments in the Arctic.

For this reason, in 2007, the critics claimed that Denmark and the four other coastal nations, besides their desire for peace, were mostly preoccupied with securing the riches in the Arctic for themselves, and that the thought of an Arctic treaty therefore was clearly unwelcome. The sceptics claimed that their peace message was merely a fig leaf for their own greed. As a diplomat with solid insight in the Arctic put it, 'At this point, the thought of a treaty spread like wildfire, and all the Arctic state governments were busy trying to quench the embers before they turned into a proper fire. China, Japan, South Korea and all sorts of nations were knocking on the door. With the creation of the Ilulissat Declaration the five Arctic states tried to make sure that they would be the only ones to sit in the place of honour.'

Later, Per Stig Møller confirmed to me that his 2007 Arctic initiative was meant also to ensure that the advantages that could be harvested in the Arctic Ocean would benefit the five coastal states. 'Yes, of course, because according to the UN's Convention on the Law of the Sea, the law is on our side. That is applicable law. It was exactly for this reason that I brought the matter before the Arctic Five. If I had brought it before the Arctic Council, it would still be discussed to this day. We had received objections from the Japanese, Europeans, Chinese and many others – I do not name and shame anyone in particular – who wanted a share of something that was not their right.'

Per Stig Møller did not share his scepticism toward the Arctic Council with others outside his closest aides. If the Arctic Council was not functional it would not make much sense to base the Ilulissat Declaration, as they did, on the Council's ability to follow up on it. The Danish diplomats kept silent and hoped for the best, acutely aware that their critics argued that others had done much better in another icy region – in Antarctica.

Scientists, politicians, and environmental champions through-out the world were inspired by the Antarctic Treaty of 1959 in which 12 states, including the Soviet Union and the United States, in the middle of the Cold War, decided to prevent a military build-up in Antarctica. The perspective was magnificent: With the Antarctic Treaty the states pledged themselves to reserve the entire enormous Antarctic continent for scientific research to the benefit of mankind. The treaty turned out to be unusually viable and still stricter rules for the protection of everything from penguins to krill have since been added. More than 40 states, Denmark inclusive, have joined and the agreement was an undeniable international success.

The Danish diplomats knew, however, that any comparisons between Antarctica and the Arctic were terribly faulty from a legal perspective. Antarctica is a continent, whereas the Arctic Ocean merely consists of water and ice. The international rules pertaining to who owns what are completely different when it comes to land and marine areas. Moreover, four million people inhabit the Arctic in clearly defined states while Antarctica was never settled or divided by legal borders. The United Nations Convention on the Law of the Sea gave the Arctic coastal states clear rights in the Arctic Ocean, and the idea that the states should voluntarily give up these rights and leave management of the entire region to the UN or others was inconsistent with all historical practice.

In 2007 and the first months of 2008, the Danish diplomats worked hard to convince their colleagues in the other four coastal states of the brilliance of Per Stig Møller's plan. The Norwegians were sceptical, but in the beginning of 2008 they yielded and from then on took part in the planning. It was decided that the Ilulissat Conference should be a one-off affair.

The United States was also sceptical, but one by one objections were removed. In late February 2008, Denmark sent the first draft of the Ilulissat Declaration to Oslo, Washington, Ottawa and Moscow. It set out in broad terms: 'The Arctic Ocean faces imminent and vital changes. The disappearance of the ice has a potential effect on fragile ecosystems and the local inhabitants' basis for living, as well as the potential utilization of natural resources.'

These were trivial facts, but the overture laid the grounds for the crucial follow-up: 'The five coastal states have special obligations to manage these possibilities and challenges in a responsible manner.' The draft stipulated how the five coastal states would enter into new and stronger agreements on environmental protection, rescue services and oil spill disasters. If the five Arctic coastal states, including the United States and Russia, signed this declaration, it would be very difficult for other nations to propose alternative Arctic treaties ever again. If the two superpowers and highly respected democracies such as Norway, Denmark and Canada solemnly promised that they would handle all threats against the Arctic environment and maintain safety at sea, then it would stick out as a grave vote of no confidence if other governments should propose other solutions. The diplomats now travelled from Copenhagen to the four other capitals to discuss the final text. In the meantime, new suggestions for an Arctic treaty were aired. In March 2008, *Foreign Affairs*, one of the United States' most influential foreign political scientific journals, published an instantly famous article by Arctic expert Scott G. Borgerson, in which he stated, 'The ideal manner in which to deal with the Arctic would be to create a universal treaty, which guarantees a peaceful and common attitude to the utilization of the riches in the region.' On 19 May 2008, a few days before Per Stig Møller would travel to Ilulissat, the World Wildlife Foundation, the WWF, published a detailed proposition for a global Arctic agreement, but again the Danish diplomats stuck to their plans.

They had secured assurance from Ottawa, Oslo, Washington and Moscow that everything was in good order. The table had been set in Ilulissat, Greenland by the most skilled hands in the Kingdom. It was time for the guests to arrive.

On Tuesday 27 May 2008, the sun shone from a deep blue sky above Ilulissat, the native town of the polar explorer and national hero Knud Rasmussen. From the small airport outside town, Per Stig Møller had a clear view of the ice fjord and the icebergs; they had never looked more beautiful. Outside the luxurious Hotel Arctic, the Russian, Greenlandic, Canadian, US, Danish and Norwegian flags hung side by side in the cool air. In town, kids were playing ball in the sun on a grassless, dusty soccer field. Summer had arrived and only on the north side of the low mountains surrounding Ilulissat were snow patches still visible. The summit was to be held in the sports centre in the middle of town.

Per Stig Møller's plan was on track. A team of officials from Copenhagen had already been in Ilulissat for several days. They had even brought a small sign in English providing directions to the press conferences. Per Stig Møller had confirmed that the other four nations played along at top level. From Russia, Foreign Minister Sergej Lavrov brought a delegation of 20. Former Deputy Secretary of State John Negroponte, a heavyweight in American foreign policy, flew in from Washington. From Oslo came Jonas Gahr Støre, and from Ottawa, Gary Lunn, the Canadian Minister of Natural Resources. It was a full house. Decisions could be made and the pre-designed message sent to the international community.

Behind the scenes, the Danish diplomats secretly celebrated the scope of the assembly, even if they had initially aimed for more. Per Stig Møller had personally tried to persuade the US Foreign Secretary, Condoleezza Rice, to travel to Ilulissat on behalf of the US administration. Now he had to settle for her deputy, the British-born John Negroponte, a former US ambassador to Iraq, who had not previously signalled any interest in the Arctic. Negroponte's attendance in Ilulissat was easily sufficient to confirm to the world that the United

States was firmly behind the Ilulissat Declaration, but for those initiated in Arctic politics it was also a sign that Washington had yet to embrace the Arctic as a truly important geopolitical issue.

From Canada signals had been received that Maxime Bernier, the Foreign Minister, would attend, but that was not to happen. Only a few days before Bernier was to travel to Greenland, the Canadian Prime Minister, Stephen Harper, accepted Bernier's resignation after a scandal that involved one of Bernier's former girlfriends. In Ilulissat, however, this made little difference. Most of those attending were well aware of Canada's firm commitment to Arctic development and the high priority that the Prime Minister himself placed on Canada's high north. Through its strong role in the establishment of the Arctic Council, Canada had a long record of Arctic engagement. Denmark was satisfied, even if Bernier had been replaced by the somewhat less illustrious Gary Lunn, the Minister of Natural Resources.

One additional decisive prerequisite was also soon put in place. Without the press the conference would not work. Ten months of intense diplomatic efforts were to culminate at this summit, but if the rest of the world was not informed, the effect would not be as desired. The PR department of the Danish Foreign Ministry had been mobilizing for months. Per Stig Møller had appeared in front of the foreign correspondents in Copenhagen, the international news agencies had received weighty omens, and several Danish journalists were assigned seats in Per Stig Møller's plane to Greenland. Danish embassies all over the world had prepared their local audiences for the news from Ilulissat.

In Ilulissat's only cinema, Per Stig Møller and Greenland's Premier Hans Enoksen called a press conference on the day prior to the summit. Behind the two was a giant ice blue photograph of the icebergs in the fjord. More than 50 people from the media, that is, from the news agencies AFP and Reuters as well as from Russian television, had found their way to Ilulissat and in front of the cameras, Per Stig Møller spelled out his central message: 'You have seen planting of flags at the North Pole, which has led some to conclude that we are supposedly close to a war in a race towards the North Pole. Others have concluded that we are in need of a new special set of rules in order to manage the Arctic Ocean. I do not see a need like that. Our ambition is to send a signal from Ilulissat showing that we are going to follow the rules that are already set and that we have a special obligation to solve the challenges that are emerging in the Arctic. The race for the North Pole is off.' Per Stig Møller referred to a conversation he had just had with Sergej Lavrov. He explained how the Russian Foreign Minister had once again toned down the significance of Artur Tjilingarov's flag-planting at the North Pole and how the American flag on the moon did not mean that the Americans wanted to claim the moon.

Wednesday morning the summit began in Ilulissat's sports centre. Lines of a handball court stood out between carpets purchased for the event. Large tables with white tablecloths were aligned in a pentagon so that all delegations could sit across from each other.

Three experts were called to present, but their interventions were designed not to cause any trouble or new discussions. It was utterly boring, just as planned. The Ilulissat summit was to signal unity and solidarity in the Arctic, not to start new debates. The central question, intensely pursued by the media, of whether peace would hold in the Arctic was not touched upon at all, even if it ran as an undercurrent alongside its unnoticed twin: A cautious incipient hope of real collaboration in the Arctic. Hopes were that the dreams of riches in the Arctic would help unfreeze old fronts between Russia and the United States and the rest of the NATO countries. The Danish diplomats noticed how Sergej Lavrov underlined Russia's interest in closer collaboration on, for example, rescue operations at sea in the Arctic. Russia was hoping to make billions on oil and gas in the Arctic, but this would only happen if co-operation with the other Arctic states continued. No one would be able to handle the tasks in the Arctic alone or operate at all if peace was not sustained. At all tables the analysis was that this need for collaboration in the Arctic would possibly allow for significant co-operation between Russia and the rest of the Arctic five, and perhaps through a spill-over effect even elsewhere in the world.

At 12:15 on the first day of the conference the ministers and the press went on an hour-long sailing trip between the icebergs. The outing to the tall icebergs in the estuary of the Icefjord served a dual purpose. It was meant to bring the five ministers closer together, but first and foremost to make them look good in the press photos. *Smilla*, the minister's tourist boat, went first and the photographers all filmed them with the spectacular icebergs in the background.

Back in the sports centre, the ministers got to work on the approval of the final declaration. Dozens of diplomats, officials and assistants were present, but later, the Danish diplomats would recall the meeting as 'intimate'. Finally, it was established that no one had any objections to the prepared text. The five governments from the countries surrounding the Arctic Ocean stood united. Ten minutes early, the ministers stood up and prepared to send their historic message from Ilulissat to the rest of the world.

It was 28 May 2008. Per Stig Møller's wristwatch showed 16:35 when he called out in Ilulissat's cinema. 'Ladies and gentlemen of the press: Are you ready for this piece of breaking news?' Hans Enoksen, head of Greenland's Home Rule and dressed in a Greenlandic anorak, sat at his right side, then Jonas Gahr Støre, and on the outer wing John Negroponte with all of his Washington authority. On Per Stig Møller's left sat Canada's Gary Lunn and then, tall and stately, Sergej Lavrov.

Per Stig Møller read out loud, 'The Ilulissat Declaration is a clear signal that the five coastal states will act responsibly in their safeguarding of the Arctic Ocean.' He explained that the five nations felt bound by existing international law, and that they would settle potential disagreements about the delineation of borders in the Arctic in an orderly fashion. As expected, he underlined that the five states saw no need for new international treaties on the Arctic Ocean. He promised intensified environmental collaboration on search and rescue services and preparedness against oil disasters. Finally, he underlined the five governments' trust in the Arctic Council.

The message was sent. Per Stig Møller had done all that he had initially intended. The image of five consenting states was clear and unambiguous. The battle for the Arctic was called off, and the whole world had heard. Anything left was diplomatic routine. On behalf of Greenland, Hans Enoksen said thank you and goodbye, and while John Negroponte studied his nails, Jonas Gahr Støre talked about climate change. John Negroponte talked about the 'joint wish to protect the Arctic Ocean' and about oil. Finally, Sergej Lavrov thanked his hosts for their hospitality. The most important thing, he said, was that the five nations had now confirmed that they would solve all disagreements concerning borders in the Arctic peacefully and through negotiation. He did not specify what the alternative to this peaceful approach would have been, and after a few questions from the reporters, Per Stig Møller concluded and said his goodbyes. It was close to 17:00. The summit was over. In the evening, a member of Sergej Lavrov's security staff got so drunk that the local police almost arrested him, but aside from that everything was quiet and peaceful.

Press coverage of the Ilulissat conference was massive. Mike Townsley, a spokesperson for Greenpeace International, was bursting with bad temper in *Kommersant*, a Russian daily. 'Anyone can see what is going on. They use the Law of the Sea to share the riches between themselves while ignoring common sense. As we know, it is fossil fuels that are causing climate change, and it is twice as disturbing because everything happens behind closed doors. They know that what they are doing is unacceptable.' This outburst was supplemented with a fierce comment from Artur Tjilingarov. In his opinion, Sergej Lavrov had been way too timid and Tjilingarov promised a renewed battle to make the North Pole Russian. From Brussels, the Vice President of the European Parliament, Diana Wallis, snapped, 'The development in the Arctic will potentially affect all the residents of the globe. Meetings excluding others are not a good signal to start with.

International coordination, and especially partnership with non-Arctic states, is necessary to meet the problems in the Arctic.'

The critics, however, were outnumbered. The *New York Times* underlined that the five coastal states had agreed to listen to reason in the Arctic. In Germany, *Der Tagesspiegel* found that peace had been re-established in the Arctic, and similar messages resonated in the *Financial Times, China Daily* and from several of the far corners of the internet.

In Denmark *Berlingske Tidende*, a daily, concluded, 'the hatchet on the North Pole has been buried'. *Politiken*, another daily, could only agree: 'The encouraging piece of news from the summit in Ilulissat is that all the five states in the Arctic now promise to be on their best behaviour, to dim their political temper, and to follow the rules of the Convention of the Law of the Sea while they await the UN. So far, so good.'

In Aarhus, Denmark's second-largest city, at the Danish Navy's Operative Command, rear-admiral Nils Wang, chief of the Danish Navy, lauded the Ilulissat Declaration as the most visionary initiative in the Arctic in recent times. In the United States, too, there was praise. Senator Lisa Murkowski from Alaska underlined the geopolitical importance of the Ilulissat Declaration: 'We have an incredible chance to develop an international policy and collaboration in the Arctic […] The way in which we seize this challenge and the way we adapt will set an example for the rest of the world. The Ilulissat Declaration provides hope that international collaboration between the Arctic States is possible.'

Seven years later, when three leading academic observers of Arctic developments summed up the recent history of the Arctic in their book *Contesting the Arctic* (2015), they described the Ilulissat Declaration as both paradoxical and decisive. Paradoxical, since the signatories basically had agreed on what they had agreed on all along, which was to follow the procedures for delineation of borders on the seabed stipulated by the UN Convention on the Law of the Sea. Decisive, because the five nations in Ilulissat had established a series of pivotal and lasting power structures in the Arctic.

2

SELF-RULE IN GREENLAND – ANOTHER STEP TOWARDS INDEPENDENCE?

In 2009, epoch-making changes occur in the Kingdom of Denmark that impact its Arctic neighbours. Greenland, a former colony, after years of negotiations, formalizes a Self-Rule arrangement with Denmark, which includes the right to secede when the people of Greenland so choose. In addition, Greenland wins full ownership of all income deriving from natural underground and subsea resources – oil, gas, uranium, zinc, iron-ore, rare earths minerals, gold and whatever else might be extracted in future. Soon, efforts to lure investors from the EU and countries like China, Japan and the United States intensify. Greenland now actively promotes a concept of the Arctic as the home of people in legitimate pursuit of economic prosperity. It discourages what it sees as over-zealous foreign attempts to protect the animals and the environment in the Arctic.

* * *

In December 2009, for the first time, the world outside Greenland learned of the visions of Greenland's newly elected political leaders.

It all began as Greenland's most famous singer-songwriter, Rasmus Lyberth, began to sing in a low-ceilinged room in Copenhagen. He sang in Greenlandic, louder and louder. His colossal voice soared while his hands jammed the rhythm on a small Greenlandic drum – the only visible acknowledgement of the heritage he sang about. He chanted powerfully; his body rocked from side to side as the massive glacier of sound washed over the dumbfounded crowd.

Danish Crown Prince Frederik was in the audience. He had moved up to the podium together with Kuupik Kleist, the recently elected new premier of Naalakkersuisut, the Greenlandic Self-Rule Government. Approximately 100 Greenlanders, Danes and foreign diplomats pressed their way towards the podium at the end of the narrow room. It was Friday 11 December 2009 in the North Atlantic House in central Copenhagen, where Greenland's official representation in Denmark keeps its offices. Greenland's new political elite had flown into Copenhagen to take advantage of the biggest political arena the international community could muster in 2009: 'The Conference of Parties', the UN's climate change conference, COP15, in Copenhagen. The Greenlandic politicians were to open Greenland's official exhibition, 'In the Eyes of Climate Change', but while the entire world was discussing how consumption of oil and gas could be limited, the Greenlandic Self-Rule Government had just launched a call for tenders of new licences for oil exploration in Greenland.

Rasmus Lyberth sang of the crux of the Greenlandic oil dilemma. It was a song which harked back to the time in 1721 when the Norwegian-Danish missionary Hans Egede brought Christianity to the Inuit. The Greenlandic hunters and their women only reluctantly received the Norwegian-born missionary, who, in his diary, wrote that the Greenlandic people were born stupid, blockheaded and violent. But Hans Egede, his family and a small group of German Moravian Brethren succeeded: The Greenlanders, within a span of just a hundred years, decided to accept the church and the Bible. The music and the singing attracted the young, and for the destitute, the weak, the widows and others, who faced an otherwise precarious existence, the church offered chances of a marginally better life. Also, and perhaps most essentially, the promise of an afterlife in a peaceful heaven offered a powerful perspective, which the Greenlanders' own spiritual world could not seemingly match.

Rasmus Lyberth sang about how the Greenlandic people gave up contact with their own world of ideas; contact with Mother Ocean and the Spirit of the Air as well as the balance with Greenlandic nature itself. Gathered closely around him were Greenland's new political rulers. After 30 years in power in Greenland, the old leaders from the Siumut-party had been swept aside by Kuupik Kleist and his left-wing fellow-partisans from Inuit Ataqatigiit (IA) and the change of government coincided with the new agreement of Greenlandic Self-Rule between Denmark and Greenland.

In Nuuk on 21 June 2009, on Greenland's National Day, the Danish Queen Margrethe II handed over the Self-Rule papers to Greenland's new leaders. The Unity of the Danish Realm was intact; foreign and defence policy continued to be controlled from Copenhagen, and banknotes were printed in Denmark, but in the Act on Greenland Self-Government it was now firmly stipulated that Greenland could secede from the Danish Realm if the Greenlandic people wished. Also, the people of Greenland had finally received acknowledgement of their right to whatever income could be made from the oil and minerals in Greenland's subsoil. The future had begun.

Rasmus Lyberth sang about the built-in dilemmas: Should the thousand-year-old pact with nature and the whales, musk oxen, fish and seals continue to make up the core of life in Greenland going forward? Or should the Greenlandic people bet hard on the oil and gas and the international corporations, which already had their feet in the soil?

Deftly, Kuupik Kleist built on Lyberth's thundering applause. He raised the microphone and presented an image of a new Greenland: 'We wish to show an image of a country in which the traditional and the modern thrive side by side – an image of a country in which everyone is strongly committed to strive for economic independence.' Officially, Kuupik Kleist was supposed to give a talk on climate, but he went much further: 'The Act on Greenland Self-Government recognizes the Greenlanders as a people under international law, with the right to self-governance. In addition, it means that it is our right to define and set our own dreams and goals. Less ice equals facilitated access to a sustainable exploitation of oil, gas and minerals. The disappearance of the ice will result in enormous volumes of water power and provide us with a unique option to establish energy-intensive industry based on clean, renewable energy. All these elements will be decisive in order to ensure our economic independence.'

The fundamental idea was simple. Each year, the Danish government transferred 3.4 billion kroner (approximately 486 million US dollars) to Greenland's national coffers. Without it, the Self-Rule Government would be hard-pressed to pay for fundamentals like hospitals, schools and pensions. The block grant represented Greenland's humiliating dependence on the old colonial power. In 2009, as Kuupik Kleist talked, recognition within his countrymen was growing that only the minerals and the oil and gas might bring enough wealth to Greenland that this dependence on Danish subsidies could end. The premier talked of an independent Greenland in which the Greenlandic people earned sufficient money to improve the lives of their children, to do something about the decrepit apartment buildings all over Greenland, and to pay for a more decent schooling system. He talked of a Greenland that the well-educated Greenlanders residing in Denmark would want to move back to, a Greenland integrated into the world economy in an entirely new way. His vision was miles from the neglected, impoverished Greenland often displayed in the Danish media. But it was also a vision gaining in strength and helped by climate change. As *National Geographic* wrote in June 2010, 'in Greenland itself, apprehension about climate change is often overshadowed by great expectations. For now, this self-governing dependency of Denmark still

leans heavily on its former colonial ruler. [...] But the
Arctic meltdown has already started to open up access to
oil, gas, and mineral resources that could give Greenland the
financial and political independence its people crave. [...] At
times these days it feels as if the whole country is holding its
breath – waiting to see whether the "greening of Greenland",
so regularly announced in the international press, is actually
going to happen.'

A few months after the climate convention in Copenhagen,
Henrik Leth, chairman of the Employers' Association of
Greenland, presented his version of the new Greenland.
He explained how small Greenlandic enterprises geared
themselves as suppliers to the foreign oil and mine companies.
In spring 2010, a prognosis from Nuuk showed how the mining
industry would create 1,500 new jobs before 2020. If this
were correct, Greenland's entire economic structure would be
overturned. Fishermen and hunters would have to enter entirely
new trades, the young must be given new skills and a range of
village communities would be turned upside down.

With the introduction of Self-Rule, the Greenlandic people
got proof of ownership to the riches of the subsoil, and climate
change boosted their hopes even further. Greenland's shipping
company Royal Arctic Line prepared for increased traffic when
the Northwest Passage around Canada opened up. Goods
would go north from Europe to Asia, and money would be
made on harbour facilities, tariffs and fuel. Greenland's economy
is incredibly small, but for potato growers and shepherds in
Narsaq in South Greenland, as well as hotels, entrepreneurs
and tourist guides, and for the young engineers from Sisimiut's
new Arctic Technology Centre in the central part of the
county's west coast, the disappearance of the ice represented new
horizons. As Greenland's Minister for Finance, Maliina Abelsen,
put it, 'I would like to remind you all that Greenland and the
Greenlandic people already have gone through significant
changes within the past 100 years. We crossed the border
to change a long time ago – and this is not merely true for
Greenland, but for the entire Arctic region.'

Greenland's political leaders had no plans to transform Greenland into an open-air museum. As Kuupik Kleist later explained to me in an interview, the entire world wanted to have a say in the protection of Greenland's pristine environment, but the first priority of Greenland's leaders was the people of Greenland. They were happy to re-open visions of a grand industrial development in the Arctic – a vision already coined by Icelandic Arctic explorer Vilhjalmur Stefansson in the beginning of the nineteenth century. In his 14 books, Stefansson persistently challenged the myth of a dark and dangerous Arctic inhabited by barbarians. One hundred years later, the Greenlandic leaders still struggled with the outside world's perceptions, but they were aided by climate change and the disappearance of the ice. The oil disasters from the likes of *Exxon Valdez* and *Deepwater Horizon* were frightening, but Kuupik Kleist and his colleagues were trying to make the world understand that those were risks Greenland would have to live with in its pursuit of prosperity.

In May 2011 in Nuuk, Kuupik Kleist experienced how the other Arctic governments were similarly aiming for swift industrial development. When the United States' Hillary Clinton and Russia's Sergej Lavrov and other Arctic foreign ministers gathered in Nuuk for an Arctic Council ministerial meeting, the whole town resounded with their common wish for economic development and growth in the Arctic. The ministers sent out a common declaration: 'First and foremost, the Arctic is an inhabited region with various economies and societies.'

This was significant. For decades, the media and government officials in Europe and the United States had presented the Arctic and Greenland primarily as the polar bears' fragile habitat, an almost otherworldly environment in need of protection. Now the entire body of Arctic governments sought to shift the world's focus onto people and economic development in the Arctic. In an historic move, the US administration had sent Hillary Clinton, the first US Secretary of State to attend an Arctic Council meeting. The tiny city centre of Nuuk was teeming with security officials, spectators and Arctic diplomats all enjoying the moment. US journalists covering Clinton's Arctic trip struggled in the snow in their delicate city shoes, but most significantly, Clinton's attendance lent crucial credence to the entire body of the Arctic Council, confirming in the process the Council's rightful place in the mainstream of international politics and as the key forum for charting the future of the Arctic. Kuupik Kleist, Greenland's premier, was overjoyed. He seemed to be smiling to everyone at once in Katuaq, the big community centre in Nuuk, and a few days later the Danish newspaper *Information* published a secret draft of the Kingdom of Denmark's first-ever strategy for the Arctic, summarized in a headline: 'People before environment in the Arctic'. Now the entire Kingdom was declaring its support for this fundamental shift of policy. A few months later, in August 2011, Kuupik Kleist, Denmark's Minister of Foreign Affairs, Lene Espersen, and the Faroe Islands' Prime Minister, Kai Leo Johannesen, officially presented the Arctic strategy in Copenhagen. Lene Espersen described the depth of the transition to the *Wall Street Journal*: 'So far, the discussion about the Arctic has been focusing on whether we should make the entire region one big nature reserve. But Denmark, Greenland and the Faroe Islands are in agreement that we want to utilize the area's commercial and economic potential. With this new strategy the door for international companies to come to Greenland and the Arctic opens. We are sending the signal that we want to welcome them with open arms. We are not nervous; we are not afraid to let in the industry in the area.'

The message from Copenhagen was crystal clear and developments continued in Greenland, even if local concerns and opposition to the lust for oil, gas and other industrial development increased. One of the most forceful young critics, the anthropologist Sara Olsvig, who was later to become a key member of the political elite, accused Greenland's new government of being in the pocket of a handful of Danish-born technocrats. Others joined in, but they did not manage to stop the hunt for investors and oil companies who would help in the exploitation. On the first page of the Self-Rule Government's strategy for the major oil areas, hope was written all over: 'There is broad political agreement in Greenland to work towards the development of the raw material industry to a principal business, which contributes positively to the economic development [...] i.e., with the purpose of reducing the significant dependency on the annual block grant from Denmark.'

Greenland faced tough competition with other nations in attracting the oil industry's investments. In 2009, Iceland set almost 100 oil fields in the waters between Iceland and the small Norwegian island Jan Mayen, 71 degrees north, up for offer. Similarly, in Norway and Russia the hunt for oil and gas was intensified.

During an interview in 2010 in his office, Kuupik Kleist told me how he tried to square his desire for economic development with his fear of a disastrous oil and societal upheaval: 'It is one of the biggest challenges we have faced. It will affect our entire society. Foreign labour! The economy! If the billions indeed pour from the subsoil how are we to manage it in order for society not to land in a coma? We have discussed this for years, and we have legislated accordingly. We have studied the experiences around the world, but theoretical preparation is one thing; it is an entirely different matter when it becomes reality. Naturally, our biggest wish is for diamonds to rain across the country so that we would not even have to face these deliberations. At the same time, however, we are driven by a very strong desire to stand on our own two feet. Why should we not exploit the same opportunities that the rest of the world already has? We fail to see the logic in this.'

About a year later, in September 2011, Sara Olsvig was elected to the Danish parliament. She had finished her anthropology studies and in all haste joined Kuupik Kleist's government party, Inuit Ataqagiit (IA), just before the election. She was known as a sharp chastiser of the Kleist government's quick hunt for oil: 'We have never looked at a map and asked each other: In which areas are we willing to risk oil pollution? Where would it be easiest to clean up? Currently, we are simply going all in to the south, east, north and west.'

Sara Olsvig was outraged that her politician colleagues were contemplating authorizing uranium mining as well as mining for rare earth elements in Kvanefjeld near Narsaq. She feared that the entire population of Narsaq would have to be relocated due to dust, noise and pollution if the owners of the mine, Greenland Minerals and Energy, got the thumbs-up: 'We have grown up listening to the saying that the oil and minerals will give us our freedom. We have never actually asked each other what the alternative could be. We have skipped a link and I am terribly sorry for that.'

In 2014, following Kuupik Kleist's withdrawal from politics, Sara Olsvig was elected chairperson for IA, also inheriting one of Kuupik Kleist's more ambitious political projects: the formulation of Greenland's first official constitution. A document spelling out the most basic visions and aspirations of the people of Greenland had been on the wish list for decades. Greenland was encompassed by the Danish constitution in 1953, and its people became fully fledged citizens in the Kingdom of Denmark. Many of those living in Greenland, however, found that the Danish constitution, developed 4,000 kilometres from Greenland way back in 1849, did not match reality in modern Greenland. In Greenland, for instance, no one can own land, but this historic trait is now challenged by the new staking on the mining industry. The basic thoughts of collective ownership to all the land of Greenland and to its riches were deeply engrained in the very soul of the nation, so how was this to be squared with the influx of foreigners and their desire to put up fences around their mining operations? Already, conflicts were brewing where the locals trying to collect berries in the mountains were chased away by foreign prospectors.

Similarly, the Danish constitution clearly stipulated that Greenland couldn't have its own foreign policy. Only through secondary laws and delegation from Copenhagen was this made to accommodate the fact that Greenland's politicians already had frequent dealings with foreign governments, including the Chinese, the Japanese and others. Greenland operated a diplomatic office in Washington and in Brussels and nurtured a wish for one more in Asia. Also, while Denmark was a member of the EU, Greenland chose to withdraw from the European Community in 1985 in order to protect its fish stocks from European fishermen. This made the people of Greenland the first people to leave the European community many years before Brexit. (In 2016, a suggestion that Great Britain might even learn from Greenland's exit from the European Community won sizeable attention in Scotland. The suggestion, made by a Danish scholar, was that England and other parts of Great Britain who wanted to leave the EU should be allowed to do that, just like Greenland was allowed to leave in 1985. At the same time Scotland and other parts of the country which did not want to leave could remain, just as Denmark remained when Greenland left.)

In 2011 when the constitutional process in Greenland was kick-started, several questions were unanswered: Should people – and foreigners – be able to own land in Greenland? Who owns the fish and the sea? Should the right to the fish and whales in the ocean be collective or sold to private companies? How should a Greenlandic constitution mirror the traditional ways of hunting that had secured survival, identity and lifestyles in Greenland for generations? What role should the Greenlandic language have in the future? Who is the government in Nuuk responsible to – and to what extent? Who could be citizens of Greenland? Which rights should foreigners – say Chinese labour in the future mines – have? Would they have the right to vote and to full-scale medical services?

At a seminar at Ilisimatusarfik, Greenland's University, Kuupik Kleist explained to me that the constitutional process was meant to clarify in particular these internal questions in Greenland: 'We are in the eye of enormous changes in Greenland, which means that it will be necessary to define our understanding of, for example, management of power, human rights, children's rights, the people's sovereignty, as well as many other fundamental matters. The preparation of a constitution can be a good way to clarify which values one's society should be built on.'

The constitution process was initiated in consensus by all 31 members of the Inatsisartut. The immediate aim was to obtain internal clarification, but Kuupik Kleist, Sara Olsvig, and many others also reminded their constituents that political independence from Denmark remained an unconditional ambition. 'My party is an independence party. Bottom line', Kleist said.

The constitutional process was now in motion, but it did not bring any clarity to exactly when Greenland would seek to secede from Denmark, and several years would pass before the actual drafting of the constitution could begin. In 2012, prior to a meeting with the Danish Prime Minister, Kuupik Kleist was asked when independence would occur, but he refrained from presenting any concrete timeline and instead resorted to his standard phrases: 'At one point, Greenland will be independent, which means that we have the total sovereignty of the country and our own foreign policy. Maybe we have a common defence policy within some sort of union with the Faroe Islands and Denmark.'

3

CLIMATE CHANGE AND THE RESHAPING OF DENMARK'S ARCTIC DEFENCE

If Greenland secedes the Kingdom of Denmark will lose 98 per cent of its territory and new questions about geopolitical relations in the Arctic will arise. What happens to the US Air Force's air base at Thule? Who will defend Greenland's sovereignty? So far, Greenland's sovereignty rests within the Danish Realm and Greenland is firmly embedded in NATO's defence arrangements. Climate change is rapidly transforming its geography and Greenland offers distinct military challenges by being so far away from the heartland of the NATO alliance. The following is an account of a three-week journey in 2010 with *Ejnar Mikkelsen*, a Danish naval ship, along Greenland's most remote and basically uninhabited north eastern coastline. A series of basic questions present themselves: How and why does Denmark patrol these frigid and lonely waters? And what did the officers onboard think of Russia's increased military presence in the Arctic?

* * *

Sixty-four degrees north, early September. A cold rain pours down over Reykjavik, Iceland's capital. Docked in the harbour, the Danish warship *Ejnar Mikkelsen* is ready for departure.

The sky is the same grey colour as the water in the harbour basin, and *Ejnar Mikkelsen*'s sharp-cut steel shell provides no contrast. At the stern and at the stem in front of the cannons the wind plays with swallow-tailed flags of the special blood-red colour that only the navy is allowed to use.

Ejnar Mikkelsen is about to leave for a three-week expedition along the east coast of Greenland, into the most northern parts of the Greenland Sea, into the world's deepest fjords, and into the open sea along the borders of the most far-flung of Denmark's territorial waters. The navy patrols along the coasts of Greenland have taken place for the last 400 years to ensure the Danish rule over the island and the waters surrounding it. As the ice disappears, this task is becoming more demanding. A new pattern of risks has to be decoded and prevented; new tasks need to be carried out. The navy ships must move farther to the north, and they must stay in the desolate and stormy waters for longer periods of time.

Shortly before departure from Reykjavik in 2010, in front of the large map of Greenland on the wall of *Ejnar Mikkelsen*'s command bridge, rear-admiral Henrik Kudsk, the director of Island Command Greenland, explains that the summer ice has withdrawn so far up towards the Arctic Ocean that *Ejnar Mikkelsen* might be able to sail all the way to Nordostrundingen, Greenland's most eastern point, only 800 kilometres from the North Pole. No navy ship has ever sailed that far up the east coast of Greenland. One of the crew members maintains that *Ejnar Mikkelsen* is not even carrying enough fuel to sail the more than 1,000 nautical miles to Nordostrundingen, but Henrik Kudsk simply points to the map once more.

Ejnar Mikkelsen is still linked to Iceland. The ropes from the stern to the bollards on the wharf are the last to be loosened. At that point, the diesel engines of the ship have already pushed the sternpost into the harbour basin and all is quiet on the command bridge save for the captain's short commands. *Ejnar Mikkelsen* is 71 metres long, and it takes precision to turn the ship in the narrow harbour basin. When fully loaded, the ship weighs almost 2,000 metric tons, and even the smallest collision with one of the other ships in the harbour of the pier could be disastrous. Reykjavik harbour is just big enough for the Danish warships, but it is far larger than any harbour on the east coast of Greenland. In not one place along the coast can one find a harbour big enough and deep enough for the Danish navy ships. Nowhere can one find fuel, spare parts or any other assistance. That is why the Icelandic harbours work as supply bases and filling stations for the Danish warships.

The disappearance of the ice, the oil, and the unresolved discussions about borders in the Arctic Ocean are forcing the navy to face the all-important questions: How will peace be maintained in this Arctic region? Will the Danish war efforts in Iraq, Lybia and Afghanistan be replaced by rearmament and militarization in the far north? Will Danish soldiers be fighting naval battles for oil, fish and borders in the Arctic? All over the Arctic, military analysts, politicians, and academics are wondering whether the tentative political teamwork of the Arctic Council, diplomacy and the civil relations of the Arctic states are strong enough to handle the changes in the Arctic. They discuss whether the new military build-up in the Arctic may in itself strike sparks. Will a deterioration of the relationship between Russia and the United States in other places around the world be transferred to the Arctic? If you look beyond the Ilulissat Declaration, if you study the military build-up in Russia, Norway, Canada, the United States and Denmark, count the Russian and American submarines in the Arctic and consider the oil, China's new role, the climate and the new freight routes to Asia, is the conclusion then that there is increased tension and potential conflict on the way in the Arctic?

Behind his desk in the VIP cabin onboard *Ejnar Mikkelsen*, Henrik Kudsk answers my question with a definite 'no'. At the time the inspection vessel departs from Iceland in 2010, he has been commander of Island Command Greenland (GLK) for five years. Up until *Ejnar Mikkelsen*'s departure from Reykjavik, he has kept a close eye on the development of the Canadian as well as the American, Russian and Norwegian military in the Arctic. He has participated in international conferences on power and politics in the Arctic, while keeping in touch with military colleagues in other coastal nations and – as he does on our flight to the North Pole two years later – he dismisses the idea of armed conflict: 'During the Cold War, the Arctic was a potential battlefield, because the Arctic lies between the two main contenders of the time – the United States and the Soviet Union. If the nuclear weapons had to be moved, they would have had to go that way. The Arctic itself had no real value. The Cold War revolved around other matters. Today, the situation is different: The Arctic has a value of its own now, but the landowners in the Arctic have common interests. At the same time, we know that only five per cent of the riches in the Arctic – oil and gas – are found in those areas where the borders are still uncertain. The rest has already been distributed. There is nothing left to fight over. In broad terms, wars always concern resources and money. If there is no financial incentive for a conflict, there is no foundation for a conflict. On the contrary, collaboration is in everyone's interest.'

Ejnar Mikkelsen departs from Reykjavik a little after 19:00. The ship has been in Iceland for 48 hours; the crew has had a few beers and blown off steam.

After 45 minutes, Reykjavik is no longer in sight. The seagulls still follow the ship, but otherwise *Ejnar Mikkelsen* only passes a few fishing boats sailing along the Icelandic coast. The swells grow bigger and bigger, and soon *Ejnar Mikkelsen* cuts though the water. The pepper shaker falls over on the table in the mess deck, and the lamps swing from side to side, but this is nothing. *Ejnar Mikkelsen* is built for the waters around Greenland and moves straight north at 13 knots. Not until persistent winds from the north gain strength during the night is our momentum affected.

Onboard, the officers from Defence Command Denmark repeat over and over that they think the risk of conflict in the Arctic is minimal, but they also know that the situation in the Arctic can change. The number of unknown factors grows in the Arctic. China moves in, and new trade patterns emerge. Oil, gas and minerals are extracted, and the environment is under threat. The Arctic coastal nations are still purchasing new military equipment, and new Arctic bases, supply ports and Arctic task forces are being planned. Military exercises are again on the Arctic agenda, or as Canadian Arctic expert Rob Huebert writes, 'The new military programs have been geared towards combat capabilities that exceed mere constabulary capacity [...] Uncertainty is the most fundamental element of the security environment that is developing in the Arctic.'

In the morning, about 12 hours after leaving Reykjavik, *Ejnar Mikkelsen* passes the northern coast of Iceland. For a short while, the flat hilltops are seen as dim silhouettes to the east, but soon *Ejnar Mikkelsen* is on the open sea. Over the radio, the captain reminds the crew of a soccer match on TV that evening. By coincidence, Denmark is playing against Iceland. Onboard, only the crew's uniforms tell us that *Ejnar Mikkelsen* is not a cruise ship, but designed to protect Danish interests. On the foredeck, the ship cannon serves as a deterrent and below deck we find heavy-duty machine guns. Off the coast of south east Greenland, the sister ship *Knud Rasmussen* patrols, and in the waters west of Disco Island lies another inspection vessel *Vædderen*.

Ejnar Mikkelsen may have a cannon on the foredeck, but it is not under preparations for war. The Russian military in the Arctic develops new and stronger forms. Russia's Northern Fleet in Murmansk plays a central role in Russia's attempt to reclaim its role as a superpower. But from his VIP cabin onboard *Ejnar Mikkelsen*, Henrik Kudsk warns me against misinterpreting his Russian colleagues. 'At the moment, no military build-up is taking place in the Arctic. Russia's build-up should not be viewed as a specific Arctic rearmament. Remember that a large part of the Russians' access to the ocean lies on their north coast. We see no military threat in the Arctic.'

In February 2011, Denmark and Russia entered into an agreement regarding increased military collaboration in, among other places, the Arctic. Three months later in Nuuk, the eight Arctic states in the Arctic Council signed an agreement regarding increased collaboration concerning rescue operations at sea – on Russia's initiative.

Seventy-three degrees north. On the fourth day of *Ejnar Mikkelsen's* expedition, the helicopter deck lies deserted in the dark of the Denmark Strait. A dense fog sticks to the ship, and the seagulls from Iceland are no longer following. Metre-high swells are a reminder of the intense storms that often rage here, and in the dark no horizon can be seen. The temperature is dropping, and the wind drains the heat out of any visitor in seconds.

Here sailed the old polar expeditioners on run-down whaling ships with the wind howling through the timber and with the railing so close to the water surface that a cross sea wave would be enough to swab the deck. Here Mylius-Erichsen, a Danish journalist turned explorer, defiantly sailed into the wind on *Danmark* in the early years of the twentieth century, preparing for one of the most important Arctic explorations of his time. A few years later, another of the great Danish explorers, Ejnar Mikkelsen, who was later to have our naval ship named after him, gazed ahead onboard the *Alabama*, a coal-powered former whaleboat with the helmsman standing outside in the freezing cold and a deck soiled by seasick sled dogs. Long before that, the navy ship *Røde Løve* (Red Lion) came on the wind to Greenland in 1605 and brought the first two Greenlanders to visit Denmark back with him – most likely by force. In 1786 the frigate *Blaa Heyren* arrived, appointed to the west coast of Greenland to scare off the increasing number of Dutch whalers. The flow of Danish ships has never since subsided.

As we continue onboard *Ejnar Mikkelsen*, Danish politicians and the leaders of Defence Command Denmark must make difficult choices. In Iraq, Afghanistan, Syria and Libya and in the waters off the coast of Somalia, plagued by pirates, Denmark has had the choice of engaging or not engaging. In the Arctic waters of the Danish Kingdom, however, Denmark cannot choose whether or not to take responsibility. They may be vast, icy and demanding but the Denmark Strait, the Baffin

Strait and the other tough waters surrounding Greenland are parts of the Danish Realm. They must be controlled, patrolled and watched over. Sovereignty must be maintained, search and rescue capacity must be established and ready every day of the year, and the tasks grow for every inch of ice that disappears. A responsible coastal state does not argue over this; it simply takes responsibility.

Seventy-five degrees north. This is where *Ejnar Mikkelsen* hits the pack ice. All night the course has been set for Shannon Island, where *Ejnar Mikkelsen* will leave provisions and dog fodder for the Sirius Sled Patrol, the Danish navy's dog sled patrol in Eastern Greenland. The Sirius Sled Patrol will arrive at the little Pantch cabin, built by Norwegian and Danish hunters ages ago, every winter – usually cold and hungry. But today the drop-off has to be cancelled. Just off the coast from the Pantch cabin lies a solid belt of compressed ice floes reaching almost a kilometre into the sea. To avoid getting stuck in the ice, *Ejnar Mikkelsen* must stay away from the coast, and neither the ship's operation vessel nor the rubber dinghies can penetrate such thick ice.

After an hour's travel farther north, *Ejnar Mikkelsen* must reduce speed to three to four knots. Here the pack ice is only broken in narrow strips. Captain Sundwall leaps to his feet and climbs on top of his chair on the command bridge to better find the open strips between the ice floes. He calls the engine room to make sure that both diesel engines are on full power. The ice is now being met with 8,000 horsepower. Heavy floes and flakes are being lifted up, crushed and pushed to the side. Less experienced shipmasters might order full speed ahead, but Troels Sundwall gently manoeuvres the ship through the ice. The pack ice from the Arctic Ocean can be several years old and three to four metres thick. With full speed ahead, *Ejnar Mikkelsen* risks sailing onto the ice and tipping over on the side instead of crushing the ice.

The trick is to catch an ice floe with the stern and push it in front of the ship as a ram, so that the fuselage will not be damaged by the constant collisions. The electronic ice map from the Danish Meteorological Institute shows that *Ejnar Mikkelsen* sails on the outskirts of pack ice that has locked up large parts of the coast unexpectedly early.

The oil industry might encounter the same type of problem. On the exact degree of latitude that *Ejnar Mikkelsen* is sailing, a group of oil companies have been singled out and given rights to explore for oil and gas; actual extraction is still decades ahead because of the ice – but the oil is there, they say. Onboard the *Ejnar Mikkelsen*, all talk of sailing to Nordostrundingen ceases because of the ice. In the evening, the crew complain because they have to couple up in the cramped cabins and because the steward and the baker have been working overtime for a long time. The number of guests onboard has been extraordinary. Danish politicians in particular have paid frequent visits spurred by all the new talk of the Arctic.

Had the men been able to look just slightly into the future, they would have seen that the visits actually led to change.

On 1 November 2012, the Queen of Denmark oversaw the opening of a new headquarters of all Danish military activity in the North Atlantic, the Joint Arctic Command in Nuuk. Also in November 2012, when the Danish parliament concluded a new defence agreement, it was decided to speed up the acquisition of a new navy ship to be deployed in Greenland with the newly established Defence Command in Nuuk. The navy's operations were re-organized according to the disappearance of the ice, the prospects of increased oil exploration and traffic, and the new security picture in the Arctic.

In 2011, the Danish Defence Intelligence Service had published an evaluation of security risks in the Arctic illustrating the complex situation: 'To some extent, it is likely that fewer military encounters will occur going forward towards 2020. These encounters could, for example, be harassment of the military forces of other states or their civilian exploration, or utilization of natural resources such as oil drillings or fishery in or near disputed areas. Even then, it is not likely that this would develop into a military conflict. The Arctic can, however, be marked by conflict, mutual mistrust and military tension, especially if the United States and Russia do not maintain their improved political relationship.'

Also, the Danish Defence Intelligence Service now, four and a half years after the Ilulissat Declaration, raised serious doubts about Russia's intent to follow UN decisions on borders in the Arctic Ocean: 'If the UN Commission on the Limits of the Continental Shelf (CLCS) does not meet the Russian demands on expansion of the country's financial zone in the Arctic Ocean, it is likely that Russia will respond by raising doubts concerning the impartiality and competence of the CLCS as well as the CLCS's recommendations in relation to demands from other countries. Russia could also react by assuming alternative interpretations of the international rules and norms.' This was the first time that Denmark officially raised doubts about Russia's intent to fulfil its own promises from Ilulissat in 2008.

The Danish politicians knew that Defence Command Denmark faces special challenges in the Arctic: The great distances, the weather, the ice and the newly peaked interests of foreign nations in Greenland. Danish diplomats were mandated to step up their efforts to ensure that the navy would have easy and extended access to Thule Air Base, since the only deep-water port in all of north west Greenland with the capacity to harbour the Danish warships is found there. Without access to this facility, the warships must sail hundreds of nautical miles to the south to Nuuk just to refuel. Furthermore, in the future, the Danish ships would have to spend weeks and months in the most northern waters off the coast of Greenland to mark Denmark's sovereignty – and because oil investigations might intensify, fishing will pick up, as will cruise ship tourism. The navy ships will be defending the oil companies against illegal actions from environmental activists, and they will have to be ready to gather evidence and documentation as well as assisting in controlling the oil in case of a spill. They will be saving tourists in distress in case of a wrecked cruise ship; they will be in place when long-distance traffic from the Northwest Passage and the number of bulk-carriers with ore from Canadian mines increase in numbers.

Onboard *Ejnar Mikkelsen* I was reminded how the actual defence of Greenland in time of war would be left to the United States. The special position of the United States in Greenland dates back to 1941 when the Danish emissary in Washington, Henrik Kauffholdt, struck a controversial deal with the administration of President Roosevelt in Washington. Denmark was under German occupation and Henrik Kauffholdt claimed that the Danish government was no longer able to make free and independent decisions. He maintained that he alone would represent in the United States the intentions and interests of the real Denmark, free of Nazi manipulations. Through his extraordinary connections in the capital he was invited to present his suggestions directly to President Roosevelt, who immediately embraced the opportunity Henrik Kauffholdt represented. The United States was not yet fully engaged in the war in Europe, but President Roosevelt and his defence department had long realized that Greenland was rapidly becoming important for the war. The British faced increasing bombardments from German planes, and in the United States fears were mounting that Britain might fall and leave the Atlantic Ocean entirely under the control of the German navy. The British were badly in need of additional power in the air, but the transfer of new fighter planes from the factories in the United States and Canada to Europe was burdensome and slow, since non-stop transatlantic flight was still not technically possible. New transfer routes were needed, and here Greenland suddenly loomed large. If landing strips and fuel facilities could be established in Greenland, modern fighter planes could fly from the United States or Canada via Greenland, onwards to Iceland and then just a short distance farther to the British Isles.

The United States needed Greenland, but Greenland belonged to the government in Denmark, which was under German occupation. Now Henrik Kauffholdt solved this problem for President Roosevelt and his military, since he claimed to represent the real Denmark, unstained by German

influence. He was more than willing to strike a deal, and the
US government decided to recognize Mr Kauffholdt as the
true representative of Denmark, ignoring the shrill protests
from Copenhagen. Single-handedly in his new capacity, Henrik
Kauffholdt negotiated an arrangement with Washington. The
United States assumed responsibility for supplying Greenland
and its population with food and other necessities during
the war. In return, the United States was granted permission
to establish the necessary military bases in Greenland and,
as means of payment for goods delivered to the people of
Greenland, also access to a crucial deposit of cryolite in
southern Greenland, a mineral essential at the time for the
production of aluminium and thus for the production of
new fighter planes. Cryolite was badly needed for the frenetic
production of American warplanes.

In rapid succession, the American Department of Defence
constructed several air bases in Greenland. The first, Bluie West
One, was built in Narsarsuaq in the very south and soon served
as a landing strip and filling station for thousands of American
warplanes on their way to battle in Europe. Today the base is
still in use as a civilian airport. In central Greenland, near
Kangerlussuaq, Sonderstrøm Air Base was established in 1941.
This air base later became part of the American and Canadian
early warning system for Soviet missiles. The American
Department of Defence used Sonderstrøm until 1992, and to
this day it functions as Greenland's only international airport.

Following World War II, Denmark and the United States
renewed their agreement in 1951 after a series of tense negotiations. At first, the government in Copenhagen assumed that the
US defence forces would withdraw their troops from Greenland
as a matter of course once the war was over. When this did not
happen a series of diplomatic exchanges began, culminating in the
visit of senior Danish officials to Washington in 1946. Only at this
stage did Denmark realize that the United States had no intention
of pulling its troops from Greenland. Instead, as mentioned above
a formal suggestion was made that the United States would simply
buy the entire island from Denmark. The United States was ready

to take over all 2.1 million square kilometres of Greenlandic rock and ice, including all inhabitants and whatever responsibilities this entailed. No price was suggested, but later investigations showed that the American negotiators were ready to offer up to 100 million US dollars in gold.

The Danes were wholly unprepared for the proposal. Denmark had no desire to relinquish its Arctic colony, even if Denmark had readily sold another colony to the United States only a few years prior. In 1917, following World War I, the government in Copenhagen sold the West Indies in the Caribbean, including the entire population, plantations, forests and beaches, to the United States for the sum of 25 million US dollars. The islands are now known as the US Virgin Islands.

No such arrangement for Greenland had been contemplated in Copenhagen, and after a short, confusing spell, the offer to buy Greenland was firmly rejected. It had, however, profoundly transformed the nature of the negotiations: Denmark now realized that the United States would not be persuaded to leave Greenland.

Instead a new arrangement was negotiated that replaced the accommodation reached by Henrik Kauffholdt and the Roosevelt administration back in 1941. In 1951 the Danish government signed the crucial accord with Washington that provided the United States with broad powers to establish military facilities in Greenland, while Denmark continued to hold and exercise full sovereignty of the entire island and its population. The accord was coupled with Denmark's accession to the newly established North Atlantic Treaty Organization, NATO, which had been facilitated by the United States. Thus, in short, Denmark, which had been criticized for not standing up sufficiently to its German occupiers during the war, was firmly re-established as a fully fledged member of the democratic world. It had retained sovereignty over Greenland, while in the process the United States – and by extension the entire NATO community – had won rights to run military bases in Greenland for as long as NATO remained in existence.

This new agreement became the foundation of the continued American presence in Greenland. In 1951, in light of increased tension with the Soviet Union, which had by now illustrated its capacity to detonate nuclear bombs, Thule Air Base far to the north was built during one short summer by more than 10,000 American soldiers. A large number of fighter planes and bombers soon flew in and out of Thule and the base area was fortified with heavy anti-aircraft artillery. The base remained essential during the entire Cold War, and in the process it became also subject of one of the most politically notorious post-colonial incidents in Greenland's history.

In 1953, a group of 112 Greenlanders who lived close to the base were forced to move. The US Air Force had plans to expand its land-based defence, and the small community of hunters and fishermen was persuaded to relocate to Qaanaaq, more than 100 kilometres to the north. This shift did not go down well. Housing prepared at the new sites in Qaanaaq proved to be constructed without proper consideration of the cold and the winds, local hunting proved inadequate so that food became scarce and over the years, speculation began as to why the Danish government was so keen to move the community just weeks before Greenland became an integrated part of Denmark and those living in Greenland were given all the rights as Danish citizens. Finally, in 1997, after a prolonged court case initiated by the Qaanaaq community the Danish Prime Minister, Poul Nyrup Rasmussen, issued a formal apology and decided to pay compensation to all involved in the 1953 relocation from Thule.

This was by no means, however, to be the end of controversy surrounding Thule Air Base. In 1957, at the peak of the Cold War, in a confidential note to Val Peterson, the US ambassador to Denmark, the Danish Prime Minister, H.C. Hansen, tacitly gave his permission to the American defence forces to store in Greenland any items, machinery or munitions deemed necessary for the maintenance of peace and for the safety of the Western world. His wording was exceedingly opaque, but his message was clear. The Danish government would not object to storage of nuclear warheads in Greenland if the US defence forces regarded that such was necessary in light of the threat of nuclear war with the Soviet Union. The note was kept not only confidential, but also completely isolated from any attention from parliament or any others except the Prime Minister's own very close aides.

The Prime Minister's decision contradicted the official policy of the Danish Kingdom. Anyone who asked at the time would be told in no uncertain terms that Denmark's policy was not to allow any storage of nuclear weapons on Danish soil, including Greenland. This policy had been the subject of much public debate and firmly established by a majority in parliament, and with the Prime Minister's own vocal support. In public the government maintained that this policy was crucial for Denmark's own security vis-à-vis the Soviet Union, which had very directly threatened to retaliate should Denmark decide to partake in any nuclear build-up by allowing, for instance, US nuclear capabilities in Denmark.

The Prime Minister's reasons for allowing US nuclear arms in Greenland were never discussed before he died in 1960, but historians have argued that he was inspired most likely by two main concerns. Firstly, he truly feared that a war with the Soviet Union was imminent and that the efforts of NATO and the United States to curtail the risks had to be supported. Secondly, he trusted that his secret could be kept at least until the risk of Soviet retaliation had diminished.

In January 1968, it almost went wrong. An American B52 bomber crashed near Thule Air Base with a load of four plutonium bombs only two days before a Danish general election. None of the bombs detonated, but a large area surrounding the crash site was badly contaminated and one of the bombs reportedly disappeared into the sea. Heated discussion of the American presence in Greenland reignited, and only through the most extravagant evasions did the secret of the tacit agreement survive.

In the end, time proved H.C. Hansen right, at least in his belief that his secret would be kept until it no longer mattered militarily. The Prime Minister's note was made public only in 1995, long after its real importance had evaporated. Even so, it instantly caused damage to relations between Denmark and Greenland. By then Greenland had established Home Rule and the political leaders in Nuuk were profoundly frustrated. For almost 40 years the US Air Force had had licence to arm its bases in Greenland with nuclear weapons, to patrol in Greenland's airspace with nuclear warheads, to store and maintain nuclear munitions in Thule – and no one had cared to inform the people of Greenland or its leaders.

Today, the few visitors to Thule Air Base can study its current main military facility, an enormous radar on a small hill a few kilometres east of the main base. The radar is one of the key elements of the American global missile defence system, designed to detect missiles from potential enemy states, in particular Russia, as early as possible, so that they may be destroyed by counter-strikes before they hit the United States. Closer to the center of the base, one will find installations where a hub of antennas receive signals from the US Air Force's military spy satellites and send them on to the United States. These installations provide critical information on anti-terrorism operations worldwide; in 2003 they were instrumental during the US invasion of Iraq. Today, some 150 American soldiers and 450 Danish and Greenlandic employees tend to the installations at Thule Air Base.

Making its way through the waters, the *Ejnar Mikkelsen* is an example of how the Danish navy has been armed in the Arctic up until now. The slim cannon on the foredeck is a 76 mm Italian-made Oto Melara Super Rapid, and navy personnel regard it as extremely effective and accurate. Below deck, the cannon's barrel-shaped cartridge belt may be armed with long grenades. In a combat situation, the cannon can be fired by pushing a pedal in the operations room. Theoretically, the powerful cannon can fire 120 grenades per minute with great precision on a distance of 15–20 kilometres. The grenades will penetrate the hull on hostile ships and then explode inside. But in 2010 *Ejnar Mikkelsen*'s cannon has never been functional. On other warships in Greenland the cannons are operational, but for budgetary reasons the cannon onboard the *Ejnar Mikkelsen* has never been supplied with the IT system that would allow it to function properly. Plus, the cannon works just fine as a deterrent for fishermen fishing illegally and others in need of discipline.

Ejnar Mikkelsen is, however, not completely without combat capabilities. Besides the Oto Melara cannon, the ship is carrying two heavy machine guns that can be mounted on each bridge wing and extra firepower can be mounted if it should be deemed necessary. *Ejnar Mikkelsen* can be armed with anti-aircraft advanced missile systems designed to neutralize anti-ship missiles, other vessels or targets on land. All these weapons can be mounted if necessary, but Captain Troels Sundwall warns against over-interpretations: 'It would be difficult to find room aboard for all the people who would be needed to effectively use two or three more weapon systems. We would also need to sail to Denmark for a period of time in order to carry out the installation.'

The operations room from which *Ejnar Mikkelsen*'s weapons would be fired in a crisis situation is situated directly behind the command bridge. But in 2010, the room was only supplied with a single worn-out IT console – far from enough to make the ship a war machine. Empty cardboard boxes lie next to the console, and the room looks mostly like a dusty storage room.

Seventy-five degrees north. After an hour of sailing through the pack ice east of Shannon Island, the *Ejnar Mikkelsen* is now moving through less icy waters in the Nordenskjold Bay. As we approach land, Troels Sundwall reduces speed almost to a halt, and finally a rattle from the massive anchor chain can be heard from under the water. A thick fog hides the mountaintops, but the rocks by the coast are clearly visible through the binoculars. The famous *Alabama* hut is said to be found here.

This was where the real Ejnar Mikkelsen, the Arctic explorer, and his engineer, Iver Iversen, had to scrape through two long years in 1910 and 1911 after an exhausting sled ride to 79 Fjord south of Nordostrundingen. After eight months on the sled, Ejnar Mikkelsen and Iver Iversen returned starved and sick to Shannon Island only to discover that their ship the *Alabama* had been crushed by the ice. The remaining expedition participants had left. The crew had built a hut from the *Alabama*'s timber on the coast, but had subsequently caught a ride with a Norwegian whaler. Not until the summer of 1912 did Ejnar Mikkelsen and Iver Iversen manage to get away in the same manner. We visit their old derelict hut and commemorate their stamina. Ejnar Mikkelsen's son and grandson later tried to reach the hut, but without any luck. At 75 degrees north, nature reigns, and only those who have visited north east Greenland understand how desolate and vast the area is.

In the VIP cabin onboard the *Ejnar Mikkelsen*, Henrik Kudsk tells me how he received a visit from the Defence Committee of the Danish parliament just a few days before our departure from Reykjavik. The politicians were told how the navy is closely linked with Greenland's civilian life.

Ejnar Mikkelsen's commanding officer talks passionately of fishery inspections, icebreaking to frozen coastal village communities, transportation of the ill and of fuel for the hunters' motorboats and rescues of distressed fishermen. Once, a warship transported a church across Disco Bay in western Greenland.

In August 2010, four members of the Presidium of the Danish Parliament were given a private lesson in this Arctic workload. The four politicians were visiting East Greenland with several of their colleagues from Inatsisartut, the Greenlandic parliament in Nuuk. The group was onboard the *Ejnar Mikkelsen* south of Tasiilaq in East Greenland when an alarm was raised from Illoqqortoormiut further north. A group of tourists on a kayaking adventure had been surprised by a powerful storm, a piteraq, and were all in mortal danger. Later on, the people in Illoqqortoormiut recounted how they found several tourists stranded on an iceberg. Two female kayakers had to be resuscitated. As the alarm reached *Ejnar Mikkelsen* in the south, the four Danish politicians and their Greenlandic colleagues were instantly dropped off in Tasiilaq, and the *Ejnar Mikkelsen* hurriedly set a course due north. The politicians from Denmark now realized that the *Ejnar Mikkelsen* was the nearest rescue vessel to the troubled tourists, even though it was 900 kilometres or a day and half's travel from the accident. Back home in Copenhagen they explained that Greenland critically needed more warships. As one of them stated, 'When Denmark has left Afghanistan, I can easily imagine that we will be able to afford more rescue vessels in the North Atlantic.' In the following months this argument became widely accepted in the Danish parliament and Denmark's military presence in the Arctic developed rapidly. In September 2012, for the first time, Henrik Kudsk, ships and crew from the Danish forces in Greenland oversaw a military exercise in north east Greenland in which all the other Arctic states were invited to participate. The contributions from the other Arctic states were relatively modest; the Russians chose to send just a single observer, but the exercise, named SAREX – Search & Rescue Exercise – illustrated Defence Command Denmark's increased scope and ability to co-operate.

Then on 1 November 2012, the Queen of Denmark oversaw the opening of a new headquarters of all Danish military activity in the North Atlantic, the Joint Arctic Command in Nuuk.

Seventy-two degrees north. September 2010. *Ejnar Mikkelsen* arrives at Mestersvig in north east Greenland. A young soldier with a sweatband around his head drives his Land Rover four kilometres along the gravel road from the washed out shacks at the rusty docks to Defence Command Denmark's hutment and the small airstrip. Once, a lead mine employed 150 men here in Mestersvig. A few of them brought their wives, and children were born here. In 2010, however, the driver of the Land Rover and one other soldier are the only inhabitants. Politicians want to close down the polluted Mestersvig, including its military airstrip, but somehow it survives.

The soldier behind the wheel apologizes for the deep holes in the road where icy water is accumulating. The two soldiers at Mestersvig are responsible for maintaining the road, but their opponent is mighty. Climate change has taken control and for the first time in history, King Oscar's Fjord just off Mestersvig has been ice-free during summer. Previously, the ice formed a solid lid on the wide fjord, even during summer. Now the powers of the fjord have been released. Tides and waves surge past the old coastline of Mestersvig all summer long and salt water erodes the gravel road. Earlier, ore carriers could barely break their way through the ice to Mestersvig. The Danish navy's cutters, the precursors of the *Ejnar Mikkelsen* and the *Knud Rasmussen*, cast anchor at Mestersvig during good years, but they always risked getting stuck in the ice. Many navy officers remember the naval cutter *Alken*, which was lost with all hands to the pack ice in 1948. Now, the gravel road is disappearing all the way up to Mestersvig.

Meanwhile, freighters, ore carriers, fishing boats and oil tankers create new traffic in newly opened Arctic waters. For Danish shipping companies and for Greenland, new trade routes to China and potential new incomes from ports, tolls and visitors to Greenland are in sight. Danish shipping companies such as Torm and Nordic Bulk Carriers are eagerly investing in ice-strengthened ships for the new trade routes north of Canada and Siberia. The shipping companies have made Denmark one of the world's leading shipping nations, and the melting of the ice in the Arctic has created new opportunities. In ten years, Asia has overtaken the United States as the largest market for European goods, and the new and shorter freight routes north of Siberia and Canada are the logical next step. A journey from Northern Europe to Japan can be shortened from 22 to ten days. New orders keep coming in at shipyards such as Daewoo and Samsung in South Korea, Japanese Mitsubishi Heavy Industries and the Finnish Aker Finnyards, which all build ice-strengthened ships. The first massive oil tankers built as icebreakers are already making their way through the ice north of Siberia.

In Mestersvig's tower, Captain Sundwall points to a one-metre-high wall map showing the coasts of Greenland. The navy personnel onboard the *Ejnar Mikkelsen* often think about how fast people die if they fall into cold water. They no longer talk about whether it will happen or not, but rather when an accident involving a cruise ship off the coast of Greenland will mean loss of life. And they know that the search and rescue operation in the extensive Greenlandic waters presents serious difficulties. If sailors, fishermen, or merchant ships are in distress the Danish navy is immediately mobilized. However, in Greenland they must deal with enormous distances, the cold and the darkness, which makes everything more difficult. More than 150 times a year, a cruise ship anchors in a Greenlandic harbour. The biggest ships carry more than 2,000 passengers and up to 1,000 crewmembers. The thought of what will happen if one of the ships is wrecked torments the Danish naval officers.

In front of the wall map, Troels Sundwall tells me how he fears the panic that would arise if hundreds of people suddenly had to be saved from the ice-cold ocean at the same time. Who should be saved – and who should not? Where will they be? Who will help the injured and the people numbed with cold? The life rafts from the *Ejnar Mikkelsen* can carry approximately 300 passengers and the ship itself maybe 200 others, but what about the rest? How will he reach the distressed on the ice? Who will provide medical attention if there are many injured? What if panic takes over? The crew is armed, but can they shoot at people in distress? As the commanding officer, Troels Sundwall envisions that he will have to lock the door to the command bridge to avoid panicking victims from disrupting the ship's operations.

Shortly before our departure from Reykjavik on Friday 27 August 2010, he and his colleagues were reminded of how disaster always lurks around the corner. At around 19:00 the Danish cruise ship *Clipper Adventurer* grounded on an underwater cliff in the Coronation Gulf in the Canadian Arctic at 69 degrees north. There were 188 passengers and 69 crewmembers onboard. The ship was immovably stuck and immediately listed 4.5 degrees. During the night and the day after, the crew unsuccessfully attempted to free the ship. Immediately after the grounding, the Canadian coastguard launched a rescue mission. However, the closest rescue vessel, the Canadian icebreaker *Amundsen*, was in the Beaufort Sea, more than 500 kilometres from the scene of the accident. Not until Sunday, two days after the accident, did *Amundsen* arrive in the late afternoon. On the same night, all passengers were evacuated. A disaster was averted, but the local news agency Nunatsiaq Online reported that several of the waterproof sections of the *Clipper Adventurer* were perforated. Later, experts from the University of New Brunswick reported how the reef in the Coronation Gulf was not as unknown and uncharted as the accident suggested. The position of this subsea obstacle had been announced in a 'Notice to Shipping' from the Canadian coastguard. However, the cliff was apparently not to be found on the nautical chart according to which the *Clipper Adventurer* navigated, most likely since the crew had not bothered to update its nautical charts.

The prospect of a catastrophic wreck torments politicians and naval officers all over the Arctic. In May 2008, when the ministers from the five Arctic coastal states met in Ilulissat, search and rescue was high on the agenda. Danish foreign minister Per Stig Møller reminded those assembled of the *Titanic*, which during its maiden voyage to New York in 1912 sank in the North Atlantic in only two hours and 40 minutes. *Titanic* was lost south of Newfoundland after colliding with an iceberg from Greenland. There were 2,223 people onboard – or approximately the same number as on the biggest of the cruise ships gathered in the fjords of Greenland today. A total of 1,571 people lost their lives.

Seventy-two degrees north. In King Oscar Fjord. From the deck of *Ejnar Mikkelsen*, East Greenland looks immensely picturesque. For more than a week, the ship sails under a close-woven gauze of clouds and fog banks. Then, one early morning the sun engulfs everything. The snow on the rocks along the coast shines, not a ripple disturbs the surface of the fjord and a bit later, out on the open sea, the stern cuts through perfectly still water. Here the touristy illusion of untouched nature still has meaning even if decision makers in Nuuk have divided the ocean in the north east Greenlandic region in oil-containing parcels. In 2010, in these extremely icy waters oil extraction is still only a vision of the far future. The reflection of the sun is blinding. The navigator on the bridge sticks closely to his nautical charts with markings from previous naval voyages. Large areas of the ocean are only marked as white voids on the nautical chart: uncharted waters. The crew talks about the risk of reefs.

Suddenly, on the starboard side, eight ringed seals appear to study this whale of steel. Like toys in a bathtub, they jump away from the ship, but for a long sunlit moment they can be followed with a pair of binoculars.

Then, for the first time since Iceland, *Ejnar Mikkelsen* meets another ship. A cruise ship, the *Expedition*, appears in Kejser Franz Joseph Fjord. The passengers onboard can be seen from *Ejnar Mikkelsen* and our naval ship politely stays in the wake of the cruise ship. Over the radio, the officer on duty communicates with the captain from the *Expedition*. There are 135 passengers and 53 crewmembers onboard.

The meeting is far from random. With an electronic signal, like any other ship in Greenland, the *Expedition* must report every six hours to the headquarters of the Danish navy in Nuuk. *Ejnar Mikkelsen* constantly knows where the cruise ship is located and the meeting serves several purposes. The cruise ship gets to see that the Danish navy keeps an eye on traffic and that search and rescue capacity is at hand. It provides respect and prevents illegal landings without polar bear rifles, illegal weapons, illegal hunting and other violations. But the naval officers also calculate that the tourists on the cruise ship will take a great number of pictures, and that photos of the *Ejnar Mikkelsen* and a swaying Danish flag will be uploaded to Facebook and the rest of the internet. The whole world will learn that Danish naval ships are in attendance here.

A few days later, *Ejnar Mikkelsen* meets the Norwegian cruise ship the *Fram*. The ship is named after the ship used by the Norwegian polar explorer and diplomat Fridtjof Nansen on his legendary expedition in the Arctic Ocean. The captain invites us for a tour of the lounge with an electric fireplace, and the steaming outdoor jacuzzis. Four rubber boats carry passengers to and from the coast for sightseeing. The best cabins with private balconies cost roughly 100,000 Norwegian kroner apiece (some 12,400 USD) for the ten-day cruise and the trip is sold out.

Seventy-four degrees north. At around eight in the morning, *Ejnar Mikkelsen* drops anchor outside Daneborg on Greenland's east coast. From inside the ship, the small and speedy operation vessel *Naja* is launched. Admiral Kudsk and a small group of people are put to shore. The 12 young soldiers from the navy's Sirius Patrol, which has its headquarters by Daneborg, have invited us for breakfast. Pancakes and rice porridge.

The life of the Sirius Patrol consists of sled rides, snow, frost, and constant challenges. But one has to view the Sirius Patrol in its historical context to understand its true nature. More than 400 years has passed since the Danish King Christian IV sent the first Danish naval ships to Greenland. Every winter, dogs and men carrying the Danish flag on the sleds patrol the desolated fjords and snow-covered landscapes in northern Greenland as a direct extension of the naval ships from the sixteenth century to today. Climate change means that the oceans are open still further north, but the northern-most part of Greenland remains trapped by ice. The ships cannot reach this far, which is why the dog sleds must claim sovereignty.

The small dog sled patrol is tremendously popular in Denmark. In August 2012, when the Danish Prime Minister Helle Thorning-Smith went on her first official visit to Greenland, she chose to visit these 12 men in Daneborg before she did anything else. This was considered an insult by the Greenlandic politicians in Nuuk but she stuck by her wish.

The 12 young men of the Sirius Patrol, wearing green sweaters with logos of a sled dog, work on two-year contracts. They build their own dog sleds and breed their own dogs. They learn how to defend themselves against polar bears and how to survive in the cold. During winter half-year, they patrol the northern-most part of Greenland from Hall Land, north of Thule, down to Illoqqortoormiut on the east coast. This extensive wilderness forms the biggest national park in the world. It is uninhabited, not easily accessible and often struck by storms and harsh weather.

Every year in March, two men and one dog team are flown from Daneborg to Hall Land by the western outer edge of the national park, a bit north of Thule Air Base. From here, by secret routes in and out of the fjords on the north tip of Greenland, they pass the military landing strip at Station North and finally take the long stretch down to Daneborg, where they will arrive in the beginning of June. A trip of approximately 3,000 kilometres. Another sled team goes from Apollo Lake close to Cape Morris Jessup at the top of Greenland to Daneborg. This is almost as far. The rest of the team conducts month-long patrols up and down Greenland's east coast.

First and foremost, the task of the 12 men is to show the flag – to be physically, perceptibly and visibly present. They must make sure that Denmark, as a nation and ruler, is perceived as authoritative and as effectively present as possible in the frozen wilderness. Their rifles and guns may only protect them against polar bears. But in the eyes of the Danish defence forces, they represent the fundamental rights of the Danish Kingdom to the immense territory. As the chief of the Royal Danish Defence College, Nils Wang, told me, 'Claim of sovereignty is a continuous process where we constantly claim the right to be an independent nation and in this case, a Realm. If suddenly, after 400 years, we are no longer present, eventually we will notice – not the day after or even a month after, but over time – that others start to ask the question: Who actually owns this place? Who has the right to this area?'

Stories of heroism in service of the nation play a central role with the Sirius Patrol. Every day the 12 men in the dog patrol pass by the grave of Eli Knudsen. At the age of 29 he was killed by the Nazis in eastern Greenland in 1943. The writing on his grave is straightforward: 'Eli Knudsen – Corporal in the Sled

Patrol – Fallen for his country – The Prime Minister's Office placed this memorial.'

After the German occupation of Denmark in 1940, it soon became clear that the east coast of Greenland was important to the war in Europe. While Hitler's troops moved further east and into the Soviet Union, it became crucial for the allies to provide weapons for the Russians. Heavily loaded convoys sailed from English harbours through the North Sea, around the North Cape and to the Russian Arctic harbour in Murmansk. The German navy brought submarines, warships and planes to stop these convoys.

In this situation, weather reports from eastern Greenland became crucial. Along the east coast of Greenland three Danish meteorological stations routinely produced weather reports for the North Atlantic and once they started transmitting in code, Germany had a problem. For this reason, in August 1942, 18 German soldiers, meteorologists and radio operators sailed from Kiel in Germany on the trawler *Sachsen* and only a few weeks later set up a weather station in eastern Greenland at 75 degrees north. The Germans built two cabins, which were quickly covered with snow, and *Sachsen* was covered with white camouflage nets. The German meteorologists sent weather reports three times a day and there was very little to threaten them. The closest Allies were far away in Iceland and Greenland's east coast was practically uninhabited.

In Nuuk on Greenland's west coast, Eske Bruun, the Danish chief administrative officer, was the Danish top authority in Greenland. The US Army asked Eske Bruun to gather the entire population of North East Greenland – 26 hunters and radio people – in Scoresbysund (Ittoqqortoormiit). They expected that if the coast were cleared it would be easier to find the enemy. Then Eske Bruun had his idea: He sent a telegram to Scoresbysund (Ittoqqortoormiit) and named the 15 men who volunteered 'The sled patrol of north east Greenland'.

This was the start of several clashes with the Germans. The sled patrol made it difficult for the Germans to operate and on 3 June 1944, after American bombardments, a German transport plane picked up the last German soldiers, records and instruments.

Seventy-three degrees north – early afternoon. Wherever the *Ejnar Mikkelsen* ventures, names on the nautical chart are a constant reminder that previously, Danish ships were certainly not the only ones to explore this part of Greenland. Our ship anchors in Myggbukta – Norwegian for Danish Myggebugten (Mosquito Bay). Other locations en route carry names such as Hansa Bay, Sabine Island, Wollaston Foreland, Emperor Franz Joseph Fjord, King Wilhelm's Land, Scoresby Land, Clavering Island, Cape Philip Broke. British naval vessels sailed here in the eighteenth century; through time, German, French, Swedish and Norwegian expeditions and whale catchers have all defied the ice, storms and great distances to explore, map, search and earn money.

Only a single time have the intruding Europeans met resident Greenlanders north of Illoqqortoormiut and told of it. In 1823, British captain D.C. Clavering anchored in Dead Man's Bay on the southern side of Shannon Island; here he met a small group of Inuit, whom he welcomed onboard. The visit went well until Clavering demonstrated his firepower and fired a rifle. The guests silently observed the demonstration, kindly bid their farewells, and went back to shore. Afterwards, no polar expeditioners of that time encountered indigenous inhabitants on the coast. In numerous locations all the way up to northern-most Greenland, evidence can be found of early Inuit settlements, but Clavering must have met some of the last early indigenous inhabitants. The European pioneers were alone and they could freely name islands, waters and mountain ranges as they saw fit. For a long time, they merely chose the names of patrons and royal supporters, or simply named places after themselves. It was not until the Europeans began to settle down that they started to name places according to their features, such as Mosquito Bay. In the 1920s, a group of four or five Norwegian hunters settled here, and it was from Mosquito Bay that the Norwegians in 1931, with a historical salute, declared the entire passable part of Greenland's north east coast to be Norwegian territory.

The black and red cabin built by the Norwegians in 1922 can still be found in Mosquito Bay. The cabin is the only in two stories on north east Greenland's coast, and it soon operated as a wireless telegraph station with connection to Norway and for all Norwegian whalers on the coast. The hunters built more than 80 cabins along the coastline and rarely had more than a day's travel on dog sled to the nearest shelter. A photograph of a merry Christmas Eve in 1926 still hangs on the wall in the living room in Mosquito Bay. Four of the young trappers, including the energetic Hallvard Devold, all dressed in rough shirt sleeves, are smiling to the photographer.

Hallvard Devold knew his Greenland history. He knew that Norwegian-Icelandic outlaws were the first Europeans to settle in Greenland around the year 900 and that they remained and prospered in Greenland for more than 400 years before they disappeared again – for still unexplained reasons.

Hans Egede, who brought Christianity to Greenland in 1721, was born in Bergen in Norway at a time when Norway and Denmark still formed a united kingdom. Following the Napoleonic wars and the Treaty of Kiel in 1814, Greenland, the Faroe Islands and Iceland remained part of the Danish Kingdom despite Denmark being on the losing side. A defeated and bankrupt Denmark grudgingly had to cede all of Norway to Sweden; the islands in the North Atlantic could have shared the same fate, but Denmark's sovereignty over Greenland, Iceland and the Faroe Islands was established in a parenthesis, most probably through British intervention. But to Hallvard Devold in Mosquito Bay and influential politicians in Oslo in the 1920s this did not constitute the end of the story. They did not accept that Denmark had the right to the uninhabited north east Greenland. In 1931, the dispute culminated, and Norway claimed that all areas outside the small Danish settlements were *terra nullius* – no man's land – and that north east Greenland in particular was not part of the Danish domain. On Sunday 28 June 1931, Hallvard Devold sent a telegram from north east Greenland to the newspapers in Norway: 'Today, in Mosquito Bay, the Norwegian flag has been hoisted. The area between Carlsberg Fjord to the south and Bessel Fjord to the north has been occupied in the name of His Majesty King Haakon. We have named the land Erik the Red's Land.' In New Norwegian, it was Eirik Raudes Land. Decades of diplomatic waffle had been replaced by open dispute.

In Oslo, the Norwegian government made the trappers' occupation their official policy. Norway made a formal claim to almost the entire accessible part of East Greenland's coast north of Scoresbysund (Ittoqqortoormiit). It was Norway's intention to own all deep fjords and the big mountain ranges stretching long leagues across the coast. In Copenhagen a feeling of shock prevailed: If Norway succeeded in winning such great parts of East Greenland, the notion of Greenland being under Danish sovereignty would no longer make sense. Other nations would immediately look upon Greenland and its affiliation with Denmark with new eyes – especially the United States. The Danish government was well aware of the view of the United States that Greenland was a strategic part of North America. In 1886, the American State Department sent people to Greenland to assess whether the island was worth buying. The United States' Secretary of State in the 1860s, William Seward, was very interested in taking over Greenland. It was solely because he had already spent seven million dollars to acquire Alaska from the Russian tsar in 1867 that the American Congress put its foot down. Since then, Washington long harboured a dormant desire to buy Greenland. In 1917, the United States bought the Danish West Indies (US Virgin Islands) in the Caribbean for 25 million dollars, so why not get Greenland as well? The thought re-surfaced during and after World War II, and in 1960 when Danish King Frederik IX met with American President Dwight D. Eisenhower in Washington, the president brought up the idea of buying Greenland again.

In 1931, the Danish government immediately took the Norwegian occupation to the International Court of Justice in The Hague. The government in Copenhagen presented the Court with excessive material to prove that Denmark for more than 350 years had defended and sustained its sovereignty of all of Greenland – not simply the inhabited colonies on the west coast. On 5 April 1933, in The Hague, the ruling was announced. There was no hesitation. The Court ruled that the sovereignty of all Greenland belonged to Denmark. In their written statement, the judges described how Danish kings, the Danish state, Danish scientists, Danish explorers and the Danish navy had made their mark in Greenland.

In 2010, as *Ejnar Mikkelsen* carefully sails towards Ella Island, the navigator spots a polar bear. Agile, muscular and a tad nervous, it turns its head and faces the ship. On this island, the bears claim sovereignty and two musk oxen are seen parading around the buildings as its guests. Not until a small team from *Ejnar Mikkelsen* has reached land and a soldier has fired his signal pistol do the bear and oxen leave. A quick inspection shows that the bear has trashed its way into a small warehouse and destroyed the wooden door to the loo outside. The old cabin of polar scientist Lauge Koch, Eagle's Nest, built in 1931 farthest up the hill, has only suffered a broken outer door.

Lauge Koch's crude dining table and spindle back chairs are still in Eagle's Nest, and on the windowsill is Koch's key with a nametag on it. In the short alcoves are thick, coarse mattresses. Enthusiastic volunteers maintain Eagle's Nest as well as other cabins along the east coast, and there are plenty of supplies of canned wiener pot and small bags of washing powder. A guest book lies on the table. Its records show that cruise ships such as the *Clipper Adventurer*, *Alexey Maryshev*, *Kaliningrad*, *Khlebnikov* and *Polar Star* have stopped by. A cheerful person has put up a handmade sign in the window: 'All major credit cards accepted', but ordinarily it is very quiet here. Behind the building in the red summer heath are fresh polar bear turds. The marine traffic is increasing, but change does not happen here from one day to the next.

A few days later, just before September turns into October in 2010, *Ejnar Mikkelsen*'s expedition to East Greenland is over.

At daybreak after two days' sailing south, the first pale lights from the Grötta Lighthouse outside Reykjavik can be seen. It has been a warm night; the weather no longer smells of the high Arctic. Shortly before we reach harbour, an Icelandic harbour pilot comes aboard and the navy's swallow-tailed flag is attached to the stern. In the navy, the Danish flag, Dannebrog, is never forgotten.

4

THE KINGDOM REACHES FOR THE NORTH POLE

In this chapter Denmark and Greenland prepare to claim huge tracts of seabed in the Arctic Ocean all the way past the North Pole to Russian waters. This move will have global consequences and yet the reasoning remains unclear. What exactly do Denmark and Greenland hope to gain? In the summer of 2012, I travel with Danish scientists for seven weeks into the polar ice to the North Pole onboard a Swedish icebreaker. The scientists collect data to prove Denmark's and Greenland's ownership of the seabed, a claim that was soon to be directly contested by Russia and which will most likely also be in conflict with Canada's upcoming claim. In addition, it clashes with a set of Chinese concepts, prevalent at the time, that describes the central sectors of the Arctic Ocean as parts of a global commons. The following is a personal account of this unique voyage to the North Pole.

* * *

On 31 July 2012, the LOMROG III expedition sets sail. The expedition is the last of three in a grand Danish project to ensure that enormous areas of seabed in the North Atlantic Sea and the Arctic Ocean fall into Danish hands. The project – the Continental Shelf Project – has been created by the country's top leaders in Copenhagen.

We set out as planned from Longyearbyen on Svalbard at 78 degrees north, but already at a quarter past three, shortly after take-off, the expedition leader, Christian Marcussen, alters the programme. He postpones his take-off briefing. The sparkling sun and the broad-nosed northern fulmars over Isfjorden have rendered the departure from Longyearbyen so spectacular that no one wants to miss it. Pointed mountains on both sides of the fjord create sharp silhouettes against the sky; the briefing simply has to wait. Such is the nature of this expedition – a constant interplay between science and the more intangible Arctic wonders.

The icebreaker's colossal diesel engines push the 107-metre-long ship towards the Arctic Ocean. With her double hull, helicopter platform, and 24,500 hp, the *Oden* is Scandinavia's most powerful icebreaker and has completed a number of polar expeditions. Everything is set and the *Oden* carries one of the Danish government's central Arctic ambitions. In addition to Captain Erik Andersson and his crew, the icebreaker is home to 17 Danish scientists and technicians from Denmark's and Greenland's so-called Continental Shelf Project. They are the core of this expedition; they are the ones who will secure the expansion of the Danish Kingdom far into the northern-most reaches of the Arctic.

The project was never up for political discussion in the Danish parliament. No one outside the project's own inner circle has been encouraged to inspire unnecessary curiosity or debate. Since its early initiation in 2000, the project has lived a protected life. The people behind it know that they have created a venture likely to bring the Kingdom in conflict with several other states including Russia, Norway, Iceland and Canada, so discretion and constant vigilance is paramount. Top people have kept the project in the government's innermost circle and now it is time for its completion. The scientists aboard are to bring about the expansion of Denmark's geography by hundreds of thousands of square kilometres. They are to consolidate and expand Denmark's influence over the Arctic Ocean. The Danish Kingdom has a chance of winning the right to the seabed and everything that should lie beneath – oil, gas and minerals – as well as the power to regulate any activity that could threaten the environment. If the expedition leads to the wanted result, the right to the seabed on the geographical North Pole itself, which represents the essence of humanity's conception and myths of the Polar world, will fall to the Danish Kingdom.

Physically, the North Pole in many respects is not very spectacular. There is no permanent land, nothing but sea and ice, but few other parts of the globe have fascinated man so intensely. And now the North Pole's most tangible element, the seabed, is to be Danish. The expedition merges with Per Stig Møller's political construction from Ilulissat to boost Denmark's stature in the Arctic, and reflects also on Danish polar explorer Knud Rasmussen's legendary sled journeys from Greenland and all across the vast expanse of Northern Canada to the Bering Strait in the early part of the twentieth century. The science of today is of course different; we have moved forward in time, but once again the ambitions of science and those of the Danish Kingdom converge in a forceful initiative with global effects.

Almost 30 sea ice researchers, genetic researchers, meteorologists, climatologists from Danish and Swedish projects, and a television crew from Denmark have been allotted seats on the *Oden*. The entire population onboard totals 66 men and women, but everyone knows that it is the collection of evidence for Denmark and Greenland that is the expedition's main purpose.

A dozen containers with computer equipment, seismic measurement tools, cables, microwave radiometers and coffee machines are fixed to the deck. Hundreds of cardboard boxes with gravimeters, plankton nets, bilge pumps, infrared cameras, bacteria filters, ice drills and electronic buoys are lashed in corners and cracks. Ahead is 45 days in the Arctic Ocean. The scientists will be in constant battle with the polar ice to retrieve data from the ocean floor some 4,000 metres down the Amundsen Basin north east of Greenland and from the massive underwater mountain range known as the Lomonosov Ridge, which runs from Greenland past the North Pole to Siberia.

If successful, the scientists will secure Denmark's geographical expansion and their efforts will enter the history books. They will be some of the first scientists ever to evoke detailed descriptions of the almost 3,000-metre-high subsea mountaintops rising from the bottom of the Arctic Ocean. They will develop new methods to measure the ocean floor under extreme conditions, and they will contribute to understanding of climate change in the Arctic. Expedition leader Christian Marcussen works for the Geological Survey of Denmark and Greenland (GEUS). For almost ten years, he has managed Denmark's collection of data off Greenland's coasts, aimed at securing the Danish Realm's expansion north of Greenland as well as in the Denmark Strait off north east Greenland and in the ocean in southern Greenland. The rest of the team on the *Oden* consist of geologists, technicians, geophysicists and three geology students from Aarhus University. Christian Marcussen has carefully calibrated the route so that the data collected will supplement the results from the two previous LOMROG expeditions. In the end, the gathering of proof must fulfil the UN's documentation requirements or the UN's experts will reject the claims of the Danish Kingdom as unfounded. Every scrap of data the scientists collect from the seabed, every measurement of the layers of sediment, every image of the subsea mountain ranges, every record of salinity and temperature are to prove that the bedrock of Greenland extends into the Arctic Ocean exactly as far as Denmark and Greenland claim. Time is of the essence. Denmark and Greenland have until December 2014 to submit their claim and prove its validity.

This time the entire nation follows the whereabouts of the scientists. This is new. During previous expeditions in 2007 and 2009, the scientists left almost completely unnoticed – only the seagulls followed. But the interest in the Arctic has exploded. In 2012, politicians, military analysts, top business people and the sharpest government officials all understand that the Arctic is the new focal point. An expansion of the Danish Realm's domain in the Arctic Ocean can have vital economic and political importance.

The expansion will provide Denmark as a nation with additional international gravity. The ability of the Danish scientists, politicians and diplomats to cope with the built-in potential conflicts of interests with Russia, Canada, the United States, and China will add positively to the respect surrounding Denmark. And then there is Greenpeace. While the scientists take in the views of Isfjorden, a press release is published by the environmentalists: 'Currently, the area surrounding the North Pole does not belong to anyone, but everyone. And so it should stay. If individual countries are allowed to claim the North Pole we risk that this unique natural area will become subject to damaging oil drillings and commercial fishing [...] Greenpeace is not criticizing science, but scientists who are participating have a personal responsibility. They should consider to what extent this unique area should be protected or whether it should be opened for exploitation and destruction.'

Greenpeace keeps probing into the global controversy: Who owns the Arctic Ocean? For thousands of years, the ice made the ocean impassable – but the ice is disappearing. Should the ocean be opened to oil drilling and other such activities? Or should it be protected as a natural park, a sanctuary for the whole world to cherish and enjoy? Can one own the North Pole? Onboard the *Oden* such political questions are not on the agenda and Greenpeace's greeting is not welcome. The scientists are engaged in keen conversation about the ice and climate change, the shape of the ocean floor, the thickness of the sediments, reference lines and geographical coordinates. They know everything about the life of the algae in the ocean's almost uninhabitable environment and they operate almost as scientific law enforcement on orders from the Danish government. But they do not talk politics.

On the first day, a feeling of unconcerned ease embraces the expedition. Preparation and planning is forgotten; the expedition is alive! Christian Marcussen walks the massive ship. He got up before five in order to ensure that crew and scientists merge without complications. The 66 people onboard need to eat, work, and live together in the polar ice without any landfall for the next seven weeks and Christian Marcussen leaves nothing to chance. Even a missing suitcase is important; one of the scientists lost clothing and gear in an airport on the way and Christian Marcussen lets the entire expedition wait until the suitcase arrives. On the first night, rock music and laughter can be heard from the *Oden's* bar.

Eighty-one degrees north, Expedition Day 2, at the edge of the polar ice. The polar bear majestically pushes forward in the water between the ice floes right in front of the *Oden*. The icebreaker has reached the first sharp floes of the polar ice just before midday, and suddenly some of the scientists see the polar bear crossing the path of the ship mere metres ahead. For a second, the ship's broad stem threatens to push the animal under water to a certain death, but luckily the bear escapes on the port side. For a brief moment, it looks back and eyes its audience on the ship's railing. Somewhat dumbfounded, the scientists all watch the bear's escape. Polar bears are frequent visitors at the edge of the polar ice where seals and other prey are plentiful, but while many of the passengers have hoped to see polar bears here, the experience is somewhat tainted. The realization that the ship almost caused the bear's death is a painful reminder that they themselves may be frontrunners for an increased amount of people, oil vessels and irreversible activity in this part of the Arctic.

The name of the expedition, LOMROG III, covers its very substance. 'LOMR' refers to the Lomonosov Ridge, the sub-sea mountain range which goes all the way from Greenland past the North Pole to Siberia. The letters 'OG' stand for 'Off Greenland'. The geology of the Lomonosov Ridge is decisive in determining who wins the right to the central parts of the ocean floor below the Arctic Ocean.

Eighty-four degrees north. Expedition Day 4, early morning. Ahead of the *Oden*, the ice now seems almost endless. It is only parted by the narrow cracks that the ship's officer is on the lookout for. The thermometer shows 0.2°C. The ship's internal information screen tells us that during the past 24 hours, we have pushed our way through the ice with an average speed of four knots (approx. seven kilometres per hour). On a regular basis, the icebreaker has to stop simply because the ice is too thick. When this happens, it reverses, gathers speed, shoots forward again and pushes its way into the reluctant piece of ice, which is eventually crushed and subdued. The shaking from these constant collisions with the ice can be felt through the ship so that cups, spoons, and all other goods are rattling. The scientists onboard live in a permanent rumbling noise.

In the polar ice, the *Oden* transforms into a heavy, crunching warrior. The stern does not have a protruding nose, no nifty forward-pointing profile like other ships. Instead, the *Oden* meets the ice with a 31-metre broad wall of hardened steel. This square steel front leans inwards below the water's surface so that the *Oden*, when moving, either forces its opponent aside or below the hull. From the railing just behind the stem, the passengers can look into the inferno of turbulent water and destroyed ice floes. Metre-thick blocks of white or blue ice shoot up close to the icebreaker's sides, hour after hour.

Such is the way of the *Oden*'s advance – at times incredibly slow, but seldom slower than Christian Marcussen anticipated. Delays are unwanted. They may cause vital data not to be collected and in the end, the UN's experts may find that Russia or Canada present better data. The scientific proof could decide how far into the ocean the Danish Realm will stretch in the future. In the enormous waters known as the Amundsen Basin (after the Norwegian polar explorer Roald Amundsen) the scientists are to measure the thickness of the ocean floor's sediments. According to UN law, the thickness of the mud layers below the ocean floor's top layer may decide to what extent the ocean floor and everything below it belongs to the Danish Realm.

Eighty-six degrees north. Expedition Day 7, 5 August 2012, in the polar ice above the Amundsen Basin. Per Trinhammer, the expedition's technical expert, dons helmet, survival suit, safety shoes, thick gloves and a headset. At the quarterdeck, he and a handful of other technicians and scientists are getting ready to ease sensitive seismic instruments into the wake of the icebreaker. During the previous night, the *Oden* finally reached the first ocean location from where Denmark and Greenland need data. Per Trinhammer knows the polar ice; one wrong move can result in the loss of equipment worth hundreds of thousands of Danish kroner. Following bitter experience from the first LOMROG expedition in 2007, the entire concept has been revised. Instead of simply ploughing through the ice with Per Trinhammer's equipment in the wake, the ship has created a channel free of ice during the night by sailing backwards and forwards; the scientists need this to collect data. Ten precious hours of sailing time have been used, but the icebreaker has created a more or less open channel of 25 nautical miles, so that Per Trinhammer's equipment has a better chance of surviving. Just after 14:00 everything is ready. Two men wearing safety vests and safety belts as well as ropes around their waists crawl onto the outermost open platform behind the quarterdeck directly facing the polar ocean. They are to guide the seismic equipment on its last metres into the ocean and secure it when it resurfaces. From the quarterdeck, one of the Swedish crewmembers controls a six-metre-high metal barrier called the A-frame, which lifts the equipment from the deck. Per Trinhammer controls the three powerful winches. With a remote control on his hip, he releases 300 metres of so-called seismic streamer. The thick plastic cable full of cords and microphones slowly winds its way into the ocean.

Instantly, something goes wrong. From the deck, the streamer cable is clearly visible – like a many-coloured snake just below the surface. That is not how it is supposed to be. A sinker and a sea anchor are not taking the cable deeper as planned, and the heavy ice floes that are pushed into dangerous commotion by the progress of the icebreaker are threatening to destroy the cable. Per Trinhammer tears at his phone. He is in constant contact with Christian Marcussen; a solution must be found instantly before the ice crushes the valuable cable.

Suddenly, a piece of the cable is seen on top of an ice floe behind the *Oden*. An ice tongue has pressed its way under the cable and forced it up on the ice itself. The risk of significant losses is impending, and Per Trinhammer makes a decision: The cable must be hoisted back up long before it has revealed any results. Annoying as it may be, it is inevitable. Time is limited and ocean floor data from this particular geographical point is crucial, but it is no good if the cable breaks.

An hour later, the cable can be re-released into the frigid ocean. Per Trinhammer has wrapped a plate of lead around the outermost tip of the cable, causing it to finally dive to the wished depth. Per Trinhammer guides the next piece of equipment, two air cannons adjoined into a cylinder-shaped construction weighing about 200 kilograms, up into the winch and steers it towards the two guides placed on the open platform. The air cannon, resembling a deformed diving cylinder, is slowly released into the ice.

Suddenly everything jerks. The air cannon hangs on a steel wire and is abruptly tugged through the air by the enormous powers of the *Oden*'s winch. For a brief moment, one of the men on the platform seems to lose his balance – for a brief second he is about to slip into the crushing ice – but he manages to regain his equilibrium.

Per Trinhammer and his colleagues retreat to their blue container on the foredeck – it is packed with computers, measuring equipment, and big monitors. From a compressor on the quarterdeck, Per Trinhammer can fill up the one-and-a-half-metre-long air cannon through a thick orange hose in the water, meaning that the pressure is 100 times higher than the pressure you will find in regular car tyres. Every 14 seconds they release the air pressure in the cannons placed under water, which causes a deafening bang. The sound is swallowed by the water, but the pressure is felt as dull pulsations throughout the entire hull. In a few seconds, the sound waves spread down into the 4,000-metre deep ocean. From here, the sediments of sand, silt, and dead algae on the bottom throw back the sound to the microphones in Per Trinhammer's seismic streamer.

The microphones send messages to the computers in the blue container and almost simultaneously, a picture of the ocean floor's various layers is created on the screen. According to the United Nations Convention on the Law of the Sea, the thickness of these layers may decide how far into the ocean Denmark and Greenland can claim the ocean floor.

For a while, Per Trinhammer's ingenious system works, but then new problems occur. The people on the quarterdeck laboriously replace the entire seismic streamer with a new one. Not until 3:00 in the morning does data again flow steadily. The following morning, a very tired Christian Marcussen examines a metre-long paper slip with fresh data and evidence. Vital data from other locations is yet to be collected, but Per Trinhammer's equipment has found thick sediments of clay, sand, and silt on top of the bedrock itself below sea. This is good news for Denmark and Greenland's claim to the UN.

Eighty-seven degrees north. Expedition Day 8, 7 August 2012, still above the Amundsen Basin. Farther to the west, Canadian scientists have mapped the ocean floor in the same way as Christian Marcussen and his colleagues, and Russian scientists onboard nuclear icebreakers, are gathering data in the ocean as well.

Christian Marcussen thinks that the idea of rich oil strikes in the central parts of the Arctic Ocean lacks scientific support entirely. He is especially aggravated when reporters link prophesies of oil at the North Pole with the non-present borders on the ocean floor, and conclude that military conflicts are likely. When he gives lectures, he stresses that the geological data all seem to indicate that oil must be found elsewhere in the Arctic. The predictions all point to waters closer to the United States, Russia, Canada, Norway or Greenland – areas where legal ownership has been settled a long time ago. More than 95 per cent of the oil which the geologists have pointed to in the Arctic is within the settled borders of the Arctic states.

Simultaneously, however, Christian Marcussen also recognizes that the existing knowledge of the ocean floor in the middle of the ocean is very limited. One of the most extensive studies was published in 2011 in *Arctic Petroleum Geology* by four American geologists affiliated with the United States Geological Studies. They confirmed that a part of the Lomonosov Ridge's geology resembles the underground in the oil-rich Barents Sea close to Norway as well as the oil-rich underground north of Siberia. In fact, the Lomonosov Ridge was probably connected with the ocean floor closer to Norway and northern Russia until millions of years ago, when massive cracks in the Earth's crust began to push Greenland and parts of the ocean floor beneath the current Arctic Ocean farther to the west – a process which continues to this day. The four experts pointed out that theoretically, oil pockets in the Lomonosov Ridge could have survived this move. They find 'a low to moderate accumulation probability' within the Lomonosov Ridge's slopes, while the prospect of finding oil in the flat ocean floor on both sides of the ridge is so low that they do not carry out an actual analysis. The scientists underline that new data could change prospects, but in general, they are not setting the stage for an oil adventure.

However, in 2012, another possible gain must be considered as well. Whether Russia, Denmark, or Canada obtains the rights to the ocean floor at 90 degrees north, the winner will be closer to 'owning the North Pole' than any other nation has ever been before. For the legal drawing of borders on the ocean floor, the actual North Pole carries no weight, but its cultural and symbolic value is difficult to overestimate. In the beginning of the nineteenth century, the American explorer Robert Peary dedicated his life to conquering the North Pole. Russian pilots were the first to reach the North Pole in 1948, several Danes have given it a try and with the spectacular submarine dive in 2007, Artur Tjilingarov illustrated the deep layers of importance which the North Pole continues to possess.

Onboard the *Oden*, Christian Marcussen will not say whether the expedition will reach the North Pole itself. The Danish scientists are not planning any scientific measurements there. No scientific data is to be added to Denmark and

Greenland's claim from 90 degrees north. Christian Marcussen knows that every hour with the Swedish icebreaker costs money, and that every second must be used to expand the size of the Realm – but he also knows that many of his people onboard are eager to reach the Pole.

Meanwhile, the helicopter drops a couple of scientists on the ice, 17 kilometres from the icebreaker. The fog blocks any view of our icebreaker and leaves behind an almost unnatural silence. Not even the faintest wind can be felt and from the west, new fog banks approach. The moisture in the air is heavy over a mosaic of light green glacial lakes on the ice and the darker furrows between the ice floes. For a moment, isolation is all we can feel. The nearest populated point is Station Nord of the Danish navy, 700 kilometres south west in north east Greenland. Towards the north west, the North Pole looms less than 350 kilometres away. Peary, Scott, Nansen and Johansen, Andreé, Højgaard, Cagni, Wellman, Sedov and all the others risked their lives fighting through these ice masses on their way to the Pole. And just as we do now, they too may have grabbed a cup and drunk from the glacial lakes' unfrozen water on top of layers of ice.

With a specially designed ice drill the scientists collect a round, oblong chunk of ice from the ice floe on which they stand. One end of the chunk consists of ice from the bottom of the ice floe, on which algae from the Arctic Ocean live: crumbled yellow-brown small creatures. The scientists are studying how climate changes affect the living conditions of these algae. The algae are food for plankton, which the fish feed on. The seals eat the fish. The seals are eaten by the polar bears. Without algae this chain will break. To the untrained eye, the ice may seem inanimate and barren. But the ice is the refrigerator from which life in the Arctic Ocean gets its nutrition. When the ice disappears, occurrence of algae shifts and the entire food chain is affected. The WWF (World Wide Fund for Nature), Greenpeace and many others are convinced that the search for oil and gas in this entire part of the world must be stopped, or at least placed under strict control until further knowledge has been gathered.

Onboard the icebreaker, opinions are divided. A young Danish geology student participating in the seismic measuring has no problem with oil drillings: 'I am proud to take part in this. I feel like a small part of history. At some point, when the ice has disappeared to such an extent that one can get here more easily, the technology will be so well-developed that we can make use of the oil in a responsible manner.'

Eighty-seven degrees north, Expedition Day 11, 10 August 2012, close to the Lomonosov Ridge. Most people onboard know the discussion concerning who owns what in the ocean surrounding the Lomonosov Ridge. The name alone suggests why Artur Tjilingarov and many other Russians believe that the preferential right of Russia is obvious. In the eighteenth century, the scientist, writer and poet Mikhail Vasilyevich Lomonosov became internationally known for his insights into the Arctic Ocean, polar ice, and the escape of the icebergs over the polar currents – 150 years before Fridtjof Nansen from Norway conducted his experiments on the ice. In Russia, Lomonosov is known as 'the Father of Science' and the country's biggest university, located in Moscow, which he founded, is named after him. As one of the first, Lomonosov broke away from the delusion of unknown land in the middle of the Arctic Ocean. In 1763, he constructed the first map of the ocean on which islands or land do *not* appear in the middle. Lomonosov created the foundation for a wave of Russian activism. In 1926, the Soviet leaders sent out a decree saying that any rock in the Arctic Ocean, from the coast of Siberia to the North Pole itself, was to be considered Soviet territory. Ivan Dmitrievich Papanin became a national hero in Russia in 1937 when he, with a team of scientist colleagues, flew to the North Pole as the start of a spectacular science expedition. With modern navigation equipment, Russia became the first country to prove that its envoys had been at the North Pole – on a mission directly encouraged by Stalin. In 2012, when the *Oden* moves us closer to the Pole, the North Pole has been visited 94 times by surface vessels. Of these, 83 have been Russian. The Russian boisterousness in the Arctic can seem intrusive to Danes, Norwegians or Canadians, but to many Russians it only confirms the long-established Russianness of the region. In June 2012, a group of scientists from the State University in Moscow even suggested that the Arctic Ocean be renamed the Russian Ocean. They believed that the long Russian coastal line towards the ocean and the proud Russian tradition for Arctic expeditions made this suggestion more than reasonable. Artur Tjilingarov does not talk to deaf ears when he says that 'the Arctic has always been Russian', but the Russian government has often confirmed that Russia will follow UN rules on all matters on borders in the Arctic, no matter how many flags are planted on the ocean floor and how many scientists demand that the ocean be renamed. Foreign Minister Sergej Lavrov has assured the world that the results of science will be decisive. Air cannons and seismic data will be deemed legitimate in the course of action, but no other types of weapons will be employed. In 2012, for the scientists onboard the *Oden*, this means that they are at the front line. Their data collection on the *Oden* will be key to the division of the Arctic Ocean.

Christian Marcussen knows all about this process, but onboard the icebreaker he refuses to voice any opinions. He knows well the difficulties Denmark might face if the wrong signals are sent from the icebreaker and decoded in the Arctic capitals. Christian Marcussen and the heads of the Russian, Canadian, Norwegian and American data collection meet on a regular basis, but they are aware that ultimately, it is the politicians who will have to deal with the final drawing of borders.

Eighty-seven degrees, forty-nine minutes north. Expedition Day 13, 12 August 2012, above the Lomonosov Ridge. The hope of seeing more bears grows. During their work on the ice, a few kilometres from the *Oden*, two of the scientists spot three ivory gulls. The chalk-white scavengers often follow the polar bears and eat their leftovers once a seal has been devoured. The scientists offer crackers and chocolate-covered toffees to the hungry birds.

Any encounter with living creatures has gained new significance after two weeks on the bleak polar ice. Two fulmars circle the ship and are closely studied. The birds resemble seagulls, but are of the albatross family; they are used to the enormous distances out here. On a sunny day, when the helicopter lowers a team onto the ice, the scientists spot a five-centimetre-long dead ice cod between two ice floes. The small fish hangs vertically with its head up as if it has frozen to death in the water column. They bring the fish to the surface and preserve it in spirit and display it on a shelf onboard. A dead ladybird from home likewise becomes the object of conversation. The few curious seals we see become sensations. As the Swedish writer Gunnar D. Hansson wrote on one of the previous expeditions:

> There, in the furrow, a seal!
> Way up here?
> Simply believe your eyes.
> It feels liberating.
> Something to attach meaning to.
> But which/what?

In the great desolation, Christian Marcussen and two experts from the Danish Cadastre in Copenhagen keep conjuring colourful electronic profiles of the submerged mountain range vertically under the *Oden*. Unlike Anatoly Sagalevitch in 2007, Christian Marcussen does not have submarines at his disposal. However, below the icebreaker, screwed into the actual body of the ship, is an oblong series of echo sounders intended for bathymetry, which make silhouettes of the ocean floor's shapes. The echo sounders are roughly one metre wide and continue through a great portion of the length of the *Oden*. If the ice cods look up, they will see something resembling a narrow bike path. The echo sounders send powerful sound signals through the ocean, where they hit the Lomonosov Ridge. The peaks and slopes of the mountains return the signals to a heavy set of computers with extra-large screens placed on the bridge just behind Captain Andersson. Peculiar, three-dimensional images of the submerged mountain ridge appear in strong colours.

This part of the job can also be challenged by the pack ice, but the hard-earned experiences from the first LOMROG expedition come in handy. Captain Andersson and his officers make the *Oden* dance in pirouettes above the Lomonosov Ridge. Despite its gravity, the icebreaker can turn itself around deftly while pushing away the ice. This makes the data collection successful despite the thick ice. Christian Marcussen must refrain from speeding up, as one would do on open sea. But as long as the images keep floating in, he is more than happy to settle for limited speed. The computers on the bridge accumulate millions of electronic signals from the flat ocean floor, from the base of the Lomonosov Ridge and farther up the steep mountainsides. On one of the first days over the Lomonosov Ridge, a simple, colourful image shows how the subsea mountains rise more than 1,500 metres over a distance of only five kilometres.

The scientists work in the middle of a paradox. The *Oden* fights its way forward with a speed that rarely exceeds six kilometres per hour, and often the icebreaker has to stop and reverse before it can move forward once again. The ice floes are thick and plentiful but the conversation onboard often turns to the disappearance of the ice. One afternoon, one of the oceanographers from the Danish Meteorological Institute (DMI) observes large amounts of 'dirty' ice. This ice has distinct brown smudges, revealing sand, dirt, and clay from the Siberian rivers Ob, Jenisej, Lena, Indigirka and others flowing from south to north in Russia. This dirty ice is less than two metres thick and must have been formed in the previous winter and travelled this far in one season only. The scientists conclude that the ice all the way to Siberia, more than 2,000 kilometres from *Oden*, must be thinner, younger, and more vulnerable than ever before.

These observations come on the heels of news which reached the expedition a couple of days earlier. While the icebreaker crawls northwards, space satellites above the ship determine that the expanse of sea ice in the Arctic Ocean has never in the history of satellite imagery been smaller than it is exactly now. A satellite photo is hung on the bulletin board amidships. North of Canada, Alaska and Siberia tremendous ocean areas are exposed. 2012 becomes a record year in the age of climate change.

Eighty-eight degrees and fourteen minutes north. Expedition Day 16, 15 August 2012, in the icy waters above the Lomonosov Ridge. For five hours during the night, the *Oden* travels through rough ice. One of the researchers has promising signs from the ocean floor. With a small echo sounder out on the ice a few nautical miles from the icebreaker, he has found indications of a previously unknown mountain beneath the water. If the mountain can be plotted onto a map it might mean that Denmark's and Greenland's claim to the ocean floor can be expanded by hundreds of square kilometres.

Christian Marcussen changes our itinerary. He juggles helicopter flights, *Oden*'s course, researchers' sleep and meal schedules, but it does not pay off. While the echo sounders under the hull listen to the ocean floor, the dream of a previously unknown mountain is turned into a modest hill on the computer screens and Marcussen returns to the original course.

Marcussen believes he will be able to support claims all the way to the other side of the North Pole. Others find the thought illusory. In 2009, Canadian law professor and Arctic expert Michael Byers presented a provoking thesis in his book *Who Owns the Arctic?* Firstly, he said, according to UN regulations Canada, Denmark and Russia could at most hope for the muddy ocean floor at the North Pole. 'The water and the sea-ice will remain part of the "high seas", meaning that ships and planes will be able to travel freely and tourists and adventurers from anywhere in the world will be able to visit without procuring passports or paying fees.'

Secondly, he foresaw that none of the three states would succeed in proving that the right to the ocean floor at the North Pole belongs to any of them. 'The Pole is unlikely to form part of any natural prolongation (of the landmasses) and will indeed fall within "the common heritage of mankind" – a technical term used to designate those deep ocean floor areas (collectively referred to as the "Area") which are beyond national jurisdiction and are administered by the UN.' Finally, he foresaw how no one would listen: 'Yet a great deal of money and effort will be spent trying to establish that the North Pole is part of one or another country's extended continental shelf, if only for reasons of nationalistic pride and domestic politics.'

Michael Byers carefully accounted for the relevant international law. First of all, Denmark, Russia and Canada must decide how extensive their claims will be (Norway is not claiming areas in proximity to the North Pole). The governments in Moscow, Ottawa and Copenhagen will then have to express their claims and document them with ocean floor data. The claims must be made to the UN Commission on the Limits of the Continental Shelf (CLCS), which is comprised of 21 geologists, bathymetry experts and experts in other fields. When the CLCS eventually gets to the claims from the Danish Kingdom, it will evaluate the scientific data: Is the evidence presented valid or are there faults and deficiencies? Have Christian Marcussen and his colleagues proven that the ocean floor of the Arctic Ocean is connected to Greenland to the extent that Denmark and Greenland claim? Not until this evaluation has been concluded will we know whether Denmark and Greenland have a valid claim to the ocean floor, and only then will direct negotiations with Russia and perhaps Canada begin. The CLCS will not decide where the borders on the seabed should be drawn. This will be a matter of direct negotiations between the relevant states.

Eighty-nine degrees north. Expedition Day 21, 20 August 2012, over the Lomonosov Ridge. On Monday 20 August, shortly after midnight, an icy polar wind is howling over the quarterdeck. For hours, technicians and researchers have struggled with 350 kilograms of iron cage while the *Oden* lies still in the pack ice. One side of the cage is fitted with jagged points surrounding its opening – just like the shovel on an excavator. With two powerful hoists, the researchers lower the cage into the sea from the quarterdeck while ice floes are kept away with gushing fire hoses and long steel rods. They lower the cage to a staggering depth of 3,500 metres and then slowly drag it up the steep slopes of the Lomonosov Ridge. The diesel engines of the *Oden* are turned off. The iron cage is dragged by the wind and the ocean currents.

After a few hours, the cage is recovered. In his survival suit, Christian Marcussen strenuously oversees the slow hoisting from a landing slightly elevated above the quarterdeck. In 2009, during the LOMROG II expedition, the cage returned empty from the depths of the ocean. This time, the tension is resolved only at 1:00 in the morning. The people on the quarterdeck have done everything right and the polar ocean releases their reward. Mud and pebbles pour out in a muddy slush and then several rocks the size of pork roasts appear. Christian Marcussen eagerly digs into the mud to feel one rock after the other; he twists and turns them in the weak morning light. His ski mask slides up over his lips and his excitement soon spreads across the deck. Still more people show up to take photos and to take part in the celebrations.

Through his ski mask, Christian Marcussen confirms the significance of tonight's catch. The Danish researchers are the first in the world to hold pieces of the Lomonosov Ridge in their hands. The rocks will now be transported to Copenhagen and analysed before any conclusions can be made, but really there is no doubt. These rocks will form tangible parts of Denmark and Greenland's evidence to the UN. If the chemical analyses in Copenhagen show what the researchers expect, the rocks will help to prove that the Lomonosov Ridge is directly connected to Greenland's bedrock. This is the essence of Denmark and Greenland's strategy. Without evidence of the Lomonosov Ridge's connection with Greenland, the chances of expanding the Danish Realm into the Arctic Ocean will fade. The Ridge is the gateway to the ocean floor and the muddy rocks on the quarterdeck might just be part of the entry ticket. Fifteen hours later, the cage reappears after another dive. This time, it is even heavier; the largest rock in the cage weighs almost 90 kilograms and has to be lifted by crane.

Now Christian Marcussen makes yet another decision. When the researchers arrive at breakfast on 21 August 2012, the *Oden*'s electronic bulletin board announces that the icebreaker will head 88 degrees north, 135 degrees east towards Siberian waters. Those skilled in navigation immediately know what this means and for the uninitiated Christian Marcussen has added a short sentence: 'During transit, the *Oden* will attempt to pass as close to the northern-most point in the world as possible.' No fanfares. No official confirmation. But the message is clear: the *Oden* is going to the North Pole.

Ninety degrees north, Expedition Day 23, 22 August 2012. At the North Pole. At 20:00 on 22 August 2012 – a few hours before the estimated arrival at the North Pole – a crowd starts to form on the command bridge. The two Swedish chefs are roaming around with cameras around their necks. Trays with tall glasses have been prepared for sparkling wine retrieved from the fridge. When the *Oden* is two nautical miles – less than four kilometres – from the North Pole Captain Andersson asks everyone onboard to join him on the bridge.

From that moment on, however, the pace is very slow and only 1,300 metres from the North Pole, the icebreaker must give up. After a day of fog, the polar sun is out and the view from the bridge is phenomenal: glimmering ice sculptures and metre-high ice pyramids. The pack ice has prepared a display more beautiful than anything the expedition has come across so far and the audience on the bridge has plenty of time to enjoy the view. The icebreaker is stuck. Captain Andersson tries to force his way through a particularly rough ice ridge, and the wine has long since gone lukewarm when he finally decides to give up. He orders a retreat and sets a new course that takes the *Oden* behind the ice ridge and onto a new angle on the North Pole.

At 23:43 on Wednesday 22 August the GPS system onboard shows 89 degrees 59.985 minutes west. The GPS receiver is now approximately 30 metres from the North Pole. Captain Andersson has manoeuvred the wide hull so precisely onto the North Pole at 90 degrees north that parts of the ship are now exactly on top of the world. The electronics cannot register closer proximity to the Pole and the captain and Christian Marcussen stand side by side in complete silence. Then, Captain Andersson speaks first. He briefly mentions that this is the ninth time that the *Oden* has reached the North Pole. Christian Marcussen offers no considerations of the metaphysical aspects, no North Pole romanticism. Instead, he praises Captain Andersson and his crew and then gets to the evening's most complex point. He emphasizes that the flag ceremony, which will take place on the ice, should not be interpreted as a political manifestation. The flags, he says, will only signify co-operation between nations 'which is the essence of being in the Arctic'. He reminds everyone not to leave anything on the North Pole – not even flags.

Five years have passed since Artur Tjilingarov planted his Russian flag on the ocean floor at the North Pole and forever changed the way a flag on the Pole is interpreted. Any new manifestations on the ice will immediately be interpreted in light of the Russian flag planting in 2007. Christian Marcussen does everything he can to debunk any hint of drama, but it is futile. Onboard the *Oden*, the idea that one may now knock down the Russian flag by dropping something heavy into the water has already become a cliché. One of the younger members of the research team jokingly suggests that the iron cage used to retrieve rocks from the ocean floor might be able to fetch the Russian flag.

A gangway is lowered from the quarterdeck onto the ice. The first to disembark are polar bear sentries, and then crewmembers carry barbecues, charcoal, soft drinks and sausages onto the ice. Last come the researchers. At first, they wander somewhat aimlessly. Where do you go when you are at the North Pole? The ice crackles under their feet. Then a number of planned happenings unfold. The ship's Norwegian helicopter pilot strips down to his underwear and rolls around in the snow. One of the younger scientists throws rocks with her name on them into the water. Two men take turns shaving each other's skulls. Someone has brought a road sign indicating distances to different places in the world: Copenhagen 3,829 km, Aarhus 3,776 km, Nairobi 10,144 km, Piteå 2,755 km, the South Pole 20,004 km. The midnight sun lights up the party and some of the Danish participants stand on their heads. They imagine how a photo of them when turned upside down will show the world placed on their heads. Before the party is over, several people undress and jump into the water between the ice floes.

Christian Marcussen supervises the most important operation. With straightforward instructions, he gathers the group for a photo. He has carried the many flags onto the ice himself, and they have now been distributed. With his effective pace, he gathers the group so quickly that a Filipino member of the research team, who has not quite understood the procedure, is too late. The next day, the group photo is examined onboard. The 63 people in the photo face the camera much like a school photo. Due to his authority, Christian Marcussen stands precisely in the middle behind one of the armed sentries, but aside from that the photo reflects no intended order or hierarchy. Christian Marcussen runs a strict and focused expedition, but not a military operation. Renting the *Oden* is expensive and since leaving Longyearbyen, he has made it clear that every hour spent onboard should be used sensibly. But he also knows that unless there is room for a little play and relaxation, an expedition will fall apart. The regulations onboard are stringent, but they do leave room for those who want to party all night with rock music and strong drinks.

Many of the Swedish participants wear jackets from the Swedish Polar Research Secretariat in the Swedish national colours of blue and yellow, but the Danes have no common characteristics. Christian Marcussen has given everyone onboard a T-shirt or a polo shirt with the expedition logo, but in the group photo from the North Pole the Danes wear no common features. Instead the many flags dominate the photo. Christian Marcussen has tried to defuse the political undertones of the North Pole visit, but the flags he cannot remove and in the following days, the group photo travels across the globe on Facebook, on Danish TV and on other media. The world now knows of the LOMROG III expedition.

The day after the North Pole, Denmark's Arctic ambassador, from his office in Copenhagen, tries to defuse the symbolism when he is contacted by Reuters: 'We do not have a submarine that can be used to plant a flag (on the ocean floor) and we would rather use our resources for gathering data.' This is Denmark's message to the rest of the world. Denmark's Arctic ambassador plays down the visit to the North Pole. It means nothing. The researchers are supposed to gather data, not plant flags. If they do leave a flag, no one is to read any intentions into it.

Such is the message from Copenhagen: Denmark does not have any political intent to convey from this North Pole encounter. The message, however, does not represent the whole truth.

Onboard, Christian Marcussen claims that the North Pole does not carry any importance. A stay at the North Pole was not included in the original itinerary and the North Pole is not part of the data collection to the UN. During a lecture in Copenhagen, he has described the North Pole as simply 'the point where the Earth's imaginary axis of rotation intersects the surface of the sea'. Again and again, he underlines that the ice at the North Pole is no different from the ice elsewhere in the Arctic Ocean. He knows how nuclear-armed Russian and American submarines patrol under the ice and how American and Russian bombers constantly flew over the Arctic Ocean during the Cold War, emptying, in his opinion, any lingering idea of a vast and untouched no-man's-land of all meaning.

He often underlines that the United Nations Convention on the Law of the Sea has given the coastal states full legal rights to claim large parts of the ocean floor. During our visit to the North Pole in August 2012, he refuses to let himself be swayed by the magic, mythology or what he calls 'North Pole romance'. But he is also painfully aware that neither he nor Denmark's Arctic ambassador have the aptitudes to defuse the powerful symbolism of the North Pole; the world is simply not ready to let go of its fascination with it.

This is why Marcussen has brought the Greenlandic flag. According to tradition, everybody onboard the icebreaker may wave a flag of their own choosing on the group photo taken at the Pole. In the photo taken on this particular visit, a large Stars and Stripes is visible since one of Christian Marcussen's co-workers onboard is American. The expedition's rugged dredging expert has brought his Dutch flag. All flags are related to at least one person onboard except the Greenlandic; there is no one from Greenland onboard. Christian Marcussen has brought the Greenlandic flag purely for political reasons.

Since the Continental Shelf Project was established, Greenland's gains from potential oil, gas and minerals in the Arctic Ocean have been publicly depicted as one of the primary components while other obvious goals have only been implied. Several of the leading government officials behind the project view the operation as an opportunity to strengthen Greenland's ties to Denmark since it will illustrate the value of co-operation with Denmark to Greenland. In this way, they hope, it will push secession from Denmark further into the future. The expeditions are fully paid for by the Danish state without contributions from Greenland, and there are no Greenlandic scientists onboard the *Oden*. When Christian Marcussen brings out the Greenlandic flag at the North Pole and hands it to a man who resides in Nuuk, but who is certainly not Greenlandic, it is a convenient solution. The flag is there to ensure that anybody who sees the photo from the North Pole – and particularly any Greenlandic politicians – will understand that the expedition keeps Greenland's interest at heart. Ironically, when the group photo is finally taken, the Greenlandic flag is hidden behind the American flag due to a light breeze. Only the bottom red edge of it is visible and only on TV recordings of the event is the flag fully exposed.

A few of those present know that the claim to the North Pole itself is more an expression of a Danish wish than a Greenlandic one. When the Continental Shelf Project was initiated, it was by request from Greenland, but only when Christian Marcussen and his colleagues' first measurements from the ocean floor became known in 2006 did it occur to anyone that Denmark and Greenland might have the right to the ocean floor all the way past the North Pole. The Danish Foreign Minister at the time, Per Stig Møller, was the first to articulate a claim for the North Pole. On 26 June 2007, at the Royal Institute of International Affairs in Great Britain, the Minister spoke of the consequences of the disappearing sea ice in the Arctic: 'These consequences include competition for natural resources that are becoming available, the right to new navigation routes, disputes over maritime zones, and areas of land that were previously covered by ice. These challenges [...] have one thing in common: They pose potential security risks. Soon we will be discussing and deciding: Who owns the North Pole? That, by the way, I think we do.'

No one in Greenland expressed a similar desire to occupy the actual North Pole. Greenland certainly had an interest in the potential riches in the Arctic Ocean, but few in Greenland expressed any ambition to conquer the very specific geographical point at the top of the world. Back in history, the people of northern Greenland known at the time by foreigners as the Thule Eskimos called the North Pole *Qalasersuaq*, the large navel. This mysterious place was situated beyond the land of people and could only be reached by those with special spiritual powers. Qalasersuaq was not a pleasant place, but a dangerous void into which the careless could fall. In 1730, when a group of Danish colonists in Greenland wanted to visit the North Pole, they unsuccessfully tried to convince a group of locals to take them there. In Greenland, the Pole itself scarcely appears in the cultural treasury of songs, myths and oral tradition. Knud Rasmussen, the Danish explorer, described how in former times the people of southern Greenland told heroic tales of the extraordinarily hardy people who lived in the north. But they were tales of people of flesh and blood, of distant relatives' feats of strength – not of the North Pole. In the records from an early Danish expedition to Greenland, the Literary Greenland Expedition in 1903, a member of the local community at Thule, Marsanguak, is quoted for a comment on the American explorer Robert Peary, who was keen on visiting the North Pole: 'He wanted to reach farthest into the north, away from the Lands. That was his wish, which we found strange since there you will find no animals and no man – only ice and no land in sight. But every man has his peculiarities.'

Some of those present at the photo session on the North Pole in August 2012 later realized that the group photo was not really taken on the actual North Pole. After the arrival at the Pole, and before anyone stepped onto the ice, all onboard the *Oden* toasted in sparkling wine and Christian Marcussen gave a speech, while Captain Andersson spent about an hour parking the icebreaker in the ice. As the sea ice drifts approximately 300 to 400 metres per hour, the group was at least one kilometre from the North Pole when the photo was finally taken.

Even so, Christian Marcussen's decision to stop at the North Pole makes him partner to a distinguished tradition. The North Pole is not part of his scientific gathering of data, and he dismisses all notion of its mystery. But by deciding that *Oden* should stop at the North Pole anyway, he lets the intangible and alluring prevail. The Norwegian national hero Fridtjof Nansen – one of the most celebrated polar explorers of all time – did the same. Christian Marcussen finds this comparison pretentious and without substance, but he is mistaken. Fridtjof Nansen also changed his plans when the North Pole came close.

In 1890, Fridtjof Nansen began his legendary three-year expedition, letting his three-masted ship the *Fram* freeze into the pack ice and drift across the Arctic Ocean to chart the drive of the ice. Prior to the journey, Nansen claimed that the North Pole itself was unimportant to him. In a lecture to the Norwegian Geographical Society, he said, 'We have not gone out to seek the mathematical point which is creating the northern point of termination of the axis of the earth. For reaching this point has in itself only insignificant value. However, it is to make inquiries in the greatly unknown part of Earth surrounding the pole, and these inquiries will have approximately the same scientific value whether the quest travels over the exact pole point or a bit away from it.'

A year or so later, during the *Fram* expedition, Fridtjof Nansen and crew had allowed, as planned, their ship to get stuck in the polar ice in the middle of the Arctic Ocean. They drifted safely in the well-insulated ship from east to west across the Arctic Ocean. Day by day, the 13 men aboard wrote themselves further into the world's history books, but they were tormented by great boredom. When Nansen discovered that the ice and the ocean currents would not carry them across the North Pole itself as expected, he changed his plans. In his extensive two-volume book about the expedition with the *Fram*, he described how an irresistible drive towards the Pole tore at him, tormented him, grew in him, until he finally had to give in: 'What an urge! Now, when I look over the ice, it is like my muscles are quivering with a desire to be allowed to start going over it for real – efforts and needs, everything will then become a pleasure. It can seem foolish that I wish to undertake this expedition; there might have been more important quiet work to be done onboard. Well, the matter is, however, that the Pole is an aim that has been tempting humans for a long time. If we do not try now (being this far north) it could happen that it will be quite a long time before we get a second try.'

Fridtjof Nansen left the ship and went towards the North Pole with only one follower and a pack of sled dogs. He was aware that the distance to the Pole was several hundred kilometres and that the journey would be highly dangerous, but that did not stop him. He had to. And he failed. Frozen and overcome by the ice, poor weather and strong currents, Fridtjof Nansen and his colleague had to return long before they reached the North Pole, but that did not alter the fact that his enterprise was charged by a strong and inexplicable desire to reach it. Their motives are not the same, but they are related: Nansen is drawn by the unknown and mysterious, exactly like Christian Marcussen allows it to draw him and the entire LOMROG III expedition towards the North Pole in August 2012. Fridtjof Nansen was personally influenced by the intangible; Christian Marcussen let the fascination of his fellow expeditioners guide him – and in the end the Pole had to be reached.

On Wednesday 22 August, on the bridge of the *Oden* and just before reaching the North Pole, one of the scientists talks about the Arctic pioneers: 'Obviously there is a connection between us and the old polar explorers. We are a continuation of that same story. It just does not physically hurt us any more. Back then it was the physique of men versus nature. Nowadays, it is the electronics that can fail in the struggle against nature.' He looks out on the last metres of solid ice before the North Pole and quotes a poem by Russian-born Joseph Brodsky, *A Polar Explorer*.

Later, on the ice at the North Pole he speaks in awe of the men who struggled through the ice on dog sleds, or on foot, a hundred years earlier. He carries out his own small ritual. He takes off his boots and walks around barefoot for a few seconds. That way, he believes, he will feel the messages from the ice more closely. Onboard, he is the only person who expresses doubt about the whole purpose of the LOMROG expedition: 'When you sail around up here it seems very abstract that someone wants to own the North Pole. It is not like you can own the South Pole either, or the Equator. I think it is evident that a foundation of several countries would be better suited to making the right decisions than one country only. Of course this area must be preserved and kept as something special.'

Onboard the *Oden*, attention is brought to the press release published by Greenpeace prior to the *Oden's* departure: 'Greenpeace does not criticize the science per se, but the scientists participating have a personal responsibility.' For a while, a few of the scientists wonder whether they ought to feel personally responsible for paving the way for oil companies into the Arctic Ocean, but as one of them says, 'If Denmark gains control of the area, you can also use that to protect the area.'

The expedition's environmental impact, however, is hard to ignore. In the struggle with the pack ice, the *Oden*'s diesel engines burn off between 40 and 60 tons of heavy, cheap bunker fuel on a daily basis. A Danish standard family utilizes 1.5 tons of far less polluting heating oil in a year. On a clear day, the acid smoke from the *Oden*'s chimneys can be seen as a fat, yellowish fog.

Eighty-seven degrees and 45 minutes north. Expedition day 26, 25 August 2012. Above the Lomonosov Ridge on the Siberian side of the North Pole. After the group photo at the North Pole, people are quickly hustled back to the *Oden*. The party on the ice is over and the next 24 hours offer little diversion. The ship ploughs through ice and dismal fog. Then, after a day and a half, late in the night, the expedition is really stuck. For the first time, almost four weeks into the expedition, the most powerful icebreaker in the whole of Scandinavia can neither move forwards nor backwards. The ship has met an especially obstinate ice ridge. The wind puffs and blows from one side, the current presses from another and ice floes are crushed and pushed on top of each other, forming tall edges and fences. These ridges of ice packs sometimes stretch so far across the polar ice that they can be clearly seen on the satellite images, which Christian Marcussen and Captain Andersson study on a daily basis.

This night, the *Oden* pushes forward several times without breaking through. Reluctantly, the captain decides to stay. He drives the ship as far up on the ridge as the three running diesel engines allow. On top of the ice ridge, he turns off the engines. He notifies a waiting team of Swedish scientists that they may now lower their equipment into the water and bring up another bit of the ocean floor. This will be used to study the fluctuation of the climate over hundreds of thousands of years. While the scientists are working, the ice packs closer around the hull. Nothing is static here. At first sight, the ice seems sphinx-like and immovable, but that is a dangerous illusion. In 1910, Danish explorer Ejnar Mikkelsen's ship the *Alabama* ended up as a wretched wooden shack on the coast of north east Greenland. In 1917, near the Antarctic, churning ice pressed Ernest Shackleton and his crew on the *Endurance* down. Fridtjof Nansen's the *Fram* only survived its tour of the Arctic Ocean because the belly of the ship was formed as a half egg which did not allow itself to be pressed down, but instead got lifted up when the ice attacked.

The *Oden* does not have the egg shape of the *Fram* and now the Swedish icebreaker is solidly stuck. The officer in charge engages the fourth and last diesel engine, but the ship does not budge. Captain Andersson is summoned in the middle of the night. He activates the last prodigious reserves of the *Oden*. With a huge pumping station in the bottom of the ship, the crew sucks water into big tanks below deck. Subsequently, they put the pumping system on full strength and in less than ten seconds 200 tons of water are moved from one side of the ship to the other. The shift pushes the massive hull down over the ice with tremendous force and with an immense creaking sound the compressed, massive pack ice that holds the icebreaker now bursts. Shortly afterwards, the *Oden* moves again. During these night hours, only a few people realize what is happening. No alarms go off. The icebreaker is not in danger of being pressed down and crushed. The ship is too strong for that to happen, but the episode causes Christian Marcussen to think. Climate change has weakened the polar ice, but it is still a formidable foe.

Later that morning the expedition continues. With the multibeam echo sounder, Christian Marcussen and his crew continue their data collection. The *Oden* is now on the Siberian side of the North Pole. Any expansion here will amplify the Danish claims in a zone which Russia likewise claims, but that does not stop Christian Marcussen. All day and all night, the echo sounder is pulsating, and slowly a colourful profile of an entire mountain appears on the computers:

This is new! This mountain has never been seen before; it has never previously been measured by man. It does not appear on Christian Marcussen's maps of the ocean floor! The echo sounder shows a mountain of more than 2,700 metres, falling steeply towards the flat ocean floor at a depth of 4,300 metres. If the data is accurate, Denmark and Greenland's claims to the ocean floor may possibly be expanded by several hundred, maybe even several thousand, square kilometres. Christian Marcussen orders supplemental investigations in order to consolidate the findings. The Danish Kingdom is expanding.

Eighty-seven degrees north, Expedition Day 37, 5 September 2012, above the Amundsen Basin. Last day of seismic measuring. Past midnight, the *Oden* has succeeded in ploughing a clean channel in the ice. Per Trinhammer and his team slowly lower the air cannon into the frigid water while heavy snow covers the quarterdeck. The thermometer shows minus two degrees. Christian Marcussen has announced that this could be the last measurement. Six hours later, the equipment leaves the water. Snow drifts lie on the deck; no one has slept; the entire team needs to rest. Christian Marcussen looks like a drowned cat, but he has discovered sediments on the ocean floor which will further support Greenland and Denmark's claim; he will not stop now. He lets the crew know that further measurements are to be executed on a stretch of ten nautical miles. Captain Andersson wants to head towards Svalbard, but that will have to wait. Not until after 20:00 on Wednesday 5 September can Per Trinhammer hoist his air cannon out of the water for the last time and start packing his equipment. Only then does the *Oden* set course for Svalbard.

Eighty-one degrees north, 12 September, close to the edge of the pack ice. The ice landscape changes swiftly. The expedition is working its way from the compact pack ice into the cut, broken-up ice known as the ice edge. All of a sudden, the helicopter is unable to fly the scientists onto the ice; the ice floes are simply too small to support the heavy machine.

The last ice floe they land on is so small that the helicopter's pontoons stick out over its edges. The next day, a polar bear runs away from the *Oden* – it is fleeing on a mosaic of floes, which are moving up and down on rolling swells, causing the bear to heave and lower with the horizon as backdrop. For six weeks, the icebreaker has sailed through great masses of ice sparing the expedition from too much rough sea – but now, at the edge of the ice, the ship suffers the will of the ocean's movements. Behind the *Oden*, a host of snowy white ivory gulls feeds in the wake of the ship. For a few hours before the ship enters open waters, black-legged kittiwakes, Arctic fulmars, lesser black-backed gulls, as well as a few agile birds that might be Ross's gulls, rally around the quarterdeck. The ship bites hard into the swells; the spray juts high into the air. The broad-backed first officer, Ivan, descends from the bridge to order all bird-lovers to clear away from the stern. Someone might get washed into the ocean.

Seventy-eight degrees north. The expedition's last day. The duty officer spots the first of Svalbard's north-facing mountains 24 hours before the *Oden* arrives in Longyearbyen. Here, the Fram Strait is mild; the expedition runs its final leg without any major seasickness. At nightfall, heavy rain starts pounding the deck and the wind makes the swells increase. For the first time after seven weeks with lots of midnight sun, the scientists experience dusk falling and small lamps are lit at the working tables on the bridge. The scientists can look forward to months of processing the gathered data, but no one is in doubt: The LOMROG III expedition went well. They have successfully managed to gather data in one of the world's most inaccessible waters. Safely stored on their hard discs are unique data sets on the Lomonosov Ridge and the Amundsen Basin. And at the very edge of the area, which Denmark and Greenland will claim, the scientists have located a new mountain, which results in an expansion of the Danish Realm, far larger than expected. Hundreds of algae tests, ice measurements, and other data can be added to existing research on the Arctic and climate change in the region.

In the afternoon, the *Oden* sails due south along Svalbard's rugged coastline. At the end of the day, the mouth of Isfjorden is clearly visible and the officer in charge sets course for Longyearbyen. Suddenly, another ship is spotted; the first one in more than six weeks. An hour later, a house is spotted on one of Isfjorden's outermost points. Then a car. A lamp post. To tourists, Longyearbyen is promoted as a wilderness station, a destination at the end of the world, wild, untamed and on the edge of the polar bears' hunting grounds. To the scientists onboard the *Oden*, however, the diminutive, coalmine city now seems like a trendy metropolis. An airstrip. Light in a window. A cyclist. The first officer seems lost in his own thoughts on the stern as he beholds land. Finally, one of the *Oden*'s massive heavy anchors is lowered into the fjord. The LOMROG III expedition is at an end.

The results are not yet final, but it appears that the expansion of the Danish Realm in the Arctic Ocean – including rights to the North Pole itself – is now more likely than ever. The political owners of the Continental Shelf Project in Copenhagen and Nuuk have reason to be pleased; there is little of what was planned that Christian Marcussen and LOMROG III have not achieved. And yet, no welcome committee is present on the quay. In just seven weeks, the scientists have made a significant addition to the long Danish tradition of standard-setting polar expeditions. Meticulously, they have adhered to instructions from the Danish government while Greenpeace has publicly insinuated that their conscience needs revision. However, as for public recognition the contrast to the expeditions of the past could not be more striking. No telegrams or greetings offering praise have arrived from Copenhagen. The Danish national flag is not to be seen on the quay; neither is champagne or any TV cameras. The *Oden* anchors undisturbed at Longyearbyen while Christian Marcussen downloads emails from home. Not even GEUS, his own organization, has found the expedition's arrival at the North Pole worth mentioning to the public.

Not that anyone onboard expected a welcoming committee. This is not the Danish way any more. Christian Marcussen and his colleagues know that the time when polar expeditions inspired awe and admiration are definitively over – and they know why. Christian Marcussen and the other participants have not personally fought the Arctic elements; they have sent emails, eaten warm food and enjoyed hot showers in the *Oden*'s cabins. They have been gone for seven weeks, not seven years. They do not live in a time when strong men who battle nature are attributed hero value. Exploration of the last white spots on the world map no longer earns scientists much respect. Indeed, the LOMROG III scientists should probably be glad that they are not rebuked by anyone but Greenpeace for their intrusion into the polar environment.

As he prepares to leave the *Oden*, Christian Marcussen has spent more than ten years on Denmark and Greenland's Continental Shelf Project. He knows every detail of the data collected, but he cannot be certain when the UN will pass sentence on his job and close the case. His own estimate is that the UN may take as long as until 2025 before it finds the time to process Denmark's claim and only then can delineation negotiations with Russia, Canada and possibly others begin. The case might not even be closed in Christian Marcussen's lifetime, but he has reconciled himself with this part of the ordeal: 'That is how it is; it is part of the process. My job is simply to deliver.'

As the scientists prepare to fly home, 12 years have passed since the Danish Prime Minister made a decision to expand the Realm northwards from Greenland. In 2000, Danish Prime Minister Poul Nyrup Rasmussen met with the Faroe Prime Minister, Anfinn Kallsberg, and the Premier of Greenland's Self-Rule, Jonathan Motzfeldt, for one of their annual, special meetings.

No one besides these three persons know exactly what was discussed, and in 2012, as LOMROG III set sail, none of them had ever publicly revealed what drove their decision.

As Christian Marcussen explained to me on the *Oden*, the geologists do not predict any commercial oil discoveries in the central parts of the Arctic Ocean, and what other possible gains the politicians might have been aiming for is not known beyond speculation.

The project was born at a time when Poul Nyrup Rasmussen had spent seven years in office and his staff presented the Continental Shelf Project as practically inevitable. If Poul Nyrup Rasmussen neglected to pursue this opportunity, the Faroe Islands and Greenland might accuse him of gross mismanagement. The UN Convention on the Law of the Seas had given the Faroe Islands and Greenland a good chance of expanding their rights to the ocean floor, and why should Poul Nyrup Rasmussen deny them this chance?

At the time, relations with Greenland and the Faroe Islands, which are part of the Danish Kingdom just like Greenland, were under significant stress. That same year, Poul Nyrup Rasmussen led a series of bitter negotiations with the Faroese political leaders who sought full independence for their island nation. Poul Nyrup Rasmussen offered the Faroese a deal so poor that the negotiations collapsed. Now, if Poul Nyrup Rasmussen were to rob the Faroe Islands and Greenland of potentially extensive areas of ocean floor, it might look as if he deliberately denied them access to oil, gas and other riches that might help them win independence. This would not only sour relations internally in the Kingdom but also make Denmark look uncomfortably like an old colonial power trying to hold on to its possession by the cheapest of means.

Greenland's political number one, Jonathan Motzfeldt, was on the verge of a political comeback. His party, Siumut, was firmly in power in Greenland and when he arrived for the meeting with Poul Nyrup Rasmussen, he was one of the strongest advocates for more Greenlandic autonomy. Ten years later, during an interview in early 2010, shortly before his death, he maintained the confidentiality of the closed meeting with the Prime Minister, but he gladly described to me the circumstances. From his modern apartment in Nuuk with its panoramic view over the Davis Strait between Greenland and Canada, he gestured towards the sea to highlight his point: Here, Greenland is separated from North America by just 300 kilometres of water. In Jonathan Motzfeldt's analysis, the quest for the ocean floor at the North Pole resulted from Danish worries over American interest in Greenland, stemming from the so-called Monroe Doctrine.

The Monroe Doctrine, named after James Monroe, President of the United States at the time, represents American thinking from the beginning of the nineteenth century. The Monroe Doctrine basically states that no foreign powers will be allowed to control territory close to the US mainland. From Monroe's time onwards, the United States perceived itself as a fortifying power and a protector of the North American continent. In this context, Greenland's landmass became a prominent protruding defensive landmass between North America, Russia, and Asia. Before and after World War II, the Monroe Doctrine led to the American Congress to suggest that the United States buy Greenland from Denmark. After the war, when the Danish government asked the American government to withdraw its troops from Greenland, the US government instead, as previously mentioned, offered to buy Greenland.

Hence, in the year 2000, Jonathan Motzfeldt was convinced that Poul Nyrup Rasmussen agreed to pursue the Continental Shelf Project primarily as a means to underscore Denmark's sovereignty over Greenland. The comprehensive scientific efforts, icebreaker expeditions, and years of scientific endeavours would bolster Danish sovereignty in the Arctic more efficiently than any warship.

For Jonathan Motzfeldt oil played an important part. The Premier and his political fellows in Greenland enjoyed close relations with the Inuits in Canada. There, fights over oil had caused heated discussions with the government in Ottawa, and Motzfeldt was eager to avoid such conflicts with Copenhagen. Motzfeldt hoped that an extension of Greenland's rights to the ocean floor could lead to oil revenue, which would bolster Greenland's ability to support itself.

They had different objectives, but at the meeting in 2000 the premiers of Denmark, Greenland and the Faroe Islands agreed to the Continental Shelf Project and no limits to its extension were set.

Publicly, no one talked of the matter, not in 2000 and not for several years to come. The idea of an ocean floor expansion north of Greenland involved Danish relations with Russia, Norway and Canada, it touched on the core of Danish–Greenlandic relations and so it might easily become controversial. No one was interested in attracting attention. Why draw attention to a project that was clearly better off without it? Initial matters were dealt with in a series of closed-door meetings within the Danish Prime Minister's Office, and only a handful of the most necessary people were involved.

On 13 May 2002, the Danish Minister of Science at the time, Helge Sander, presented an overall plan to the inner circle of the government. As prime minister, Poul Nyrup Rasmussen had been replaced by his liberal successor, Anders Fogh Rasmussen.

Helge Sander's presentation consisted of one and a half pages plus a 12-page technical note. The one and a half pages plus the note on ocean depths and other technical details were one of the few documents, or perhaps the only official document, stating why the Danish government involved itself in the Continental Shelf Project. The one and a half pages have never been published. The text is not signed, nor is its author indicated. Technically, the papers came from Helge Sander's ministry, but the text reveals a broad circle of stakeholders. At the top of the first sheet, it is indicated that negotiations had already included department heads of the Danish Prime Minister's Office and the Danish Ministry of Finance.

In the short document, only four lines of the text were designed to motivate the ministers to all that would later be carried out at sea, on land, and on the sea ice. These four lines are the only available written justification of the entire project, written down for the government's decision makers: 'To the extent that Denmark's demands are accepted by the

Commission on the Limits of the Continental Shelf (CLCS), an exclusive right to the area and the ocean floor's living and non-living resources as well as the opportunity to establish environmental criteria for the use of the area is obtained.' That was all. This was the political basis for the decision to carry out the project to which Christian Marcussen would subsequently dedicate more than ten of his best working years. The Danish Kingdom could win exclusive rights to the underground as well as the opportunity to protect the environment against the activities of other actors. As a government official recalls, 'We could not have the Russians polluting the Arctic Ocean.'

The Continental Shelf Project was described as 'unavoidable'. According to the anonymous authors, there was no way around it no matter what the gathered ministers might think. Denmark's obligations towards Greenland and the Faroe Islands were portrayed as a central point of the entire project and any potential objections were dismissed with reference to Denmark's constitutional responsibilities for the welfare of the Faroe Islands and Greenland.

For some of the project's key players, the case was simple. One of the government officials who followed the Continental Shelf Project during its first years told me that the officials involved were inspired by a common, unfocused, but powerful force: 'In history, I do not think that you can find any examples of a nation-state that did not attempt to acquire all areas it could. This is the main point: We can obtain new rights in a new area as a nation-state. Even though it might not look like it is worth much, it might turn out to be worth something later.'

The short document from the Danish Ministry of Science exposes this fundamental desire to expand, defend and maintain the country's territory at any cost and at any opportunity, a force that was much evident in the fifteenth and sixteenth centuries, but which also in 2012 inspired the inner circles of decision makers.

Without further hesitation, the Danish government's finance committee granted 150 million kroner to whatever research necessary. The underlying motive was not discussed for long, and the desire to conquer the actual North Pole itself played no role. The government officials' best estimation at the time was that the North Pole was situated too far north to be part of any realistic claim Greenland and Denmark might make.

In the years to follow, the project was quiet but active – as seen in Christian Marcussen's picture from the North Pole in 2012. The collection of data was thriving and the public could follow the *Oden* step-by-step through the researchers' reports. It was more difficult to ascertain what drove the politicians.

When Christian Marcussen returned home in late summer 2012, conquests and explorations of the Arctic had played a central role in Denmark's perception of itself for more than 400 years. Battles were fought, heroes were praised, dozens of popular books were written by researchers and explorers and now Denmark, Greenland and the melting of the ice cap were suddenly vital parts of international discussions. Climate change had made the Arctic relevant across the world. But it is still unclear which thoughts are behind the Danish government's attempt to claim the North Pole and the floor of the Arctic Ocean.

Is it all to please Greenland and avert the island's secession? Will the conquest further 'deflower the Nordic myth of inaccessibility' as Danish author Christian Grøndahl writes? Does the Danish government have an opinion on the cultural significance of the great Arctic ice for 'the human mind in its most noble fight against superstition and darkness' that Norwegian explorer Fritdjof Nansen wrote about?

If the Danish politicians have any deeper thoughts on the disputed areas in the Arctic Ocean they have never been published. But in 2011, in the Kingdom's first Arctic strategy, it was officially stated that the incorporation of the North Pole into the Danish Realm is part of the Kingdom's Arctic ambitions.

Then a precarious dilemma developed. In August 2011, a few days before the publication of the first-ever Arctic strategy, the Premier of Greenland's Self-Rule, Kuupik Kleist, presented his own view in the Greenlandic media: 'I would prefer that the area surrounding the North Pole remains international waters. I appreciate the symbolism of certain areas not being commercially exploited. Instead, the area could serve as a common research area where climate change could be monitored, since the Arctic is one of the places in the world which is most exposed.'

For a few precarious hours, the Kingdom was divided. A potential diplomatic mess was threatening, but then the diplomats in Copenhagen stepped in. After a public presentation of the new Arctic strategy, which did not mention Kuupik Kleist's point of view, Lene Espersen, the Danish Foreign Minister at the time, made a surprising statement on TV: 'We could not agree more. I think that Kuupik Kleist's vision of a special reserve is a very beautiful vision. In a perfect world, it would be great if we established a common natural reserve under special protection. But in order to avoid conflict, we first have to agree on where to establish the borders. Conflict is to be avoided at all costs.'

This was news – apparently, the Danish government supported the establishment of a natural park at the North Pole! But in fact, it was only diplomacy at play. When Lene Espersen elaborated on her statement in the *Wall Street Journal*, it became clear that her aim was merely to pacify Kuupik Kleist and avoid a public show of disarray: 'When the borders have been drawn, we hope that it will be possible to agree on a permanent nature reserve with the neighbouring countries.'

In other words, the idea of a natural park would only be pursued if the entire Arctic community agreed. The plan was not mentioned in the Kingdom's official Arctic strategy and when Kuupik Kleist left politics a few years later, the idea quickly disappeared into thin air.

By 2012, it was a well-known fact that Russia, just like Denmark, would make claims to the ocean floor at the North Pole. Already in 2001, Russia sent its claims concerning the borders on the ocean floor to the UN. Russia wanted an area which ended in a triangular point at the North Pole.

This allowed other countries to also claim triangular pieces all the way up to the North Pole. Denmark and Greenland's claims, as the LOMROG III expedition illustrated, would, in contrast, include the entire North Pole and a large piece of the ocean floor surrounding it.

In the end, the experts of the UN Commission on the Limits of the Continental Shelf (UNCLCS) may approve the claims of all three countries even if the claims overlap. Several countries might well have legitimate claims to the same piece of Arctic Ocean floor just like two countries divided by a river might have claims to the same river bed. Importantly, the UNCLCS will *not* decide the matter if more countries have justifiable claims to the same piece of ocean floor. In this case, Christian Marcussen and his colleagues' data will be boiled down and used in political negotiations directly between the relevant states.

No one knows when this matter will be decided. There is a long queue at the UNCLCS in New York, so it might take ten to 15 years before the commission has examined Russia's, Denmark's and Canada's claims and only then will direct negotiations between Copenhagen, Ottawa and Moscow begin.

(For the story of Denmark's and Greenland's final – and surprisingly gigantic – claim to the UN Commission on the Limits of the Continental Shelf, see Chapter 12, '2014–15: Greenland and Denmark claim the North Pole – and more'.)

5

FEARS OF CHINA

In 2012, a controversy between Denmark and Greenland over relations with China makes waves all the way to Beijing. In Greenland, many yearn for Chinese investments. In Denmark, fears grow that China through its vast financial powers will win political influence in Greenland. Again, Greenland's increasingly global significance is underscored. Copenhagen worries that a Chinese presence in Greenland will unhinge the complex accommodation with Greenland and the United States over Thule Air Base and Greenland's place in the Arctic security complex. Digging for a solution, Denmark and Greenland disagree dangerously on the final powers over Greenland's strategic minerals – uranium and rare earths.

* * *

Cui Hongjian did not beat around the bush: 'It may be so that countries closer to the Arctic such as Iceland, Russia, Canada and a few other European countries wish for the Arctic to be private property, and that they would have first claim to develop the area. However, China insists that the Arctic belongs to everyone, just like the Moon.'

Cui Hongjian was in charge of the study of European relations at the China Institute of International Studies in Shanghai. His remark came just as the Premier of the State Council of the People's Republic of China of the time, Wen Jiabao, began a high-profile trip to Europe with a visit to Iceland in May 2012. At the time, Chinese officials and academics frequently aired their understanding of the Arctic as part of a global commons. When Zhou Jingxing, a political advisor at the Chinese Embassy in Washington, received a Danish visitor in June 2012, he explained, 'Our politics is that the Arctic should be a joint property of humanity. Therefore, we also believe that it is crucial that we carry on negotiations and conversations concerning this.'

Earlier that same month in Nuuk, the head of operations at Greenland Mining and Energy A/S (GME), Ib Laursen, pointed to a large colour photograph on his office wall, not far from Nuuk's industrial port. The photograph was taken from a helicopter. It shows parts of the Kvanefjeld, a broad-backed mountain close to Narsaq in southern Greenland. In the foreground are the undulating swathes of mountain where Laursen and his colleagues envision a large open-pit mine. The photographer's focus is on a dozen dome-shaped hutments in which the drilling crew has lived and worked during test drillings. At the right side of the photograph is a sheep farm, the closest neighbour, at the foot of the mountain. In the back, a vaguely discernible creek runs down the bedrock and out in a crystal blue, partly ice-covered bay. Six or seven kilometres farther away one sees the houses of Narsaq, homes of Narsaq's 1,400 inhabitants.

Deposits of the so-called rare earth elements are seen as clear, bright patches on the mountain with no vegetation. Plant life here does not like the rare earth elements, but that does little to quell the otherwise very popular nature of these minerals. They are essential to numerous modern high-tech products such as mobile phones, windmills, fibre optics, television screens, laser technology, and modern weapon systems, missiles and night-vision binoculars. For four years, extensive test drillings have, according to Laursen, confirmed that the Kvanefjeld contains the largest known deposits of rare earth elements outside of China. For this reason, intelligence agencies, industrial strategists, the Confederation of Danish Industry, the Danish government, Chinese mining conglomerates, the EU, Naalakkersuisut (the Greenlandic Self-Rule Government) and many others all have a profound interest in Laursen's test drillings.

The rare earth elements have gained global significance, and everywhere in the equation is China. By the end of 2012, the Chinese producers of rare earth elements controlled around 96 per cent of the global market. Previously, China had used its near-monopoly to pressure Japan in a dispute about fishing rights, and in 2010 when the United States wanted to sell weapons to Taiwan, it was suggested in the Chinese press that China should retaliate by freezing all deliveries of rare earth elements to the United States. In 2009, when Chinese investors wanted to buy a majority holding in Lynas Corporation, an Australian mining company, which extracts rare earth elements, the Australian government interfered and prevented the acquisition.

In 2012, as the head of development of the GME mine at the Kvanefjeld, Laursen operates in the middle of this global discussion of the Greenlandic rare earths and China and Arctic geopolitics. To top it off, GME also wants to extract uranium from the Kvanefjeld. In this particular mountain, uranium will be an unavoidable by-product from any extraction of rare earth elements and both substances are controversial, globally as well as locally. The population of Narsaq is pining for new jobs and the entire Greenlandic nation lacks income, but critics fear that an open, dusty mine at the Kvanefjeld will cause so much exposure to unwanted substances and pollution that the actual existence of Narsaq is threatened. They fear that the entire village may have to be relocated. Besides, the idea of Greenland as an exporter of uranium has divided Greenland for years and the government in Denmark is similarly concerned, since uranium impacts the entire nation's international relations and security politics.

For 24 years, Laursen has lived in Greenland. His children have gone to school in Narsaq; he has lived in Narsaq for many years. He believes that Greenland will benefit greatly from a mine in the Kvanefjeld. He avoids much of the politics, but as a businessman he explains how Greenland should approach the Chinese monopoly: 'If you want to make money you must break a monopoly, not take part in maintaining it. If Greenland takes part in breaking the Chinese monopoly, a lot of money can be made. Imagine if we contribute with all the rare earths from the Kvanefjeld! We can deliver 20 to 25 per cent of the consumption of the global market.'

In 2012, there is no clear evidence that Chinese producers wish to control the Greenlandic deposits. But fear that such an interest should emerge is thriving and growing, particularly in Denmark and the EU. Already in 2009, the European Commission entered into negotiations with the authorities in Greenland to ensure that China does not gain control of Greenlandic minerals. In June 2012 in Nuuk, the Premier of Greenland's Self-Rule Government, Kuupik Kleist, signed a mutual declaration of intent with Antonio Tajani, the Vice President of the European Commission. With this declaration, the EU promised economic support for research and education which will help Greenland build a stronger mining industry. With his signature, Kuupik Kleist guaranteed that Greenland will do its utmost to ensure that Greenlandic minerals 'are brought to the market under full consideration of internationally passed legislation on fair market access'.

Shortly before putting his signature on this declaration, Kuupik Kleist explained to me how he had just discussed China and the minerals of Greenland directly with American Secretary of State Hillary Clinton when she visited Copenhagen early in June 2012.

He underlined that the joint EU–Greenland declaration does not prevent Chinese companies from making money on extraction of rare earth elements in Greenland, since the declaration is solely about how the minerals are offered for sale on the global market. Kleist believed that it will be impossible to exclude Chinese investors from mining projects in Greenland, even if the Greenlandic politicians wanted to make an attempt: 'Who are Chinese today? How about the Australian companies? Are they not Chinese as well? Who are their shareholders? How far does one have to go back in the food chain to see if there are Chinese investors or owners involved in a given company? Today, financial institutions finance a globalized industry. They do not have a flag on their logo. It will be an impossible task to find out how the ownership of these companies is arranged.'

In the middle of Nuuk's city centre, Kaj Kleist embodied the Premier's point: Who is not a little Chinese today?

For a number of years Kaj Kleist was head of Greenland's central administration, but now at the end of 2012, he had worked for three years as Information Manager and connecting link to Greenland's political elite for London Mining, a mining company planning to deliver iron ore to the Chinese steel plants.

London Mining Greenland A/S was owned by the British parent company London Mining, which was on the lookout for investors in China for an iron mine in Nuup Kangerlua, formerly known as Godthaab Fjord. In 2012, the potential investors included Chinese conglomerates such as Sinosteel, China Communications Construction Corporation and the China Development Bank. In May 2012, Kaj Kleist sized up the global financial crisis and explained to the Danish financial newspaper *Børsen* that in his opinion, no one besides the Chinese had the necessary funds to finance the iron ore mine in Nuup Kangerlua. Kaj Kleist explained that London Mining was waiting to spend 14 billion kroner on the mine.

In 2012, when London Mining submitted its application for permission to establish the mine – it ran for a staggering 6,000 pages – the Danish newspaper *Politiken* claimed that the company was 'controlled by the Chinese'. Rear admiral Nils Wang, head of the Royal Danish Defence Academy, offered a comment: 'Greenland is of great interest to China, because it holds a lot of the raw materials and minerals. These are a condition of continued Chinese growth. Both the EU and the United States have been inattentive when it comes to foreseeing future possibilities. The Chinese are thinking far ahead. That was how they gained monopoly of the rare earth elements before anyone in the West discovered the value.'

The iron mine in Nuup Kangerlua was controversial in Greenland, just like Laursen's plans for uranium and rare earth elements in Narsaq. In 2012, it seemed that the iron ore mine would be Greenland's biggest industrial project ever. The prospect of close to 2,000 Chinese mine workers, whom London Mining was planning to import for construction work, was the cause of heated controversy. London Mining suggested paying the Chinese workers a salary below Greenlandic standards and public debate was intense.

During the debate, it also transpired that London Mining had transferred ownership of their Greenlandic subsidiary to two shell companies on Jersey Island, a well-known tax haven, and new thoughts arose on how Greenland's oil, gas and mineral profits might perhaps be better ensured if Danish or Scandinavian actors were put in charge of the extraction.

The fear of substantial Chinese involvement in Greenland initially established itself in Denmark when Ove Karl Berthelsen, member of Greenland's Self-Rule Government, was dispatched to a mineral conference in Tianjin in northern China in autumn 2011. Here he was invited to meet China's Vice Premier at the time, Li Keqiang. In Denmark, *Politiken* covered the meeting, and suddenly questions were asked about why such a powerful Chinese politician would spend time with a representative from Greenland – a tiny semi-nation with only 56,000 inhabitants.

Then, a few months later, the first-ever Chinese ministerial delegation arrived in Greenland when China's Minister of Land and Resources, Xu Shaoshi, visited Nuuk. He and his entourage of eight spoke with the Premier of Greenland, Kuupik Kleist, and also visited the Greenland Institute of Natural Resources. Xu handed over a model of a Chinese submarine and through his interpreter he invited the institute to participate in a science expedition off the coast of Eastern Greenland in 2013. The visit reinforced the impression that China was actively seeking a role in Greenland and it also collided with an even more notable event.

On Friday 20 April 2012, as already mentioned, China's Premier at the time, Wen Jiabao, flew to Reykjavik in Iceland for a two-day visit as his first stop on a major European trip.

Wen travelled with a delegation of almost 100, including 11 ministers. On TV, the Icelanders could watch Wen posing with an Icelandic lamb and in two days, Iceland and China signed six agreements on everything from energy and development aid to Africa to climate research.

A look at a map will explain why: In the years to come, shipping through the northern sea route from China to Europe will increase and Iceland is located right on this emerging sea lane. In 2011, Icelandic Minister of Foreign Affairs Ossur Skarphéðinsson dubbed the North-East Passage the 'new silk route in the Arctic Ocean' with Iceland as an important transport hub on this route. Iceland, on the verge of national bankruptcy in 2008, dreamed of becoming the Arctic Singapore, with constant income from hundreds of cargo vessels in search of service, ports, and fuel. Wen Jiabao's visit fit perfectly into this Icelandic strategy and Iceland secured Wen a useful Arctic platform. China's diplomats in Reykjavik had already established the city's largest embassy, with room for 30 cars in the basement.

Wen Jiabao ensured the Icelanders that China would respect UN's Convention on the Law of the Sea and thus share the Arctic states' perception of sovereignty in the Arctic. Wen did not compare the Arctic with the Moon.

Then, in June 2012 in Copenhagen, the debate about China's potential influence in Greenland reached new heights. The Chinese president, Hu Jintao, visited Denmark on a three-day official visit on his way to a world summit in Mexico. In Copenhagen, trade agreements and industrial contracts worth billions were to be settled. The Queen, the Prince Consort and Denmark's two princes with their royal wives received President Hu and his wife at the airport.

The planners, however, had forgotten Greenland. Already prior to Hu Jintao's arrival, the media noted how Kuupik Kleist was dissatisfied that he had not been invited to the talks with the Chinese president, since the Arctic and Chinese interests in the region were very likely subjects on the agenda. The Danish government explained that the Arctic and Greenland were not even on the agenda, but the rare earth elements, an iron mine at Isua in central Greenland and the new Arctic shipping routes were all there to indicate that this was not in any likelihood the full picture.

The editor-in-chief of *Politiken*, Bo Lidegaard, a leading expert on Greenland, summarized China's priorities in his newspaper: 'If you look from Beijing towards Denmark, Greenland is the first thing you see.' Two days later, on 12 June, the front page read: 'China to make billions on raw materials in Greenland's underground'.

In an editorial in *Weekendavisen*, readers were advised that 'it is essential to know that the Chinese are completely indifferent to native peoples' rights; they murder and suppress their own people. They will not hesitate to press the Greenlanders with the influence they already have or are given. Moreover, China will not hesitate to exploit any raw material monopoly. The country is currently the world's number one spender on arms, and it is both stupid and dangerous to play at their game'.

Simultaneously, a serious dispute escalated between Greenland and Denmark. The government in Copenhagen claimed that it had the right to exercise control over the uranium and rare earth elements in Greenland since they held security implications. In Nuuk, Premier Kuupik Kleist and his staff were furious. From their point of view, this interpretation conflicted with the Act on Greenland Self-Government from 2009 as well as with the subsequent agreement that Greenland, as of 1 January 2010, had taken over full responsibility for the administration of all raw materials, including the issuing of research and extraction licences.

All of a sudden, it became clear that the relationship between Greenland and Denmark was founded on very muddy grounds. In September 2012, the Danish newspaper *Berlingske Tidende* scrutinized the 609 pages that summarized years of negotiations between Greenland and Denmark prior to the 2009 act on Self-Government. The journalists found not a single word of guidance about uranium or any other security issues posed by Greenland's minerals.

At the Royal Danish Defence College in Copenhagen, this dilemma had long tormented the College's chief official, Rear Admiral Nils Wang. In 2011, he was on an extensive study trip to China, and in June 2012 he appeared on national television in full uniform. He explained that the uncertainty over who exercises control of the raw materials in Greenland presented a growing weakness in the Danish Realm's relations with the rest of the world. He also wrote an op-ed in *Politiken*: 'It is an open question whether the Realm is ready to manage the gigantic pressure which is settling on Greenland's rare minerals ... Seeing that China's need for raw materials seems to grow relentlessly, there is no doubt that China will continue to approach all strategic important raw materials anywhere in the world. This includes Greenland, which besides the rare earth materials also possesses other minerals that are vital for China's growth [...] Neither is it a coincidence that Greenland's Minister for Mineral Resources is received on the red carpet by Vice Premier Li Keqiang – as if this was the most natural thing in the world.'

Finally, in August 2012 in Igaliku, Greenland's Premier Kuupik Kleist and Danish Prime Minister Helle Thorning-Schmidt reached an interim solution. They agreed that Greenland and Denmark should hold high-level meetings more frequently and that the uncertainty concerning the control over strategic minerals must be addressed and sorted out.

As Kuupik Kleist said, 'There are aspects of the activities surrounding the minerals which also touch upon foreign and security policy. This means that we will now initialize a process whose aim is to determine what projects are exclusively Greenlandic and what projects will have to be discussed.'

The global ramifications were easily detected. As French researcher Damien Degeorges commented in a Danish journal, *Ræson*, 'Greenland will become the new rendezvous point for the world's two biggest superpowers, the United States and China. In Greenland, the level of debate on international politics can be very low at points. It is necessary to discuss how to handle the raw materials on a global policy scale – not local policy. In Greenland, there is not enough focus and attention on the possible global political consequences which arise when you hand over access to your raw materials. This aspect entirely escapes the Greenlanders' interest, which basically is to earn money.'

Simultaneously, the international community's awareness of Greenland's emerging relations with China grew. Russian diplomats in Copenhagen worried, for instance, how Denmark and Greenland openly supported China's wish for a seat as Permanent Observer in the Arctic Council. Russia's urge to understand Denmark's attitude was part of the reason why a researcher from Copenhagen University, Timo Kivimäki, was sentenced to five months in prison for espionage. Accepting monetary rewards, Timo Kivimäki had helped Russian diplomats understand, among other issues, Denmark's position in the Arctic.

Two American experts on China analysed Denmark's role in the *Wall Street Journal*: 'Denmark has made a strategic decision to prioritize its economic relationship with China and is now becoming the key gateway for Beijing's commercial and strategic entrée into the Arctic. Copenhagen administers Greenland's foreign policy and will likely dangle the island's rich geological potential in front of Beijing as it works to bolster the China-Denmark trade relationship.'

The analysts noted how Denmark's ambassador to China, Friis Arne Petersen, clearly acknowledged China's 'legitimate economic and scientific interests in the Arctic'. They stressed how Greenland, and not Denmark, was interesting to China. 'The minerals that lie under Greenland's snow are the real prize, worth far more in both monetary and strategic terms to China than the imported goods or export market Denmark itself can provide.'

In Denmark, the debate became still more heated. In November 2012, *Politiken* wrote how 'Greenland is threatened by the world's most hardcore imperialistic nation'. In Nuuk, a disgruntled member of the Self-Rule Government, Ove Karl Berthelsen, pointed out how Chinese investments in Denmark were often described as a major win and that they should be regarded as such in Greenland as well: 'If the iron mine project succeeds it will become a milestone for Greenland. Our aim is to become a mining nation and the iron mine project is the first step in this direction.'

Thus, in the summer of 2012 in Nuuk, while Ib Laursen pondered his rare earth mine in Kvanefjeld, Greenland's politicians had to consider not only their own nation's future, but also China's potential role in it.

6

GREENLAND – AN ARCTIC OIL STATE

The ocean floor beneath Greenland's waters holds immense oil and gas deposits, or so the geologists say. For decades, Greenland has dreamt of sudden riches, but so far none of the foreign companies operating in Greenland's waters have found oil or gas worth extracting. Meanwhile, the quest for oil and gas is changing Greenland and frustrating millions outside the country. They fear catastrophic oil spills, degradation of Greenland's pristine environment and accelerated climate change. Again, Greenland takes centre stage in a global debate. Some argue that Arctic oil should not be extracted at all; others ask why Greenland and its less than 60,000 people must be the first on earth not to exploit its natural resources.

* * *

Jørgen Hammeken-Holm points to a dot on the map showing potential oil fields off the coast of north east Greenland. He explains to me that even the northern areas, which have for millennia been inaccessible because of the ice drift from the Arctic Ocean, will soon be accessible to the oil industry. We are in 2012. The number of ice-free days enabling ships to sail untroubled along the north eastern coast steadily increases. Despite the fact that this number can vary significantly from year to year, Jørgen Hammeken-Holm has no doubts – oil rigs can be established even off Greenland's north eastern coast within the foreseeable future. He points to the map: 'Look at this! Here you can easily see how the concentration of ice continuously decreases.'

As head of the Bureau of Minerals and Petroleum's licence office in Nuuk, Jørgen Hammeken-Holm has been centrally placed during Greenland's negotiations with the world's biggest oil companies for years. In August 2012, he became the Bureau's principal manager. Jørgen Hammeken-Holm was one of the authors of the 2009 strategy, which outlined Greenland's oil reserves and how Greenland intended to manage them.

By the end of 2012, Greenland has entered into agreements with American ExxonMobil and Chevron, Norwegian Statoil, Danish DONG and Mærsk Oil, Scottish Cairn Energy, Swedish and Canadian companies – and more were lined up. No one has located a single drop of oil in Greenlandic waters and most minerals also remain unexploited. However, the astronomical expectations along with a determined political focus on oil and minerals has already changed Greenlandic society.

In particular, two areas off Greenland's coast illustrate this development: On these locations, the oil industry will be working offshore farther north than anywhere else on the planet. Among specialists, the two areas are known as KANUMAS, Kalaallit Nunaat Marine Seismic. Nobody knows the magnitude of the oil reserves in these areas for certain, but the oil industry is used to the unknown; it is vital for them to secure access to the large – and largely unknown – reserves in the Arctic, as they are perceived to be some of the last ones on the planet. The mere potential of oil is enough to keep stock prices high.

On 1 December 2009, an international auction on the 14 concessions in the KANUMAS area off north west Greenland was launched by the Self-Rule Government in Nuuk. Six months later, the oil industry had submitted 17 proposals and a press release was dispatched from Nuuk: 'The Baffin Bay oil tender round is the most successful licence round of its kind in Greenland. Never before have so many proposals from the oil industry been received.' Seven companies were given access to explore potentials for oil and gas off the northern-most coast of West Greenland, and in December 2012, three consortiums had filed 11 applications for permission to explore the seabed off the coast of north east Greenland.

The media often portray such events as a result of the oil companies' insatiable hunger for oil and gas. There are, however, other interpretations. One of the critical analysts of the oil hunt in the Arctic, Alexander Shestakov, who heads the Arctic Programme of the World Wildlife Foundation, WWF, argues that the Arctic governments – including Greenland's – often pressure the oil companies to develop the Arctic oilfields at a pace which exceeds the companies' own ambitions. Danish and Greenlandic politicians co-operated for decades to make Greenland an attractive investment for the oil companies and the trend continued when Greenland took over full ownership of the raw materials underground in 2009. Critics say that in this process, the most serious questions have never been answered. They say that the risk of oil catastrophes is too great considering Greenland's extremely harsh conditions, and that it will be impossible to clean up oil spills so far north – in particular the KANUMAS areas. The critics consider collisions with icebergs plausible and regard the industry's emergency response plans as hollow. Lastly, they are unconvinced that Greenland's small administration can tackle the multinational corporations.

These heavy dilemmas are pressing matters in Greenland. And so, in 2012, the public in Greenland discusses whether oil and gas will bring corruption, inflation, and prostitution. Shall they embrace the oil and the risks it causes such as pollution and social and cultural atomization? Is the potential revenue from oil and gas that necessary or should Greenland pursue a different course?

In the KANUMAS areas, the oil industry's Arctic pioneers will be facing the masses of ice in the long, dark polar winter as well as environmental activists from all over the globe, who will be eagerly guarding the whales, polar bears and seabirds. Even the oil industry acknowledges that an oil spill this far north would be extremely challenging or simply impossible to deal with because of the ice, the wind, and the great distance to float locks, helicopters, other equipment and expertise.

In 2012, sceptics wonder if the small administration in Greenland could handle the challenge. When Jørgen Hammeken-Holm talked to me in June 2012, however, no critics had yet presented concrete evidence that the manner in which Greenland handles oil lacks in competence when compared to more experienced oil states. The Greenlandic politicians insist that their oil industry applies the most advanced technology and the strictest security standards, inspired especially by the Norwegian oil industry, known for its stringent precautions.

Also, if large earnings from oil should ever emerge, this revenue will be deposited in a fund established in 2009, following Norway's example. The main idea is that only the interest on the money will be available for government spending, while the bulk of it is safeguarded for the benefit of future generations.

Jørgen Hammeken-Holm believes that the Greenlandic oil administration, which is composed of less than 30 people, is strong exactly because of its small size: 'It makes us flexible. We are not experts in technology and construction of oil platforms. We hire the experts we need and only when we need them. That gives us the opportunity to find the best available.'

Accordingly, advisors from the Norwegian and Canadian oil industries were brought in to advise Nuuk when the Scottish company Cairn Energy carried out oil drillings off the Greenlandic west coast in 2010 and 2011. Every morning, Jørgen Hammeken-Holm's experts and officials participated in Cairn's internal briefings to oversee that operations went according to plan.

In the preceding years, the pace in Greenland's oil sector had been very high. From 2007, the oil companies' concessions in Greenland grew from 7,000 to 130,000 square kilometres within two years and in September 2010 news arrived: Cairn Energy had found evidence of gas and two types of oil on the test drilling site Alpha-1 S1 in the Davis Strait, roughly 170 kilometres west of Disco Island on the west coast of Greenland. Cairn published a press release: 'The presence of oil and gas confirms an active and functional petroleum system in the basin, which is very encouraging at this very early stage of our investigation in the Sigguk block and other areas.'

Cairn's find was the first find of oil traces off the coast of Greenland. The prospect of a true jackpot suddenly re-appeared in full force, but the find also brought intensified controversy. In the summer of 2010, activists from Greenpeace in fast-moving rubber dinghies stopped Cairn's test drillings for 36 hours, and they returned in 2011.

The activists, however, had little ground to worry. While the media played up Cairn's discoveries, Cairn had in fact only found traces of oil in one of their four test drillings. In Nuuk the managing director of the Self-Rule Government's oil company, NUNAOIL, Hans Kristian Olsen, issued a warning: 'A commercial find cannot be proved by a single drilling. The needle in the haystack has been found, but we cannot know how big a find this is.'

In September 2010, Cairn stopped their test drillings because winter was approaching. They returned in the summer of 2011, but did not find any more oil. Cairn had spent billions of the shareholders' fortune, they had no commercially viable oil and they have not drilled in Greenland since. In the oil industry, the consensus is still that there are rich deposits of oil off the coast of Greenland, but activity remains low.

Interest grew in 2000 when the US Geological Survey (USGS) published the first landmark analysis and it swelled again in 2008 when a follow-up report offered details. The prognosis is that 30 per cent of the Earth's unused deposits of natural gas and 13 per cent of its unused oil are located in the Arctic area and that up to five per cent of this oil and gas is located off Greenland's north western coast and 7.6 per cent off Greenland's north eastern coast.

The critics believe that the oil hunt in Greenland has been too fast; for the hopeful the process has been terribly slow.

(The sceptics predict that falling oil prices will make the companies back out long before the oil starts flowing, a tendency that became widespread in 2013 and 2014 when several oil companies left Greenland completely. This exodus continued in 2015 and 2016 when oil prices continued to drop.)

In 2012, the threats to the environment posed by the search for oil have already become better understood. Off the coast of north west Greenland, for instance, a famous part of the ocean is known as the North Water Polynya or Pikialasorsuaq. This is one of the most biologically productive waters in the Arctic. In 2009, it was carefully described by experts from DMU, Danmarks Miljøundersøgelser, a Danish environmental research institution. The North Water Polynya is one of the peculiar ocean areas which, due to currents and warmer water from the ocean floor, remains free from ice during large parts of the year.

The North Water Polynya attracts colossal amounts of life, from small fishes to baleen whales, king eiders, walruses, seals and finbacks. This is where the entire orchestra of living creatures, from plankton and algae to whales, breeds and hunts in ice-free lagoons while the rest of the Arctic waters are clasped in ocean ice. On the coast, not far from the North Water Polynya, large colonies of small black guillemots breed. They dive up to 200 metres below the ocean surface. Scientists believe that 80 per cent of all black guillemots on the planet breed on the rocks near Qaanaaq in northern Greenland. They will be in the danger zone should an oil spill occur anywhere nearby.

The scientists described how some of the waters covered by oil concessions west and east of Greenland make up rare retreats for endangered species: For the polar bear hunting along the edges of the ice in north east Greenland and for the fin whale and the blue whale, known for the deepest voices in the world of animals. Off the coast of north east Greenland, the 20-metre-long sperm whale and the world's last Greenland whales of the Spitsbergen type forage. The whales do not like the noise from ships, helicopters or planes. Oil drillings and subaqueous explosions can change the behaviour of the whales, destroy their hearing, disturb their communication and prevent them from finding food. They will be affected by wastewater and oil leaks. The oil can damage the eyes of the whales and their intestines, as well as their baleens, used to filter fish and small fry from the ocean water. The polar bears will face similar threats. Ship traffic through the ice will affect the bears' hunting grounds and an oil leak could kill them. Polar bears hunt between the ice floes where the oil would gather, and a polar bear with oil on its fur will try to lick it off and may die from oil in its intestines.

All this, however, does not necessarily mean the oil exploration in Greenland will be the end of animal life. The scientists also described how the bangs from seismic examinations might affect the ways of whales and Greenland halibuts, but hardly permanently. Drilling ships will scare the whales, but the whales would most likely still find their way to wherever they are going. Oil drilling rigs may discharge large amounts of polluted water, but new techniques can diminish the damage. Norwegian platforms are subject to such tough environmental rules: 'Zero discharge and total fluid management' as Statoil calls it.

Nobody, however, has yet come up with a clear answer on how to deal with any major oil spill in ice-covered water in Greenland.

The responsibility for fighting an oil disaster will lie first and foremost with the relevant oil company itself. Jørgen Hammeken-Holm and his colleagues in the Ministry of Natural Resources had, prior to Cairn's drillings in 2012, ensured that the preparedness of Cairn also consisted of considerable money reserves to be used for a potential clean-up. The exact amount remained a secret, but the insurance group Lloyd described the financial demands to the oil companies who wish to operate in Greenland as 'especially stringent'.

If the oil companies cannot deal with an oil spill themselves the responsibility lies with the authorities in Greenland and/ or Denmark. The emergency response close to the coasts falls under the responsibility of the Greenlandic Self-Rule Government, but in open waters the responsibility is with the Arctic Command of the Danish Defence, headquartered in Nuuk, approximately 1,000 kilometres from the prospective oilfields in north west Greenland and more than 2,500 kilometres from the potential oil drillings in north east Greenland. In the event material and experts would be mobilized from a special environmental unit with the Royal Danish Navy. Minor equipment inventories have been constructed in Greenland and a co-operative agreement with Canada opens the possibility of help from the west. Exercises with transfer of personnel and equipment have been executed, but none to deal with a major oil spill.

The weakness in the emergency systems in the Arctic became a global theme in the early summer of 2010 when *Deepwater Horizon* was shipwrecked in the Mexican Gulf off the state of Louisiana in the United States. In a matter of hours, 11 of 126 people onboard lost their lives. Many were injured. Enormous amounts of oil – some guessed 62,000 barrels or nearly ten billion litres per day – discharged at high pressure from the hole in the ocean floor directly into the ocean.

Within a few days, skilled observers framed the catastrophe in an Arctic perspective. A press release from Word Wildlife Foundation went out: 'However horrible the situation may be, the consequences would be far worse had the accident occurred in the harsh and distant environment of the Arctic. An oil discharge in the Mexican Gulf is like having a heart attack in New York City, a place with all thinkable resources near at hand. An oil discharge in the Arctic is like having a heart attack at the North Pole. If Santa Claus himself does not show up, one cannot count on getting help for a very long time.'

7

NEW PREMIER IN GREENLAND – 'INDEPENDENCE IN MY LIFETIME'

In 2013, hard-hitting nationalist Aleqa Hammond wins a landslide victory and becomes the most vocal advocate for independence in the history of Greenland. 'Divorce is a matter of time', she says. Her reign is short, stopped in its tracks by her own mishandling of public funds, but before then and still as Greenland's Premier, Aleqa Hammond, fluent in several languages, openly discusses her plans for independence with international audiences. She expresses what many in Greenland feel and enrages in the process parts of the Danish populace. In her short, tumultuous tenure relations with Denmark are set on fire and bitter internal fights ensue in Greenland over whether to mine uranium, how soon to separate from Denmark, and over what it truly means to be Greenlandic.

* * *

The camera caught Aleqa Hammond from the front and a little to the right. If she was nervous, it did not show. She smiled self-confidently as she sat bolt upright, dressed in a black angular jacket, next to Iceland's president, the experienced statesman Ólafur Grímsson. There she sat, in the front row, with 1,000 people in the audience waiting for her. She had been in office as Greenland's Premier for exactly 200 days, and in seconds she would address the largest group of decision makers ever gathered in the Arctic.

Hammond's address, from the brightly lit stage of Harpa Centre, Reykjavik's gleaming new concert hall, was one of the most important of the day. As the first keynote speaker she would literally set the stage. She would explain to hundreds of decision makers from Russia, Canada, China and the United States where the Arctic world was headed. They were all waiting for her to explain this Arctic in transition, the Arctic so famous now for its climate change, its oil and for being home to a whole new ocean, the Arctic Ocean, that humans – not least the Chinese – could now sail through, fish and drill in. Hammond, the elected leader of the 56,756 people in Greenland, had been handed the responsibility for the speech that would get this international gathering off to a proper start.

Grímsson had launched his plan for this momentous gathering to sizeable fanfare long in advance at Washington's Press Club. Invitations to the Arctic Circle, as he called it, were sent out a year in advance to an audience of people who wielded direct influence over the future of the Arctic. His plan was to inspire a broad, global discussion about the Arctic region and the new shipping routes from Europe to China, the prospects of oil, gas and minerals and who had the rights to it all. Here were fisheries rich enough to meet a large part of the world's exploding needs for protein. Climate change would ease access to the riches, even as it created havoc and fear in other arenas.

While preparing for the conference, President Grímsson had allied himself with Alice Rogoff, the editor-in-chief of the *Alaska Dispatch*, her billionaire husband, and others with access to the global business elite. Seated in the front row were now the president of COSCO, China's largest shipping line, the chair of Google's board of directors, the president of the International Council on Mining and Metals, representatives from the oil industry and from deep-pocketed investment firms like Guggenheim Partners and from American think-tanks. The South Korean deputy foreign minister was there, as was Russia's Arctic ambassador and a long list of other VIPs. The conference started with a taped greeting from UN Secretary General Ban Ki-Moon, and then it was Hammond's turn. Rising, she took the stage and prepared to speak.

Back in Greenland, Hammond's landslide victory in the 2013 general election had been credited to her ability to accentuate the importance of everything Greenlandic – the language, the culture – and to her insistence that she would lead Greenland towards independence. Hammond was a charismatic figure, to the point of being arrogant, and she was controversial, both in Denmark and in Greenland. She clearly defined a way to be proud and Greenlandic, she was outspoken and she identified a recognizable opponent. On election day, 12 March 2013, a TV crew from the Danish Broadcasting Company covering the election in Nuuk asked Hammond what her priorities were and her answer came without a second thought: 'My dream is the nation of Greenland. My dream is a Greenland that is politically and economically independent of Denmark, and I think it is enormously important how the two talk to each other in the time to come. We need to improve our ability to talk to one another. As long as we are a part of the Kingdom, we are both obliged to do something about that.'

Even before the election, Hammond made it clear that in her opinion Greenland should declare its independence sooner rather than later and her statement to the TV crew was soon repeated to other news outlets in Denmark. 'I have always said that I will live to see the day that the UN recognizes Greenland's independence. On that day, we will sing our national anthem and we will raise our flag around the world. What better goal than that can a little country have?' she told the media. Other statements underscored her personal commitment: 'My personal goal is that the current government will take the steps that make it possible for Greenland to obtain its independence in my lifetime.' She had just turned 47.

'In my lifetime!' Historically speaking, Hammond wanted independence in the blink of an eye. She talked of soon ending hundreds of years of dependency on Copenhagen. She wanted the people of Greenland to step onto the world stage, rich and free, as members of the UN and participants in the Olympics and any other international event. In Denmark, newspaper front pages told their readers to get used to the thought of Greenland leaving the Kingdom. The loss of Greenland – and some 98 per cent of the Kingdom's territory – would be yet another step in a process that first saw Denmark lose Norway in 1814, and then the German-speaking provinces of Schleswig and Holstein in 1864. Without Greenland, Denmark would lose much of its clout internationally; the Danish Prime Minister might no longer have the ear of world leaders. Aleqa Hammond was heralding great upheaval.

Also, she was tearing away the historic narrative that Denmark had nurtured about itself for so long, a story of polar explorers, and of Denmark's meeting with an ancient Greenlandic culture so outlandish that it was hard to imagine that their descendants now used iPads and talked about oil, uranium, and independence 'in their lifetime'.

Aleqa Hammond's timing was crucial. The Danes were just beginning to understand that Greenland was entering a new era. In the media, at schools and universities, in literature, in boardrooms, in the military, at art museums and in parliament – throughout Denmark – everyone from academics to editors was busy seeking to grasp Denmark's new role in the Arctic. The global attention to developments in the Arctic breathed new life into old discussions about guilt and the merits of Danish colonial rule. The more enterprising tried their best to urge the government in Copenhagen to seize the new opportunities in the Arctic before it was too late, and many Danes still had trouble accepting that all the mineral wealth of Greenland, as stipulated by the new Self-Rule Act, did now belong solely to Greenland. It was in the midst of this emotionally charged discussion that Hammond emerged. Her message was clear: Greenland would be independent.

Soon. She got under the skin of Danes in a way that none of her predecessors ever managed. The deadline she had set for independence was sufficiently far away so as not to be relevant in her own political tenure, but it sent a signal of urgency and of her own deep personal involvement. It also instantly put Denmark at odds with Greenland. Hammond obviously saw it as her job to write the last chapter of the history of relations with Denmark, and it was clearly a task she would carry out with pride.

In Reykjavik, she immediately excited the gathered decision makers, investors, and analysts. She told the audience, 'Greenland has significant unexplored mineral, oil and gas resources, including an estimated 25 per cent of the potential supply of rare earth elements globally.' She also predicted how Greenland's parliament, the Inatsisartut, would, just a few days after the conference, vote to allow uranium mining in Greenland. 'This will pave the way for Greenland in a not-so-distant future to become a significant uranium exporter – among the world's top ten or possibly top five.'

This was news. Could Greenland really become one of the world's largest exporters of uranium? Many of those now following Aleqa Hammond's words very carefully had barely heard of Greenland before. They might have listened as she spoke of climate change and its sizeable effects in Greenland, but it was uranium, rare earths and all the other mineral wealth Greenland was sitting on which really caught the audience, and Hammond masterfully conjured up the power Greenland had been granted over its own underground. 'In 2009, Greenland achieved "self-government status" within the Kingdom of Denmark. Amongst other things, the "self-government" law recognizes that the Greenlandic people are a people under international law and therefore have the established right to self-determination [...] In 2010, Greenland took over the sole competence from Denmark over oil and gas and mineral resources.'

She thrived in the spotlight. She did not wear any Greenlandic jewellery, no brooches made of narwhal horn or any of the other symbols Greenlandic politicians often tend to wear in public. Hammond was not there to represent an ethnic minority. She was there as a head of state and she delivered her address in faultless English.

No one present could have been left in doubt: Greenlanders now made the decisions in Greenland. Denmark and the Danes had skilfully been removed from the equation. Greenland's relationship with Denmark was complicated; few in either country fully understood what the division of powers really was, but in Hammond's version everything seemed clear: In Greenland, the Greenlanders were in power! If you want to do business or talk about oil, minerals, uranium, fishing, partnerships, please come directly to me!

Far south of Reykjavik, in Copenhagen, Hammond's repeated chest thumping was not going down well in the corridors of power. Greenlanders' aspirations to be free and independent had long been recognized and to a certain extent respected, but the rhetorical power in Hammond's message and her single-minded focus on ending Greenland's relationship with Denmark as quickly as possible resulted in confusion and palpable irritation. Meanwhile, her critics found a certain satisfaction in the fact that she was also divisive in Greenland. Her wish to lift the ban on uranium divided her own people as much as the Danes, as did her proposal to establish a reconciliation commission that would investigate past conflicts with the Danes. Some welcomed this reckoning with open arms, while others saw no reason to revisit painful events of the colonial past. In Copenhagen, Prime Minister Helle Thorning-Schmidt ruled out any Danish participation in the work of a reconciliation commission.

Søren Espersen, a member of parliament and spokesperson for the Danish People's Party, called on Thorning-Schmidt to reign in her Greenlandic counterpart: 'Aleqa Hammond's recent statements, not least when it comes to uranium, reveal that she and her party, Siumut, have an unpleasant side. It has almost become something of a habit for her to lash out at Denmark and constantly challenge the Self-Rule Act and the constitution.

Consequently, I would ask the Prime Minister to address this change in Greenland's official behaviour.'

Veteran Greenland observers found Hammond to be out of line; some said she bordered on racism. In her first live appearance on Danish television, she courted controversy again. 'I do not look Danish. I do not speak Danish. Danish is not my native language. And Greenland is far away from Denmark. You can compare the Kingdom of Denmark to a marriage, but right now this marriage has been put on hold. Now we are talking about the likelihood of an amicable divorce. It is only a matter of time.'

Hammond's political message was rich, but her personality won the hearts of many in Denmark and Greenland. She was at once effective, charismatic, well-dressed, and eloquent and she offered an insight into a cultural battle in Greenland that grew more intense after she and her allies came to power. As divisions between Greenland and Denmark were growing, so too were Greenlanders finding themselves increasingly divided. Should they pursue development of oil and minerals at a breakneck pace, or should they take their time? Would it be wiser to put Greenland's money on tried-and-true industries like fishing and tourism? Should the nation allow uranium? Should it let people go on living in the smallest hamlets along the coast, or were these tiny communities too small and too costly to be sustainable in a modern world? Aleqa Hammond made all of these issues more poignant and current, and she also threw herself into the most sensitive issue of them all: She often spoke about the Greenlandic language, and suddenly an intense debate was raging in Greenland. Did speaking the language correctly make you more Greenlandic than others? Are you less Greenlandic if you have lost some – or all – of your Greenlandic because you have a Danish father or mother? Are some Greenlanders more valuable than others? To many it was a painful debate.

In both Greenland and in Denmark, difficult dilemmas were mounting and new questions were asked. Does Greenland need the Kingdom of Denmark? Does Denmark need

Greenland? Is there a middle way – an acceptable alternative
to independence? Can the Kingdom be reformed? Is it only
natural that Greenland heads in one direction while Denmark
heads another? What do Greenlanders mean when they talk
about independence? What kind of society do they want for
themselves? And what will Copenhagen do?

In March 2013, when Aleqa Hammond was handed the
keys to the Premier's Office on the ninth floor of Nuuk's new
mall, the first thing she took note of was that she could still
make out the faces on the street even from this lofty height.
Then she took in the view: She could see the fjord, the old
colonial harbour and the low wooden buildings built by
the first colonists. To the east, she could see the modern new
apartment complexes built on the lower reaches of the 'Store
Malene' mountain. She could see the hills on the other side of
the airport. Behind her desk she had hung an old gold-framed
oil painting of a proud Greenlandic hunter stalking birds.
Spear raised, dressed in kamiks and polar bear fur trousers, he
was the epitome of the honourable hunter, forever in harmony
with nature. Behind him the mountain of Uummannaq was
clearly recognizable, as if to emphasize that Hammond had
grown up in the real Greenland: The cold, distant northern
part of the country. The rest of her office was furnished with
a hypermodern ash-grey sofa set, flowers on the windowsill,
candles and a smallish snow-white polar bear carved out of
soapstone and polished to a high shine.

A year later, in February 2014, back in Nuuk after a trip
that took her to Paris, Brussels, Tromsø in northern Norway
and Copenhagen, Hammond explained to me during a two-
hour interview in her office why she had made her vision
of Greenlandic independence from Denmark her political
trademark. She explained why independence, for her, was about
much more than the subsidies from Denmark, and why she
insisted that Greenlanders distance themselves from their past
as a colony and the 300 years under Danish dominion. 'I find it
only natural to discuss independence. It is only natural that we
want to be independent. It is only natural that our people want

to be responsible for all that affects our lives. We want to chart our own course; we – as a people, country, culture and citizens of a globalized world – feel that is the way it should be. About 80 per cent of all Greenlanders voted in favour of self-rule in 2008. The people of Greenland voted for greater autonomy and for taking the next step in building our country. I am proud to come from a country where people are not in doubt.' Within a year of being elected as Greenland's political leader, Hammond had managed to establish herself as Greenland's biggest proponent of independence from Denmark to date. In November 2013, she told *Information*, a Danish daily, 'I think as the leader of an independent nation'.

She also, however, maintained that Greenland's fate would be forever tied to Denmark's. She was never afraid to address this apparent contradiction. 'All my life, Greenland has been a part of another country, and I am very aware of that other country. I do not look at things just from a Greenlandic perspective. There is a Danish part of me, and there is a Greenlandic part of me. The Danish part of me is not something that I have chosen, but it is still a part of who I am. It was not my choice to learn Danish; I was told to. I could not, not take Danish classes in school or choose another language. We have Danish norms, Danish laws, our school calendar follows the Danish one, we have Danish doctors, teachers and traditions, and our public holidays and our religious holidays are those of Denmark. I have no problem interacting with Danes even though I have never lived there. Denmark has an enormous influence here. I am a subject of another country, and that has affected me personally, just as it has affected us as a people.'

Even before she was elected, Hammond used carefully selected elements of her past as the foundation of her political message. She was fond of recalling how she, when she was 12, asked her mother if she could stop using her given Danish name. The vicar in Uummannaq agreed to a name change, and since then she has only used her Greenlandic name.

At the election that brought her to power, Aleqa Hammond received 6,818 votes, far more than any other Greenlandic candidate ever had. Her party's second biggest vote getter, Hans Enoksen, himself a former premier, received just 632. The aforementioned opposition leader, Kuupik Kleist, garnered 4,369. Greenland's urban elite, who by and large had supported Kleist and his cadre of educated candidates, barely knew what hit them, but Hammond herself saw her victory as a mandate to push Greenland farther down the independence path. 'My mother grew up at a time when all the important decisions were made in the Greenland Ministry in Copenhagen: her schooling, her work and her place in society. I, on the other hand, grew up at a time when we had our own parliament and our own government. Today, we are shaping a society based on our own ambitions and norms. We dare to do more, and we want to do more. We demand more of ourselves. I like that. I am part of a movement, of a people on the move. We no longer need to live on fishing and hunting alone. We focus on education, diversity, working together with other countries, greater responsibility, taking responsibility for more areas of public administration. Greenland is setting the agenda, both at home and abroad, and people are becoming more politically aware. I am not the leader of this movement; I am a part of it. I am just the first premier who has dared to be so open about it.'

As the new head of Naalakkersuisut, Greenland's cabinet, Hammond quickly waded into controversy. Her critics felt she was hideously populist. She pursued her goals with a fervour that bordered on the brutal, and when she formed her first coalition government with the largely liberal Atassut and Partii Inuit, a newly formed nationalist protest party, their common manifesto included a controversial promise to address the perceived traumas of the colonial era: 'In order to distance ourselves from the colonization of our country, we must engage in a process of reconciliation and forgiveness. An action plan to accomplish this will be drawn up.' A few months later, her coalition put forward a budget that included financing for a Reconciliation Commission. Hammond told *Sermitsiaq*, Greenland's most widely read newspaper, a weekly, that the commission would include a historian, a psychologist, an anthropologist, a sociologist and quite possibly a church official, and that their job would be to 'address the issues that were preventing basic reconciliation with the colonial period, the relationship between Denmark and Greenland and our people'.

The precise aim was not perfectly clear, and for many the Commission was as irritating as a bug in the ear. Hammond's critics accused her of demonizing the Danes in order to win electoral support. Others feared that she was comparing Greenland's colonial past with Apartheid in South Africa. Among these was Uffe Ellemann-Jensen, a former Danish foreign minister: 'You would think that Greenland had an abysmal past on par with Apartheid. But it was never like that. Why do we not come back to reality? A reconciliation commission is something you set up after years upon years of abuses and you really have something you need to address. That is just not the case here.' Mogens Lykketoft, another Danish former foreign minister, and the acting president of the Danish parliament, was also bearish on the idea: 'I have a different point of view than Aleqa Hammond. It is correct that mistakes were made in the past – by both Danes and others. But the people of Greenland were never intentionally mistreated. You will find few examples of colonial powers that have had less of an interest in profiting from or a greater interest in developing their colony. As far back as I can see – at least as far back as the 1920s – Denmark's distinct aim has been to raise Greenlandic living standards to the same level as in Denmark. Denmark might have been overly paternalistic, but everything was always done with the best of intentions.'

Lykketoft and Ellemann-Jensen's statements were typical Danish reactions to Hammond's plans for reconciliation. Both are considered close friends of Greenland, sympathetic to many of Greenland's aspirations, but during a March 2014 interview, Lykketoft told me how he disagreed with Hammond's opinion that a majority in Greenland supported independence. 'We have intermarried and formed families for 400 years. A lot of Greenlanders have ties with Denmark – not just mentally, but also personally. There are a lot of

Greenlanders in Denmark, and there are very few pure-blooded Inuit in Greenland any more. That's why I do not think you are going to see a firm majority for dissolving the Kingdom for the foreseeable future. You might see a temporary majority every once in a while – just like we have seen it in the Faroe Islands – but when it comes down to it, the majority is not there. Personally, I am happy about that. Being three countries together in a single Kingdom enriches us all.'

Greenland's 2014 budget set aside 9.6 million kroner to fund the Reconciliation Commission for the next four years, or half of the 20 million kroner Greenland had set aside to bring down cancer rates. Nevertheless, in her new year's address, Aleqa Hammond defended the costs: 'We have progressed so far that we Greenlanders are now recognized as a people with the right to self-determination. This recognition is a right the Greenlandic people are granted according to international law and the UN. But as we have taken steps to develop our country and ourselves as a people, we have neglected to discuss what was happening. I dare say that some of the biggest taboos in our society have emerged as a result of our history and the relations between the various groups in our population. We must break these taboos and make people more aware of the relationships that exist between them. We must also be ready to make a change if we come across something that is unjust. There were situations where people's feelings were hurt. These sentiments need to be addressed, and reconciliation is the next logical step. We must reconcile ourselves with the past, as well as with different population groups and with ourselves. We must take responsibility for our own country and take the next step forward as a people, and in so doing give more people the chance to take responsibility for their own lives and to contribute to our society.'

It was not immediately clear whether Hammond and her staff would let Greenlanders who wanted to make claims for wrongs suffered at the hands of the colonial authority do so as individuals, or whether it was the nation of Greenland as a whole that, like so many other former colonies before it, felt the need to write its own history. The Danish government, though, rejected the whole Commission out of hand.

Ulrik Pram Gad, a University of Copenhagen political scientist, summed up the debate in *Europa*, an online magazine: 'The constant refrain repeated by Danish lawmakers about a "kingdom of equals" has always rung hollow in Greenlandic ears. New generations of Danish politicians can have all the best intentions to speak and act politically correct, but it is not clear in what respect the relationship is equal, or how far that equality extends. Greenlanders can point out any number of incidents from both the past and present in which Copenhagen has said one thing but done another. They can also relate examples of how equality was something they had to fight for.'

For many Greenlanders, it remained unclear what Hammond expected the Commission to achieve. But during the interview at her office, she readily explained her thoughts. Her aim was not to blame Danes or to get Denmark or the Danish state to apologize for the past, she said. 'I am not trying to make anyone responsible. I cannot ignore that Denmark is a part of Greenland's history. But this is not about getting rid of Denmark; it is about us moving on as a people.' Hammond was not looking for an apology. Instead, what she envisioned was historians and others identifying what wrongs Greenlanders feel were done to them and then taking a look at what actually happened. 'Denmark and Greenland did not agree on everything. If you believe that you are lying to yourself. We did not make thousands of Greenlandic children legally fatherless together. We did not decide together that the Thule people in the north of the country should be forcibly relocated overnight just so someone could build an airbase. We did not decide together that the mining town of Qullissat should be shut and its people moved. All these events are a part of our experience as subjects of the Kingdom. We need to reconcile ourselves with that history before we can move on. There is a lot that we cannot talk about today, but I find it natural to discuss something that is such a big part of who I am.' Hammond described how she expected that the colonial past would be dredged up by the Reconciliation Commission in public meetings, in televised debates or in radio broadcasts, and that this would lay the foundation for reconciliation. The process, she felt, would give many Greenlanders the peace of mind they need in order for them to be able to begin the arduous task of preparing the country for its independence – be it in the mental, political, or economic sense. 'We know this works. It is not the first time a former colonial power and the people it colonized have sought to reconcile with each other.'

One Danish Prime Minister had already once issued a formal apology on behalf of the Danish state. In 1953, as described above, a little more than a hundred people living near Thule Air Base in northern Greenland were forcibly relocated. When a Danish court, in 1999, found that the relocation had been unlawful, Poul Nyrup Rasmussen, the Prime Minister at the time, paid the group 1.7 million kroner in compensation and issued a formal, measured apology – in Greenlandic. 'In the spirit of the Kingdom, and out of respect for the people of Greenland and the people of Thule, the Danish government, on behalf of the Danish state, apologizes – *utoqqatserpugut* – to Inughuit, the people of Thule and the entire nation of Greenland for the manner in which the relocation was decided and carried out.'

In reality, the apology was not just a Danish apology. It was a joint Danish–Greenlandic apology, co-signed by Jonathan Motzfeldt, the head of the Greenlandic Home Rule government at the time, thus signalling just how difficult it often is to draw a clear line between what Danish lawmakers were responsible for and what their Greenlandic counterparts were part of.

During the interview at her Nuuk office, Hammond mentioned that the Canadian state had long since apologized for forcibly removing thousands of Inuit children from their biological parents. The Sami of Norway and Sweden were apologized to by Oslo and Stockholm for past transgressions, just like Australia's Aborigines got an apology, but the idea never gained traction in government circles in Copenhagen. A leading member of Denmark's governing coalition in 2014,

Christian Friis Bach, explained the decision to reject Aleqa Hammond's Reconciliation Commission: 'We have never been at war with Greenland or in a conflict with them. We have co-operated with them, for better and for worse. Of course there were things we should have done differently, but there is no point in apologizing for what was done in a different time and by different people living in a different situation.'

In Nuuk, the setting up of the Commission continued. An administrative head was found, and a number of professionals offered to assist as experts. Among them was Jens Heinrich, a Greenlandic historian, whose 2012 doctoral dissertation examined the political development of modern Greenland. He found Aleqa Hammond's initiative promising: 'We know that many of the unfortunate circumstances we see in Greenland today can be traced back to the errors of the past. If we confront modern Greenlandic history, it will allow us to move forward more confidently and quite possibly debunk some of the myths of Greenlandic history. One of the things that it will be particularly important to look at will be to what extent Greenland's lawmakers have been responsible for what happened.' Speaking with *Jyllands-Posten*, he lashed out at the Danish refusal to take part in the process. 'A people need to know and write its own history. That is how we must see the Reconciliation Commission. It is not an attack on Denmark and Danes or an attempt to get an apology out of them.' Shortly afterwards, Jens Heinrich was appointed as one of the five permanent members of the Commission.

For Hammond the issue was a hornet's nest. When the debate over reconciliation and Danish colonialism started to gather speed in 2013, she found herself under fire for raising a divisive public discussion about who is a 'real' Greenlander when she linked her quest for independence to a wish to strengthen the Greenlandic language, culture, and tradition.

Some Greenlanders who did not speak fluent Greenlandic felt as if they were being made inferior to 'full-blooded' Greenlanders, or, worse, that they were somehow suspicious if they did not fully support Hammond's positions on independence, culture, or reconciliation. Hammond, as always, brushed criticism aside. 'I am not a nationalist', she told *Kristeligt Dagblad*, a Danish daily. 'Wanting to strengthen Greenlandic culture should not be seen as a nationalistic project. It should be seen as a natural desire to strengthen Greenlandic identity.'

Kuupik Kleist, Hammond's predecessor as premier and leader of the opposition until March 2014, found it hard to express his frustration in diplomatic terms: 'The political climate is not very good for the time being. She uses independence as an excuse for avoiding political discussions about more down-to-earth issues. At the first sign of resistance, she bristles and takes it as a sign that you are anti-independence.' Kleist cared little for Hammond's approach. 'My party is a pro-independence party, but I have always maintained that we need to build up a country that can stand on its own two feet first. If you say that we can become independent by your 70th birthday or before you die, you risk creating a society that lacks in areas like democracy, economics, and foreign affairs. Independence might be feasible in the next 40 or 50 years, but right now nothing is happening because of the rotten political climate and the long list of disagreements between Greenland and Denmark which Aleqa Hammond has caused.'

Not long after, Kleist announced his own resignation as party leader. During a press conference, he explained that it was time for a new generation to step in and get ready to take on the challenges that awaited them – including the next election. In the government headquarters, in the office directly under Hammond, her Environment Minister, Kim Kielsen, explained that he, in principle, was behind the Premier's political project, but that he personally felt it was unrealistic that independence was conceivable in his own lifetime. 'We are all passionate about independence', he said, thumping his chest. 'We should be able to decide for ourselves in Greenland, but we have different points of view internally in our party. I would like to see the next generation get better educated so that they can decide for themselves if they are ready for independence or not.'

Little did he know, of course, that he himself would soon be head of the government.

On the economy, Hammond was at odds with many economists, who found it unrealistic that the independent Greenland she dreamt of would be able to support itself any time soon. During our talk in her office, however, her rhetoric took on a less immediate tone. 'It is not as if we are saying that we want to break away right now. Before we can do that we need to wean ourselves off the Danish block grant. The Self-Rule Act lists 32 administrative areas that we need to overtake before we can get that far. Only when that is done can we negotiate what needs to happen in order for Greenland to become independent. When we reach that point, on the other hand, is up to us.'

She smiled. 'You know what? In 1979, when Home Rule was established, I did not know that a Greenlander could become a pilot or a doctor or an executive. Today, I can hire a Greenlandic solicitor if I want. I can go to a Greenlandic doctor or specialist. When I fly on an Air Greenland flight to Copenhagen, the pilot speaks Greenlandic. It is fantastic what we have been able to accomplish in the span of just 30 years. No other indigenous group anywhere has been able to accomplish so much. Our educational level is still too low and I admit that we face major economic challenges; in 20 years there will be twice as many pensioners as there are today, and we are going be facing a billion kroner deficit each year. Foreign economists and experts say this constantly, but they are not telling us anything we do not already know. That is exactly why we are trying to do something about it. I am upbeat and I am optimistic about the future of our people and of our economy.'

Aleqa Hammond was equally unconcerned about Greenland's dependency on the block grant: 'I see us gradually moving out of its shadow. In 1979, before I could vote, the block grant made up an outrageously large part of the budget. Look it up yourself. When we moved to Self-Rule in 2009, the block grant's proportion of our national income was far less. As we educate ourselves more, our reliance on it decreases. The importance of the block grant will decrease over time.'

There were plenty of obstacles. Nine months into her term in office, all but two of the permanent secretaries leading government ministries had either quit or been fired. The situation reached a climax in January 2014, when Tom Ostermann, Hammond's domestic partner and a former police officer, was hired as special advisor for Hammond's fishing and hunting minister. The media claimed that it was a blatant example of nepotism. Tom Ostermann was let go after three days, and not long after the minister was gone too. Hammond had appeared as an incompetent leader and her advisors as badly lacking.

Aleqa Hammond seemed to thrive on adversity and she was not snobbish. At her office she discussed recent meetings in Copenhagen with Denmark's Queen Margrethe. Danes often claim that Greenlanders are heartfelt supporters of the monarchy, but Hammond's comments on the queen's relationship with Greenland were blunt. 'She has to visit us, whether she wants to or not, because she needs to keep an eye out for the state's interests in Greenland and the Faroe Islands.'

She also claimed that the decision to give Prince Vincent and Princess Josephine, the youngest children of Prince Frederik, the heir apparent, Greenlandic middle names should be interpreted not only as a sign of the royal family's love for Greenland. Giving the royal twins Greenlandic names – Minik and Ivalo – carried an ulterior message, she said. The royal family, she believed, was using the Greenlandic names as part of an effort to strengthen the bonds between Denmark and Greenland. 'These two names have not been chosen at random. They are using the monarchy to show that Greenland is important to Denmark. The monarchy has a Greenland policy.' Also, the royal name-game was not without precedent, she explained. In 1940, when Queen Margrethe was to be christened, Iceland, at that time a Danish colony, was close to declaring its independence. Her father, who later became King Frederik IX, gave her the Icelandic name Thorhildur.

8

TO BE OR NOT TO BE INDEPENDENT

A majority of the 57,000 people in Greenland embrace independence as a warm, if distant, vision but some want to distance themselves from Denmark more fervently than others. As in other former colonies, opinions in Greenland differ widely on how to relate to the old colonial power, and in Denmark most struggle to understand what Greenland's quest for independence is all about. In the town of Sisimiut on Greenland's west coast I explore everyday life in Greenland with a true nationalist; in Narsaq in the south I talk to one of the rare fans of permanent statehood with Denmark.

* * *

Ulrik Lyberth sends me an email with a challenge to come interview him in Sisimiut, Greenland's second largest town, with about 5,000 inhabitants, on the central stretch of Greenland's west coast. He indicates that he has views that differ substantially from the mainstream in Greenland. On a tour of Sisimiut on a cold February day some months later, he points out the sites. 'Look over there! During the colonial period, that was where the Danish governor lived. He was called Naalagaqq, the one-and-only-ruler', he says.

The icy road up the hill from the old harbour passes a small shopping plaza, not unlike those you might see in Denmark. He turns right and enters the municipal office, takes a number and waits by a potted plant. He needs to pay the fee for the right to use a tiny plot of land where he stores his boat during winter. 'Now we are headed into Danish territory', he says, holding out the bill. 'See, it's written entirely in Danish. Not a word in Greenlandic.'

The previous weekend, Lyberth had been in Nuuk attending the newly formed nationalist Partii Inuit's first annual congress to show his support for preservation of the Greenlandic language and for independence from Denmark. Out in the Aqqartarfik neighbourhood in Sisimiut, he counts 15 concrete tower blocks, all built in the 1970s. One is boarded up and cordoned off, ready for demolition. I note how the scene could just as well be from suburban Denmark and Lyberth smiles. 'That's exactly it.' He sees the Danish imprint everywhere: in the brutal tower blocks, in the kindergartens, at the schools, in Pisiffik – the supermarket 'owned by a Danish firm'.

There are no sled dogs to be heard. Most houses in Sisimiut were built far enough apart so that there was room to keep packs of dogs, but modern people need their sleep and so they keep their dogs out of town, past the hotel looking out over Kangerluarsunnguaq, or Scuplin Bay. Modern-day dog sledding, Lyberth explains, is mostly an expensive hobby, often practised to keep the tradition alive. There are only about 100 teams of dogs left in Sisimiut, while an estimated 700 snowmobiles roam the snowmobile trails. Lyberth himself is more inclined to fish and hunt seal at sea. This allows him to bring home traditional food. 'We hardly ever eat Danish food', he says as he enters Qimatulivik, the little shop with all manner of fresh meat: seal, reindeer, muskoxen and fowl.

Over at Pisiffik, the supermarket, Lyberth picks up coconut biscuits and checks out the deals. Three packs of pork mince from Denmark are on special offer. Back at home, in his terraced townhouse overlooking the Davis Strait, he explains his frustration with Greenlandic society.

Since 1721, he finds, Greenland has been run only to profit Copenhagen. Everything in Greenland – fisheries, hunting, tax collection, education, schoolbooks – is based on Danish rules, regulations and an administrative structure wholly unsuitable for Greenland. 'At one point, the officials in the town of Nanortalik wanted to make their public administration more efficient, so they hired someone from Denmark to help them. He had never been to Greenland, but from the moment he got here he was giving advice about how to make changes. You just cannot do that.'

'Denmark ought to apologize for the things that happened: forced relocations from Qullissat, Thule and Ivittuut, "fatherless" children. We have been talking about all this for 50 years without anything coming of it. It still hurts that we have not been apologized to. If Denmark apologized, it would put our minds at ease and we could move on. The media always make all our problems out to be the Greenlanders' fault, but there is a reason why things are this way. We need to drag it all out into the light and treat it like your dentist would treat a rotten root canal.'

To Lyberth, independence from Denmark cannot come soon enough and unlike most Greenland politicians he is ready to cut spending on welfare if that is what it takes to become independent. 'The Danish block grant is a crutch for us Greenlanders. As long as it keeps coming, the Danes can keep telling us that we cannot live without it. But we can. There are vast riches in this country, and we have got a privileged position between East and West that we can exploit. What I would really like to see is a calculation of how much of Greenland's value is shipped off to Denmark each year. My guess is that the 3.6 billion kroner we get from the Danes each year is peanuts in comparison.'

The belief that Denmark is turning a profit on Greenland has long been held by many in Greenland and it came back in a new apparition thanks to Partii Inuit. Lyberth had the party's version laid out for him during its first annual congress by August Thor, the head of the Faculty of Law at the University of Akureyi in Iceland and an expert in North Atlantic relations. August Thor made two points. The first was that since becoming a colony in 1721, Greenland had, in his opinion, been a cash cow for Denmark. Greenland ought to have independent experts calculate how much Denmark made off Greenland since the arrival of Hans Egede, he explained. The calculation should include everything Denmark earned from the sale of pelts, whale oil, and all other commodities. It should include the value of whatever Danish tradesmen, teachers and vicars brought back with them to Denmark – including their pension savings. The experts should calculate the profit Danish firms made in Greenland and also measure how much Denmark saved as part of a deal with the United States, which many in Greenland believe exists, that allowed Denmark for many years to increase its defence spending at a slower rate than other NATO countries in return for allowing the US military to have bases in Greenland. If you put everything together, Thor said, it will far exceed the amount that Denmark has put into Greenland. The conclusion, he says, would be clear as day: Denmark still has a responsibility to support Greenland, even if Greenland chooses to secede from the Kingdom. 'The economic problems Greenland has today can be blamed on the decisions the Danes made well before Greenlandic lawmakers gained influence. That, combined with 300 years of economic exploitation, gives Denmark an obvious responsibility to aid Greenland, regardless of whether Greenland remains in the Kingdom or not. At least until Greenland can support itself economically.'

This may take a while. The Danish block grant represents about half of the annual income of the Self-Rule Government. August Thor's other point was therefore that Greenland should secede as quickly as possible. Only as an independent state would Greenland be able to make the most of free-trade agreements or other economic co-operation agreements with other countries. 'True, Greenland negotiates directly with oil firms and foreign investors, but Greenland does not do so as an independent country. In the first place, Denmark is always at their backs, and, in the second, they know that whatever profit they make has to be split with Denmark. If there is oil, or if a mine turns a profit. Denmark controls Greenland the same way you would control a child.'

August Thor argued that Iceland's own secession from the Kingdom of Denmark was an obvious example for Greenland to follow. Iceland never accepted the Danish constitution and finally cut all ties to Denmark in 1944.

Not far from Lyberth's home in Sisimiut, Ove Rosing Olsen, a doctor, disagrees heartily with many of Lybert's opinions. In the 1980s, when Greenland took over responsibility for the health service from Denmark, Olsen was named the country's first health minister. He left politics in 1995 and now serves as the chief medical officer for the Qeqqata local council, which includes Sisimiut, the town of Maniitsoq, and the area's smaller settlements. He thinks Hammond is right to highlight the progress Greenland has made. 'It is amazing what we have accomplished these past 30 years. In 1978, I became the first doctor with two Greenlandic parents. Today, there are about 30 of us. When we said we wanted to take over responsibility for Greenland's healthcare, people were pessimistic. "There's no way it will work", they said. But we have shown them. In my hospital, the vast majority of our nurses are Greenlanders, I have five Greenlandic doctors and the quality of care we can provide is far, far better than what it was when I started as a doctor.'

This type of sentiment can be heard in all corners of Greenland. The long-term goal of independence is a mantra in the halls of government, among members of Inatsisartut, among the young and old, teachers and fishermen, stylish teenagers and wizened hunters. Which path to choose in order to reach this new phase of Greenland's development is a topic of heated discussion, but there is broad agreement on the underlying premise.

One of the rare dissenters is Josef Petersen, 38, from Narsaq in the far south. He moved to Narsaq with his parents when he was seven. After leaving primary school, he got an education, married, had kids, started as a teacher and was promoted to head of the local employment centre and its 45 young jobseekers. In 2013, he was elected to the Kujalleq municipal council, which covers all of southern Greenland for Atassut, a liberal party that used to be known for its belief in strong ties with Denmark. 'I want to keep the Kingdom together', he says. 'Greenland and Denmark have been together for a long time and we have close ties. My mother has a Danish father and my wife's father is Danish. I follow Danish politics, and when Denmark plays football or handball, people in Greenland root for them. Yes, we need to have responsibility for our own affairs, but I think it should be as part of the Kingdom.' Petersen has never lived in Denmark, yet he still feels a strong connection to it. He feels at home speaking Danish.

'I know there are a lot of people in my party who say that as long as it is financially responsible then we should declare our independence, but they are only saying that because they know it will take so long, that it will never happen. If it did happen, and I hope not, we would need to take over responsibility for the courts, the police, civil aviation, maritime authority, and a lot of other things. I do not even want to begin to think about what it would cost. The Kingdom gives us the leeway we need. We can count on having Denmark there if we get into financial trouble, or if we need specialized help at some point.'

The debate on relations with Denmark is heavily intertwined with the debate about the Danish language and its role in Greenland. In the government preceding Aleqa Hammond's, a number of cabinet members, including the finance minister, spoke only limited Greenlandic. Some Inatsisartut members do not speak Danish well, but debates in the legislature were often carried out in Danish and interpreted into Greenlandic.

The language dilemmas are everywhere. At Sisimiut's Cafe Taseralik, I overheard stylish young mothers chat over coffee in a mix of Greenlandic and Danish, and many children of mixed marriages prefer Danish. There are about 5,000 Danes in Greenland who get by without speaking Greenlandic. Only a handful of Danes speak Greenlandic fluently, even though many hold key positions. Meanwhile, about half of all Greenlanders do not speak more than very patchy Danish, and anyone travelling to Greenland quickly finds out that the only way to speak to people is often through an interpreter unless you master Greenlandic. Important discussions on the radio are inaccessible to Danes, and also among the rapidly growing group of educated Greenlanders, there is mounting frustration over the linguistic divide.

9
PROSPECTS OF URANIUM

In 2014, a controversial decision by Inatsisartut, Greenland's parliament, to lift a ban on uranium mining in Greenland creates a deep rift with Denmark. The government in Copenhagen fears that Greenland's uranium might jeopardize Denmark's long-standing commitment to the global efforts to curb nuclear proliferation, but Greenland's governing elite claims exclusive powers over any raw materials in Greenland, including uranium. In the tiny town of Narsaq, the residents tell me how promises of a uranium mine less than ten kilometres from the city centre cause fears of contamination, but also new hopes of jobs and prosperity.

* * *

Two ravens fly aimlessly in the golden winter sky above Narsap Ilua, a bay just outside the town of Narsaq opening out into Brede Fjord in southern Greenland. Two fishermen jig the lines they have dropped through holes in the ice; lumpfish roe is in season. Out at the end of the bay, frost is starting to form a layer of thin ice in the dim afternoon sunlight. The water on the other side of the point is like glass; the gulls' wings nearly touch the water as they fly over. A wire fence winds its way up the mountain. Kunanersuit, also known as Kvanefjeld, is just opposite the bay. It rises slowly, forming a grey-white bow. Farther up it becomes steeper, making it harder for the snow to stick. Up where rock meets sky, the mountain flattens out in the direction of Erik's Fjord, named after Erik the Red. It was here, over 1,000 years ago, that Erik, exiled from Iceland for murder, led the first group of Norse settlers to Greenland. They had the banks of the fjord to themselves as they settled, planted crops and hunted. They harvested the land's bounty, exploited the minerals and worked the seas. When new groups of Inuit then migrated east and south from North America the two peoples traded, argued, and intermarried – just as Greenlanders and Danes did some 300 or 400 years later.

In the snow at the foot of Kvanefjeld, at the end of a road that has been cleared of snow, Pavia Rohde calls up a map of the mountain on his iPhone. 'Look, there, on the plateau beyond the peak – that is where the mine is to be. And there, Tileq Lake – that is where the tailings are to be deposited.' Rohde, a blacksmith, who for years operated one of the big separators in the gravel pit outside the town, was hired by Greenland Minerals and Energy (GME), the mining firm, to keep an eye on the company's equipment and supplies until the digging actually begins. 'Tailings' is the mountains of rock leftover when the miners have extracted what they came for.

More ravens glide along the mountain. Out on the water, a lone boat makes its way through the cold. Thin bushes poke through the snow down by the creek, while off in the direction of Narsaq Rohde can see the old gravel pit where he once worked. Kvanefjeld is not physically remarkable, but as anyone who follows Greenland politics has long since understood, the mine that might be established here is phenomenal in many ways. A vision of a uranium mine has divided the Greenlanders and driven a hard wedge between Denmark and Greenland, while the promise of riches is key to some people's dreams of the future. Kvanefjeld holds one of the world's richest deposits of uranium, and buried with it is one of the largest deposits of rare earth minerals outside of China. In Greenland's political circles this is important. Without this mine, without the mine at Kringlerne, some 15 kilometres to the south, without the new gold mines farther south, without the iron ore near Nuuk and without the rubies and the zinc in the north, the vision of an independent Greenland will be harder to sustain.

In Narsaq, Kattie Nielsen points at a small group of houses. 'My grandparents lived there, in the blue house, with their five sons and their daughter. Now my aunt lives there. The house on the left, the one with the scaffolding, is where my husband and I are going to live. It is my uncle up there fixing it. The big grey house belonged to my parents, and now my brother owns it. My other uncle lives in the other grey house there to the left and my sister and her kids live in the yellow one.'

Kattie Nielsen is back in Narsaq with her family after a decade in Iceland. She and her husband are taking over the hotel in Narsaq. Her father, Karl Olesen, dressed in overalls and gumboots, stands in the doorway of his shed, cutting up seal meat and putting it in plastic bags so he can send it to a brother in Denmark. In the shed, a butchered reindeer hangs from the roof, and there is a bow saw for the bones, two rifles, an old VHF radio, plastic bags, two garden gnomes, cardboard cases and a Carlsberg advert. Inside, Jørgen Olesen, Kattie's uncle, also in overalls, speaks in a deep, rumbling voice as he takes off his boots in the hallway. The three exchange small talk in Greenlandic over coffee, bread, cheese and Danish pastry. Karl Olesen stays close to the stove's exhaust hood as he smokes; it is too cold to smoke outside.

The two brothers, both in their fifties, started fishing the fjords near Narsaq when they were still boys. They had children and their children had children. Karl points to a picture and counts nine grandkids. The brothers recall the years they fished from their own boats, when the prawn plant kept three shifts busy around the clock. That was before the fish disappeared, rules changed, and the processing plant reopened as a sheep abattoir on subsidies from the government in Nuuk. Back in the old days, the plant kept 100 people busy producing processed seafood for Danish consumers. Then the big trawlers took over prawn fishing, and the processing jobs were shipped off to Poland, Denmark, China, and Japan. Today the Olesen brothers make their living fishing big crabs. Their legs get sold abroad, but they do not bring in what the prawns once did.

Kattie Nielsen, already the diplomatic hotel concierge, does not want to have an opinion on uranium, but she and her husband have a plan: They have made no long-term commitments to stay in Narsaq. If the mine turns out to be dangerous they will move again.

Kvanefjeld has been a topic of debate in Narsaq for decades. It started in the 1950s, when Danish conscripts were sent up in the hills with Geiger counters. In the 1970s, technicians from Denmark's Risø nuclear research lab mined 20,000 tons of ore from the mountainside, taking a good portion of it back home with them. In Denmark, young Greenlanders marched in protest, and a few years later protests started in Greenland. Juaaka Lyberth, an author and singer, composed songs about Poul the Greenlander, an eighteenth-century figure who wrote about the poor, greedy Danes so thirsty for gold and minerals they had to sail across the most ferocious seas imaginable.

Eventually, everyone in Narsaq knew that their surroundings were packed with minerals. The local dentist said the kids had exceptionally strong teeth thanks to fluoride in the water. Fishermen and schoolchildren listened side-by-side as scientists spoke about thorium, radon, uranium and zinc, and in 2005 GME bought the old lumberyard and set up office in the red building by the church. GME took on local hires and set up tent camps on the mountain, and heavy equipment was lifted onto the mountain by helicopter. GME distributed brochures and held community meetings throughout southern Greenland. They bought one of the bigger houses in Narsaq for their drilling crews and townspeople learned how the rare earth minerals from Kvanefjeld would be used all over the world in wind turbines, mobile telephones, hybrids and advanced missile systems. GME sponsored the local football club and put on parties in the community centre. A lot of people were excited, but there were just as many who feared the worst, including Jørgen Olesen. Nowadays, he's solidly against the mine. 'If the wind blows from that direction will it carry radioactive dust this way? Why should we let them ruin our lives? Are they just going to close in 30 years and shove off again? They told us the olivine mine up north was going to remain operational for a hundred years, but it closed down long ago. Same thing with the gold mine in Nanortalik. They said that would be open forever, but it closed last year. None of that does anything for the country. We would be better off fishing. That is something we will always be able to do.' There is a sticker on the fridge that says, 'Urani? Naamik' (Uranium? No thanks). Karl Olesen expects that most of the mine's jobs will go to foreign workers.

Kvanefjeld is visible from all corners of Narsaq. Like a backdrop, it's there as you come out of the supermarket and when you go to church or drop off children at the kindergarten. The berries on the slopes of Kvanefjeld are a staple of most people's diet. In the summer, the locals stock up on trout from the stream from Kvanefjeld. Sofus Frederiksen's farm and the sheep and cows that he raises on the mountain are famous throughout Greenland. Fishermen work waters not far from Kvanefjeld, and everyone in town knows that GME wants to dump their tailings into Tileq Lake. Representatives from GME have explained that the mine will be an open pit mine; unlike underground mines, where all you can see is a small opening in the surface, everything here will be exposed. Critics warn that poisonous dust can blow down over Narsaq, the kindergarten, the school, the waterworks, while GME claims that it rarely blows from that direction. The mine might need to use acid to separate the various minerals and it is not yet clear where this acid will go. And what about the water-soluble fluorine that will be released as dust? Will the citizens of Narsaq still be able to drink the local water? Gert Asmund, a chemical engineer from the University of Aarhus in Denmark, told the newspaper *Ingeniøren* that he is concerned about the tailings, some 56 million tons of it, going into the lake. Asmund expects the tailings will be rich in uranium, thorium, fluorine and other heavy metals, creating a health hazard for humans and animals alike.

In 2014, however, plenty of people in the town are still confident that the environmental problems can be taken care of. GME plans to build dams and install water filtration to clean any water leaving the lake. Josef Petersen, one of the town's most dynamic people (and the one who wants Greenland to remain part of the Danish Kingdom) thinks the mine has big potential. 'It is not just a matter of mining jobs. Before you know it, there will be enough people to support new businesses here. Maybe a barber will open up shop. Right now, there are no restaurants, no take-aways. Tradesmen, people in the service sector, families – they will all get a new life.'

The population of Narsaq has fallen in recent years, but the town is still home to about 1,400. There were 92 break-ins and ten sex offences in 2013. The local police chief talks a lot about dope, but the school up on the hill is being renovated and expanded. The town's little toy store has a giant sign proudly announcing its address on Niels Bohr Square, a tip of the cap to the Nobel Prize-winning nuclear physicist and honorary Narsaq resident.

In 2014 the Kvanefjeld is already famous. Politicians, intelligence experts, military brass, officials from Copenhagen and Nuuk, envoys from Brussels and stock traders from around the world are all aware of what is under the Kvanefjeld. While the Olesen brothers and Kattie Nielsen told their stories, Greenland's environment minister was in Australia to learn how uranium is extracted and refined there. Others have studied how Canada handles its uranium mining. GME says that a mine, complete with crushers, waste depots, roads and port facilities, can be completed over a couple of years provided the authorities in Copenhagen and Nuuk issue the necessary permits. During construction, an estimated 1,000 workers, mostly foreigners, will be necessary, but once the mine is running, about half of the 700 permanent employees will be Greenlanders and the economic benefit will, the company says, have a major impact on the country. Critics, however, still say the mine and the impact it will make on the environment could cost Narsaq its existence.

For most Danes, the fact that Copenhagen and Nuuk did not see eye to eye on uranium became apparent on 29 August 2013 when Aleqa Hammond, Danish Prime Minister Helle Thorning-Schmidt, and Kaj Leo Johannesen, the Faroese Prime Minister, gathered for their annual national meeting in Denmark. The morning was spent at Thorning-Schmidt's summerhouse south of Copenhagen, but by the time the afternoon press conference rolled around, the group appeared to be on the verge of a fall-out. Hammond and Thorning-Schmidt clearly disagreed over uranium. Thorning-Schmidt seemed uncharacteristically dour as Hammond addressed the press. 'I think that we can look forward to having some enlightening discussions. The three of us have come to the conclusion that there are aspects of the uranium question that we disagree about.'

It was unprecedented. A press conference about so important a question and the leaders could only agree to disagree. What was more, it was almost as if Hammond was enjoying the moment.

At the heart of the dispute was a simple but deep divide. Thorning-Schmidt's government maintained that uranium, since it may be used in nuclear weapons, was a defence and security issue. As a result, the Danes felt that Copenhagen had the right to step in to prevent, for instance, the uranium from being sent to North Korea or Iran, or if it felt that the way the uranium was handled in other ways constituted a threat to national security.

Hammond and her associates in Nuuk argued that the uranium stems from their country's underground, and that underground resources clearly fell, according to the 2009 Self-Rule Act, under the Greenlandic administration. They agreed that uranium should not wind up in the hands of rogue states or terrorists, but they maintained that in all these matters Nuuk has the final say.

In September 2013, I interviewed Jens-Erik Kirkegaard, Greenland's Minister for Mineral Resources, on Danish television. He accepted that uranium mining was a matter of national security. He accepted that Copenhagen was committed to preventing nuclear proliferation. Greenland, he said, was more than willing to sign all relevant international agreements on responsible handling of uranium. His only issue with Copenhagen was that he wanted Greenland to have the final say on all these issues. Almost concurrently, Hammond's government released a memo that mentioned the possibility of involving the Supreme Court in order to solve the dispute. According to the Self-Rule Act, the court's members can be asked to mediate if Denmark and Greenland give up on negotiations.

Hammond's indication that she might involve the Supreme Court was unprecedented. Speaking with the Danish newspaper *Information*, Bárur Larsen, a lawyer, explained that such a move would be a clear sign of an actual constitutional crisis between two members of the Kingdom.

In October, Thorning-Schmidt talked of the growing conflict in her opening address to the Danish parliament. She offered no solutions.

In Greenland, fears were mounting that Copenhagen was in fact preparing to somehow undermine Nuuk's legal right to decide over its own underground and that leading decision makers in Copenhagen regretted that the Self-Rule Act of 2009 did not provide Denmark with some sort of veto right over the handling of Greenland's minerals. The understanding in Nuuk was that Denmark was now using national security as an excuse to take back control over Greenland's oil, gas and minerals.

On 16 September, not long before Inatsisartut, Greenland's parliament, was to vote on the moratorium, Villy Søvndal, Denmark's Foreign Minister at the time, met with Aleqa Hammond in Nuuk in one last effort to find a compromise. It was to no avail. The likelihood of a negotiated solution had vanished.

Then the joint Danish–Greenlandic group of officials dealing with the uranium issue released its report, 'Consequences of Ending the Uranium Mining Moratorium'. A comprehensive review, it laid out myriad complications which uranium mining would cause for Copenhagen and Nuuk. Among them were potential health risks, maritime security issues, radiation protection, and the need for an agency to oversee the mining. The report cited the agreements which Denmark had signed with the International Atomic Energy Agency and EURATOM. It explained the type of laws that would need to be passed in both countries and the extra administrative and expert staff that would be needed. But as thorough as the report was, it failed to rule on the most important question of them all: Who had the right to decide? Instead, it found an administrative measure that made it possible to move forward without compromising Copenhagen's control over foreign policy and without dealing with the root of the power struggle.

This turned out to be a stroke of genius. The idea was simple: Denmark and Greenland would now negotiate all practical details and divide tasks and responsibilities on all the many issues related to potential uranium mining, while the disagreement about final authority would be left for future talks – and only dealt with if ever necessary. The plan was to remove all practical obstacles to uranium mining and then hope that the power struggle would meanwhile prove to be irrelevant in the real world.

On 24 October 2013, Aleqa Hammond got her victory and the world got itself a potential new uranium-producing country on top of the 19 existing ones. Inatsisartut voted 15 votes to 14 to lift the moratorium on uranium mining in Greenland. Ahead of the vote, 400 protesters took to the streets of Nuuk to urge lawmakers not to lift the moratorium and the evening before the vote, Hammond kicked Partii Inuit out of her coalition after it emerged that its sole member of parliament was going to vote against the bill. The outcome remained as Hammond wanted: The moratorium that had been in place for 25 years was lifted and it was now possible to mine uranium in the Kingdom of Denmark.

Then, in early 2014, Hammond made an unexpected move that forced Helle Thorning-Schmidt, the Prime Minister, to accept that the power struggle continued. Hammond was in Copenhagen and due to meet with Thorning-Schmidt to discuss uranium. The day before the meeting, the Greenlandic government released, without warning, a comprehensive legal evaluation that found that Greenland had the right to decide over its underground – including its uranium. It was a clear provocation. Thorning-Schmidt received the evaluation at 16:30 in the afternoon the day before the meeting. There would be no way she would be able to do anything but scan it and Aleqa Hammond herself admitted that the timing was intentional.

The evaluation was written by Ole Spiermann, one of Denmark's leading experts on Greenland and constitutional interpretation, and his conclusion was clear. The Danish government's argument 'lacked legal argumentation' and 'control and safeguards were not, in and of themselves, foreign policy matters'. Over the course of 30 pages he deconstructed the Danish position. He rejected the arguments of the Ministry of Foreign Affairs and the Ministry of Justice. 'As a general principle, the Danish government cannot use its foreign policy competency for the purpose of recalling or limiting the Self-Rule Authority's executive or legislative authority in powers that have been devolved to it, such as mineral resources.'

During her meeting with Aleqa Hammond, Thorning-Schmidt then raised the stakes. She informed Hammond that Copenhagen would also demand to be kept fully informed about all Greenland's negotiations involving rare earth minerals. Danish officials had come to the conclusion that both uranium and rare earths were of such importance to national security that they would need not just to be informed but to also be given the authority to stop negotiations, mining activity or export if it ran counter to national interests.

To the Greenlandic officials, this was poison. What would be next? Would Copenhagen ask for a right to veto oil explorations? And what about zinc, or iron ore that was to be exported to China?

Soon after, it was clear that the Danish Prime Minister was ready to make development of a mining industry in Greenland all but impossible if Aleqa Hammond did not give in. In the spring of 2014, when a bill was introduced in Copenhagen to make it possible for foreign labourers to work in Greenland's mines, it contained one crucial clause: The law, if passed, would not take effect until Nuuk accepted Copenhagen's right to veto decisions about uranium or rare earth elements. Only in 2016 was the matter resolved, and only after prolonged and difficult negotiations. In the end, the Danish government and the leadership in Nuuk signed a three-pronged set of agreements that settled the matter – at least for the time being. In essence, Denmark retained the right to deny exports of uranium from Greenland, if Copenhagen finds that the buying party is unlikely to handle uranium according to internationally agreed standards and conventions. On its part, Greenland in this complex set of agreements retained the right to decide when, how, by whom and at what price any mineral deposit, including uranium, can be mined in Greenland.

10

A COLONIAL PAST COMES BACK TO HAUNT

Greenland's desire to reconcile its colonial past with its quest for self-reliance raises hard questions: Was Denmark a brutal and exploitative colonial power in Greenland? Should the Danes apologize for the past as other colonial powers like Australia and Canada have done? Some argue the missionaries and the merchants from Scandinavia came to Greenland as a blessing. Others, as we have seen, still blame the Danes for many ills in Greenland. Most, meanwhile, agree that understanding the past is crucial for understanding the present. As the Danes mobilized, British and Scottish explorers also went north and established communities in New England, Newfoundland, and Nova Scotia, while the French built what is modern-day Quebec. Denmark enviously watched as foreign whalers made huge profits in Greenland's waters. Whale oil from Greenland fuelled the streetlamps of London and Amsterdam, and Denmark was missing out. Norse settlers had established themselves in Greenland already in the days of the Vikings, so the rulers in Copenhagen claimed historical rights – as some still do today.

* * *

Most visitors to Rosenborg Castle in central Copenhagen will find their way up the worn stone steps of the spiral staircase and into the throne room. There, two silver lions, each standing a metre high, slender and vigilant, greet visitors with expressionless gazes, as if ignorant of what stands behind them. Majestic, dominant and elevated slightly above the rest of the room is the Narwhal Throne, or, as it was known when it was created, the Unicorn Throne. It was the throne of King Frederik III, Denmark's first absolute monarch, who became king by divine edict in 1648 upon the death of his father, Christian IV.

It was inspired by the new king's fascination with the Old Testament's throne of King Solomon. Frederik, looking to add his own touch, ordered his court artisan, Bendix Grodtschilling, to create a throne of the most precious material available, the tusk of the Arctic narwhal, which grows to a length of three metres. The Arctic ivory was known to Copenhagen already at the time of the Norse settlers and whalers still made good money from it; in Denmark and in the rest of Europe, the tusks were commonly believed to stem from unicorns.

Today, the throne may help answer a question increasingly asked in both Denmark and Greenland: What was Denmark's original plan for Greenland? What is the plan today? Why did the early colonists head there, and how have their motivations changed over time?

When the throne was completed in 1671, it outdid anything ever created by a Danish king to symbolize his power. From the armrests four narwhal tusks shot upwards towards exquisitely carved panels of narwhal ivory; its back was dominated by two golden angels, both with halos made of more narwhal ivory. Each of the armrests rested upon nine pieces of tusk, and each of the front legs stood upon its own pedestal of narwhal ivory.

Choosing narwhal tusk was a stroke of genius. In 1662, unicorns and the power of their twisted horns would have been familiar to Europeans from the Bible, various bestiaries and from Marco Polo's reports from his journey to Asia in the thirteenth century (he had probably seen a rhinoceros). It was believed that a single hair from a unicorn could restore fertility or improve harvests. The horn itself was ascribed powers of healing; trapping a unicorn could only be done by a maiden and trade in the tusks was a lucrative business on European waterways as far south as Constantinople. In the eighteenth century, Hans Egede, the missionary who spearheaded mission and trade in Greenland in 1721, wondered whether the unicorn of the Bible was not actually the Greenlandic narwhal reinterpreted as a horse-like animal. As late as 1940, scientific experiments were still being carried out to determine whether the horns actually came from unicorns. In the time of Frederik III, unicorns were a fact of life, and news that he had fashioned an entire throne out of their horns spread quickly throughout Europe. It was unparalleled. The majesty of the throne was shown to envoys from the royal courts of England, the Hanseatic League and from kingdoms throughout Italy, France, Russia and the rest of Europe. Frederik's status, and the status of his kingdom, grew.

Frederik was, in other words, very much aware of the riches of the North. In 1611, his father, Christian IV, then in his twenties, undertook the most dangerous and most ambitious expeditions any Danish-Norwegian king had ever executed. The goal was simple: to show that Denmark controlled the seas of the far North, extending to the northern-most tip of Norway. The strategy, named *Dominium Mares Septentrionalis* (Dominance over the Northern Seas), was envisioned as a massive display of Danish naval power in the northern seas. The young king threw everything he had into it. Half of his fleet escorted his ship, the *Victor*, as it sailed north of Norway and deep into the White Sea, in modern-day Russia. The signal sent to the other powers of the day was unmistakable and modern-day military commanders would have been impressed: Without firing a single shot, Christian IV managed to display willingness and ability to defend the farthest reaches of his kingdom. Greenland was at this point hardly more than a myth, a legend from the time of the Vikings, but Norwegian waters were under Danish control. The Swedes had to rethink their own ambitions in northern Norway, and the English, Dutch and other seafaring nations were forcefully reminded that the Danish king meant business when he demanded taxes in his

North Atlantic from Norway to the Shetlands, the Faroe Islands and Iceland.

For the Samis and other local populations of northern Norway, life under Danish rule was not pleasant. The king's henchmen ruled with a heavy hand; the territory was now theirs and they intended to keep it.

In 1629, Christian sent Captain Jens Munk, an experienced sailor, on another ambitious venture west to find the Northwest Passage. The expedition failed, and Munk had to winter in Hudson Bay. Most of the crew died from hunger or scurvy, but the voyage underscored again how serious Christian IV was about expanding his kingdom.

Christian's ambitions taught his son Frederik and succeeding kings that the North was a land of opportunity. In 1665, an image of a Greenlandic polar bear was added to the Danish royal coat of arms, and to this day, in the basement of Rosenborg Castle, on display together with the crown jewels, visitors can study numerous items made of narwhal tusk: jewellery boxes, walking sticks, and carved figurines of Inuit hunters. Craftspeople who carved figures out of tusks, including Frederik III's wife, Juliane Marie, knew the stories of Erik the Red and the Norse settlers in Greenland. From 984 and through over 400 years, these settlers, who arrived from Iceland, made a name for themselves as suppliers of narwhal and walrus tusk, hides, and other prized goods. In 1327, one Norwegian church emissary returned with 650 kilograms of tusks as the Norse contribution to the holy crusades. In a stroke of marketing genius, Erik the Red gave Greenland its name; at times, there were 4,000 to 5,000 Norse settlers living in Greenland, rivalling in size the population of Copenhagen. The Norse were skilled merchants, hunters, farmers, fishermen and shepherds, and they thrived in the mild climate in the fjords of southern Greenland.

The Norse legends, of course, took on colour as time went by, but they always retained a grain of truth. The Icelandic sagas described the rich farmlands in Greenland, no farther north than the rich pastures in Norway. What, then, in the seventeenth century, when Frederik took power, should prevent the king in Copenhagen from trying to re-populate Greenland? Well into the twentieth century scientists were still theorizing about forests on the inland side of Greenland's coastal mountains; only with surveys from aeroplanes centuries later were these fantasies buried. The spectre of land at the North Pole also prevailed for long, as did the notion that Greenland was perhaps connected to North America. In the seventeenth and eighteenth centuries, perceptions of the Arctic as a trove of valuable minerals, mystical animals, and boundless treasures were common in London, Hamburg and, of course, Copenhagen. British and Scottish explorers had long gone north to find riches. They established far-off communities in New England, Newfoundland and Nova Scotia, while the French created New France in what is now Quebec. By the seventeenth century, Copenhagen found itself watching as Basque, Dutch, French, English, and Scottish whalers turned huge profits on whales off Svalbard and in the Davis Strait. The baleens from the largest whales were popular in Europe, where they were used to stiffen women's corsets. Whale oil, obtained by melting blubber, was an irreplaceable ingredient in soap and indispensable as a fuel in the streetlamps of London, Amsterdam and other cities. Whaling made Greenland the eighteenth-century equivalent of an oil state, and it served as the foundation of major trading companies in London, Amsterdam and Hamburg. Copenhagen, despite its efforts to establish itself as a northern power, found itself on the sidelines of this booming trade.

In 1721, things took an important turn. Three ships – two merchant vessels and a whaling ship from the Bergen Company in Norway – sailed from Bergen with the king's blessing to begin the colonization of Greenland. (Norway and Denmark were united at the time under the King in Copenhagen.) At the head of this expedition was a 35-year-old Norwegian by the name of Hans Povelsen Egede, a recently appointed royal missionary, his wife, Gertrud Rask, and their four children. In all, some 80 people were aboard the three vessels. For the first years, Egede and his family stayed on the islands off the coast of modern Nuuk. After seven years, they moved farther into the fjord, when a royal governor established Godthåb as a colony. The governor had brought marines and about twenty small-time convicts of both genders. The convicts had been forced to marry before departure, and now tried to establish a life here – that is, those who survived the winter. Once Godthåb was settled, the plan was to build a fort at Nipisat, close to the Dutch whaling settlement near modern-day Sisimiut, but like scores of other designs by the king's strategists in Copenhagen, the fort never materialized.

Step by step, however, Greenland was influenced. Over a period of 80 years Danish-Norwegian merchants, missionaries, and soldiers were dispatched by the king to Greenland, where they established 14 colonies on Greenland's western coast. Small batteries of signal cannons were set up. Churches and trading stations were established along 2,000 kilometres of rocky coast. Royal interest in the Greenlandic colonies varied; often there were bigger fish to fry in Europe and the king's fortunes fluctuated. For long, the gospel played a key role; the merchants were Christians and wholeheartedly supported the work of the mission, its imported vicars and their Greenlandic apprentices. With time, however, this fine balance became difficult to maintain and trade became the central element of attention. For decades, the king left all trade in sealskin, oil, furs, baleen, walrus tusk and the legendary narwhal tusk to private merchants, who had to fend for themselves, although with guns and other necessities provided by the king. In 1736 and 1737, the *Blaa Heyren*, a heavily armed frigate, was sent to patrol among the Dutch traders in Disco Bay, and, in 1776, King Christian VII granted the Royal Danish Greenlandic Company a monopoly on trading in Greenland and the right to defend its trading monopoly with arms. Out of fear of the great whaling nations, Britain and the Netherlands in particular, foreign ships were permitted to continue whaling and to come ashore for fresh water, but they were not allowed to continue their trade with the natives.

How then, to describe the true intentions of the Danish
colonists now, 300 years later? Why were – and why are – the
Danes in Greenland? Was colonization designed to improve the
lives of Greenlanders through the Christian message, literacy
and civilization? Should Greenlanders be thankful for what the
Danes did, for Christianity and the missionary schools? Or did
the merchant Danes exploit Greenland and its people – by force,
when necessary? Was the Danish colonization, as Greenland's
veteran diplomat Finn Lynge later claimed, uniquely mild; no
one was ever executed on the king's order. Or is that a far too
mild picture-postcard version of a much harsher reality?

All these questions have bearing on the present. If the Danes
only intended to assist as the people of Greenland developed
their society and found enlightenment, then there would be
little reason to seek reconciliation, as Aleqa Hammond did.
If it is true that the Danes came primarily to save the souls of
the Greenlanders, does it make sense at all to call Greenland a
former colony?

In Aarhus, Denmark's second largest city, I called on one of
the country's leading specialists in order to understand better
what drove the Danes back in the early days of colonization in
Greenland. 'How are you with Gothic letters?' Ole Marquardt
looks up, smiles and turns back to his computer, which shows
a list of individuals employed by the Royal Greenlandic
Company dating back to the nineteenth century. One
particular detail has caught his attention. Next to one man's
name, it says 'can do odd-jobs as a cooper'. Marquardt looks
pleased. A historian, he has spent years going over observations,
lists, details and other historic documents, and has become one
of the Kingdom of Denmark's leading experts on Greenland's
colonial past. Between 1999 and 2007, he was the rector of
the University of Greenland. He continues to be a part of the
university's staff, and he is certain that he knows why the Danes
went to Greenland in the eighteenth century. 'They had clear
economic interests', he says.

'Godthåb – present-day Nuuk – was no farther north
than Trondheim in western Norway, and the colonists knew

there was money to be made. Greenland has not always cost Denmark money, even though that has become a common belief. During some periods, the Royal Greenlandic Company was a highly profitable business. They did not always record their earnings in very transparent ways; often money was spent on, for instance, churches and therefore not recorded as profit, but Greenland was just like any other colony that ever existed: It was there to turn a profit.'

Marquardt does not believe in the myth that the Danes implemented a unique, humanitarian version of colonialism. Unlike in North America, where Native Americans could be replaced by white farmers, and where African slaves could be replaced by other African slaves, the few Inuit in Greenland were indispensable for the seal hunting that formed the economic foundation of Danish colonialism in Greenland. In order to make sure that the basis for their business in Greenland stayed in place, the Danes made sure that the Inuit could maintain their lifestyle and multiply. 'They were irreplaceable at sea. If the Danes had been able to do without the Greenlanders, they would have been dealt with far more heavy-handedly. The Danes showed that they were no strangers to slavery and the whip in their colonies in the West Indies, Africa, and elsewhere. The Danes were not focused on the well-being of the Inuits when they did their best to keep them alive. If they could have replaced them, we would no doubt have seen the same situation as we saw in North and South America.'

Seal blubber was melted down into oil; hides were exported to Europe and fashioned into knapsacks, capes, and other necessities. When the Danes suffered military defeat at the hands of the Germans in 1864, the wheels of their cannons were lubricated with grease made from seal oil and ash. The order of business in Greenland – controlled by the Danes – was focused solely on seal. The 'Hans Egede Principle', it was called, and it required that the Greenlanders kept hunting seal and a highly professional administration if it was to turn a profit. The Royal Greenlandic Company employed hundreds of Danish administrators, clerks, and auditors in Greenland. Marquardt's research shows that during some periods, the Company had one Dane in Greenland for every seven Greenlanders working to bring in the seals. Each trading station had to have a staff to purchase, control and administer what the Inuit could catch, and each town had, on average, four Greenlandic settlements that the firm could sell supplies to. Sealers were active along 1,800 kilometres of coast, from Upernavik in the north to Qaqortoq in the south. It all required manpower. In the nineteenth century, there were only about 10,000 Greenlanders living in Greenland, but the number of Danes and Norwegians dispatched to the island by the Royal Greenlandic Company grew and grew.

Trade also meant a steady supply from the outside, and a market for goods like sugar, tobacco and coffee quickly developed. With the introduction of firearms, the Greenlandic hunters became more effective and trade grew while the Danes made sure focus remained on seals. As late as the early twentieth century, influential voices in Copenhagen were working to ensure that Greenlanders remained focused on fur and blubber, even if a number of people both in Greenland and Denmark argued in favour of fishing and mining. Or as Marquardt puts it, 'Seal hunting was the only thing Danes considered to be truly lucrative. Danes did not want Greenlanders getting too accustomed to eating figs or drinking coffee. They did not want them going soft, you know. It was important that they keep hunting. Despite the high death rates.'

Marquardt's understanding has its detractors. Thorkild Kjærgaard, who taught history at the University of Greenland, sees the relationship in an entirely different way. Greenland, as he sees it, was never a colony in the strict sense of the word. Colonies are basically repressive, exploitative constructions, he argues, and neither was ever the case in Greenland. In fact, the opposite was true, he argues: The Danes and Norwegians who went to Greenland in the eighteenth century did so with the permission of the Danish king, and with the intention of re-establishing what was once an old Norwegian empire and to spread Christianity. They regarded the people in Greenland as part of the nation – countrymen on a par with those living in the rest of the Danish Kingdom.

In 2011, Kjærgaard put forward the basic idea behind this theory in a publication that mapped the rapid establishment of settlements on Greenland's western coast in the eighteenth century. He took issue with the assumption that the colonizers went to Greenland for economic reasons. If that had been the case, he argued, they would not have bothered to build towns. They would have done what Britain's Hudson Bay Company did on the other side of the Davis Strait, in Canada, less than 400 kilometres from Greenland. The Hudson Bay Company did not establish settlements. It operated trading posts where Inuit could sell hides and it did not bother with religion, missionary work, or the like. This approach was profitable; according to Kjærgaard, there were times when the Hudson Bay Company posted annual growth rates of ten per cent. On average, it was far more profitable than Greenland was to the Danish merchants. In Kjærgaard's interpretation, Copenhagen had entirely different objectives. Firstly, it wanted to rebuild Norway's long-gone North Atlantic Viking Empire. Secondly, they were looking to carry out their *Dominium Mares Septentrionalis* strategy that would allow the Danish-Norwegian kingdom to control a vast maritime territory from the White Sea to Vinland in North America. Lastly, they had religious motivations that were totally unrelated to profit. 'The Christian Danish-Norwegian kings who ruled over large, multi-ethnic territories – including Inuit – were regarded as modern incarnations of Old Testament kings. The Danish-Norwegian Narwhal Throne was seen as every bit as majestic as Solomon's ivory throne. The Christians and the Frederiks who ruled Denmark, Norway, Iceland, the Faroe Islands, Greenland and the German-speaking duchies of Schleswig and Holstein were considered the Davids and Solomons of the High North. The Christianization of Greenland and Greenland's spectacular integration into the Danish-Norwegian state structure through the creation of a chain of coastal towns were a part of God's divine plan.'

Seen that way, Greenland was no colony. According to
Kjærgaard, Greenland was not colonized but re-incorporated
as an integral part of an immense national and religious project
that included Greenlanders as active participants and citizens.

In short, for Kjærgaard, life in Greenland before the time
of Hans Egede and Christianity was basically unhappy, while
the church offered hope and enlightenment. In the eighteenth
century, the church and the educational system were inseparable,
and Kjærgaard explained to me how the missionaries brought
not only God's words but also the ability to read and write
with them to Greenland. Egede published the first primer in
Greenlandic in 1739. His son Poul completed a Greenlandic
translation of the New Testament in 1766. Not long after, Bible
reading became a beloved pastime all along the coast. Hinrich
Rink, a Danish geologist and later administrator in Greenland,
founded the Greenlandic-language newspaper *Atuagagdliutit*
with Greenlandic friends, the world's first paper to feature colour
illustrations. By the nineteenth century, literacy in Greenland
was ahead of literacy in rural Denmark, and Kjærgaard argues
that Bible reading had 'created a standardized Greenlandic
language, shared by all Greenlanders, which led to the creation
of a distinct national identity that did not exist previously.
Greenlandic national identity, the reformed Lutheran church
and Bible-reading were all different facets of the same thing'.

This version of Greenland's history places credit for much
of what underpins today's Greenlandic society squarely at the
feet of the missionaries and the societal order introduced by
the Danish and Norwegian colonists. As Thorkild Kjærgaard
puts it, 'Of all the indigenous American languages, including
some which were spoken in highly developed cultures, only
Greenlandic remains as a language that is still widely used –
thanks to the Danish–Norwegian missionaries. What is more,
Greenland is the only country in the Northern Hemisphere
where the aboriginal population makes up more than just
a minority of the overall population that continues to exist
thanks to their government's half-hearted efforts. In Greenland,
they constitute *the people*.'

In Nuuk, down in the old colonial harbour, Hans Egede's statue still stands, looking out over the fjord. At the National Museum, just a few hundred metres from this tribute to Egede, Daniel Thorleifsen, the museum's Greenlandic director, offers me his own interpretation of the past. A visiting journalist from the *Financial Times* once noted that everything in Thorleifsen's museum was written in Greenlandic and English, not in Danish, and the journalist left with the impression that the museum was hell-bent on portraying Danes as brutal and insensitive, but Thorleifsen has no such aims. He stands astride the two main conflicting interpretations of the history of the Danes in Greenland as they are represented by Ole Marquardt and Thorkild Kjærgaard. Denmark's colonization of Greenland was economically motivated, but also influenced by Christianity and altruism, he tells me. He rejects the idea that Denmark saw Greenland as a source of endless wealth. 'If that were the case, they would probably have got here sooner. Hundreds of years passed between the Norse disappearing and colonization beginning. In the start, they came so that Hans Egede could preach. A number of years passed before the king really took an interest.' He finds it indisputable that the Danes treated Greenland as a colony, even if the process of colonization in Greenland does not compare in any substantial sense to what happened in African or Asian colonies. Danes and Greenlanders were not equals; power and wealth was not in any way shared in equal measures. Greenland was a colony. 'That is how Greenlandic academics have always seen it. We were a colony, just maybe not a colony in the classic sense. Denmark always held the belief that they could not just abandon Greenland after they had got involved, so they tried to make it profitable. At times, they considered whether it would be best to pull out of Greenland entirely, but then the state got involved and that is the way it has been to this day.' Danish colonialism, in Thorleifsen's view, was fundamentally different from colonialism in other parts of the world. Ever since the nineteenth century, he says, Greenlandic authors and thinkers have sought to explain how the Danes were truly interested in the development of Greenland and its people even when they were colonizing, and how they slowly involved Greenlanders themselves in the island's administration.

In 2012, Thorleifsen contributed to *Naboer i Nordatlanten* (Neighbours in the North Atlantic), a seminal work about the history of Greenland, Iceland and the Faroe Islands. He tells me how he senses a recurring trend in Danish–Greenlandic relations. Just like Denmark tried to encourage enterprising businessmen to get involved in Greenland in the eighteenth century, the modern state of Denmark has also tried and failed to encourage businesses to get more deeply engaged in Greenland in recent decades. 'The constitution was changed in 1953 and Greenland was made a part of Denmark. Businesses went to Greenland to try to industrialize the fishing industry. When that went downhill in the 1970s, the state took over again, exactly the same way the king gave himself a monopoly on trade with the island in 1776. It was not a matter of aggressive state-oriented policies, but there was no other solution so Denmark just took charge – both then and now.' He smiles. 'Maybe the state really saw Greenland as a necessary evil.'

11

DREAMS OF OIL AND GAS BURST WITH A BANG

The global rush for Arctic oil, gas and minerals hits Greenland with a vengeance. As the quest for independence intensifies and the world turns its spotlight northward, prospects of riches transform the politic debate in Nuuk. A national strategy, adopted by Inatsisartut, the Greenlandic parliament, promises oil and minerals that will help Greenland assume its rightful place among other independent nations of the world. In Houston, Beijing, Perth and other foreign centres potential investors are briefed and invited and Greenland teems with foreign prospectors. Then suddenly, the shiny projections meet heavy resistance. Greenland's leading scientist spearheads research to prove the heavy projections overly optimistic. The clash between optimists and realists is not pretty.

* * *

In the autumn of 2013, senior government officials in Nuuk responsible for Greenland's mining, oil and gas put the finishing touches on the final draft of a document that was to chart the course to Greenland's future.

The minerals strategy, if approved, was to codify once and for all plans to develop the country's vital oil, gas and mining industry. The most immediate effect would of course be felt in Greenland, but the strategy would also affect Greenland's relations with

Denmark and the rest of the world. The strategy was intended to show how oil, gas and minerals could put an end to Greenland's economic slump and shorten the path to independence.

The authors first struck up an alarmist tone. 'Since 1995, net emigration has amounted to 7,019 persons. [...] A considerable number of emigrants were resource-rich persons. If recent years' net emigration continues in the medium to long term, this will mean a very considerable loss of human resources for Greenland and may significantly limit the country's possibilities of increasing self-sufficiency. Net emigration therefore poses a very serious problem for Greenland.'

On the subject of mining, the strategy walked a fine line. On the one hand, it needed to accommodate the new premier Aleqa Hammond's wish for a speedy process towards independence, yet on the other it needed to avoid giving false hope. The report was expected to offer hard facts about something that was far from certain: How interested were oil firms in exploring for oil in Greenland? Would they find oil? How much? Where? Would the mining firms be able to lure enough investors from China or other countries to get their ventures off the ground, and by when? How much could the country expect to profit from its mineral resources? Should Danish firms be given special preference?

When a draft of the strategy was made public at the end of December 2013 it presented a superbly optimistic outlook. 'At the time of writing, it looks as if three to five mines may be opened in the period from 2014 to 2018, and it is estimated that every second year there will be one to two offshore drilling projects. It is not unrealistic that the number of mines in operation will increase in five years and that more than 1,500 people will be employed in proper mining jobs. Over a 15-year period, a simultaneous launch of these mining projects may generate more than 30 billion kroner in tax revenues.'

The strategy also predicted that a significant oil discovery would be made not too many years into the future. Similar predictions were put forward in 2011 by Greenland's Tax and Welfare Commission, which made the assumption that by 2020 'a small drilling rig will be set up for a 500-million-barrel field'.

Other firms were expected to continue production, and by 2025 'a big drilling rig will be set up for a two-billion-barrel field'. If these assumptions held true, and if Greenland's profits were wisely managed in a sovereign wealth fund, the fortune would, according to the strategy, amount to more than 435 billion kroner by 2060.

Nothing was set in stone, but for readers who shared Hammond's dream of 'independence within my lifetime', the message was clear: Even the most conservative estimate of the draft made the dream appear quite realistic.

Jørgen Hammeken-Holm, head of the key minerals office of the government and one of the authors of the strategy, confirmed to me in an interview in early 2014 that there was good reason for optimism. As the long-time head of the Bureau of Minerals and Petroleum, Hammeken-Holm was a veteran negotiator who had sat across from representatives of oil majors such as Shell, Chevron, Statoil, Conoco-Philips and BP, as well as smaller firms like DONG, Maersk Oil, Cairn Energy and Husky.

Hammeken-Holm did not rule out the prospect of an oil discovery off the western coast in time for a start to production by 2020. 'It is not something we can rule out at this point. It all depends on how much drilling activity there is in 2015, and where it is done. If drilling is delayed, then a production date will also be delayed. The one thing I know is that if someone offers evidence of a commercial oil find, we would see a flood of companies showing interest.'

The strategy also discussed the potential for an even larger find – one containing two billion barrels and developed to the point of production by 2025. A find of this size, however, is most likely off the north eastern coast, and that made the prediction dubious. Drifting ocean ice and extreme weather conditions in the waters off north eastern Greenland have kept oil firms from presenting any proposals for how they would drill test wells. The Arctic was still a highly volatile frontier for the oil industry and when officials in Nuuk drafted their strategy, none of the oil firms had yet found any real oil in Greenland.

On-shore activities are more predictable, and here, too, Hammeken-Holm defended the strategy's optimistic outlook. 'There has been a slow-down in the global commodities market, but it is realistic to expect that within six years there will be five or six mines operating.'

The strategy listed the projects furthest along and for the average Greenlander, minerals had come to be understood as key to the country's future. At the mining school in Sisimiut, the first class was working its way towards graduation, and outside stores in Narsaq and the rest of southern Greenland, flyers offered classes in 'miner's English'. The prospects were all still birds in the bush, but they were very fleshy birds indeed.

Meanwhile, GME was moving forward with its exploration of Kvanefjeld. On the road to the mountain, at the end of a stretch cleared of snow, a little wind sensor stands atop a tripod. It is one of three aggregators posted in Narsaq; a second one has been set up outside Pavia Rosing's green private house in the centre of town, while the third is on the point out towards the fjord. GME is collecting environmental data about the entire area, and the wind sensors give an indication of which areas might find themselves downwind from the mine and at risk of having radioactive dust blown at them. The findings will contribute to the environmental risk report that officials in Nuuk require before considering a final approval to GME and its plans to extract uranium and rare earth elements.

In early 2014, sitting in his office in Nuuk, Ib Laursen, GME's project manager, explained that the company expected to have the required studies completed by early 2015. They included an environmental impact assessment and a study of the overall impact the venture would have on Narsaq. If all goes as hoped, he believes the mine can be operational by 2017. 'We can learn from those before us so that we do not repeat their mistakes. Mostly the decision whether to do it or not is a political one. As far as I see it, there is no practical reason why we cannot do it.'

The way Laursen sees it the Kvanefjeld mine would benefit Greenland in a number of ways. The sale of uranium based on 30-year contracts with friendly countries that would use it in their atomic energy programmes – France, the United States, China – would ensure a steady stream of capital over the long term. The rare earth elements would be sold on the more volatile commodities markets, providing investors with their return. The whole operation would be subject to taxation, making sure that Greenland got its share.

In 2014, sceptics point out that the price of rare earth elements has tumbled. This means, they say, that GME will have trouble finding investors willing to put up the money for port facilities, a crusher, barracks for the workers, dams and all the other infrastructure required, but Laursen brushes these concerns aside. 'Rare earths are irreplaceable. Businesses that develop environmental technologies are not going to overlook the opportunity that global warming presents them. The market will rise again. Mark my words.'

In one respect, the draft of the mineral resources strategy quickly became outdated. In October 2013, just after public hearings about the strategy began, Naalakkersuisut, Greenland's cabinet, moved to grant London Mining, a British mining company, the right to mine a part of the Isukasia area in central Greenland for iron ore. The Isua project is located at the foot of Nuuk Fjord, some 150 kilometres from the capital.

In 2012, as mentioned above, the Isua project had been the source of a hefty political dispute in Copenhagen and several disagreements remained unresolved. Danish labour unions wanted to ensure that foreign mine workers in Greenland were treated properly and the Danish intelligence community was worried about Chinese involvement in what promised to be the largest industrial project in the history of Greenland.

Difficult questions remained unanswered. Who would be responsible for the children the expected Chinese workers would have while in Greenland? How many would settle permanently in Greenland? The government in Copenhagen was caught flat-footed. Isua had been in the works for decades, but the Danish government did not have a plan.

PwC, an auditing firm, estimated that during the first 15 years the mine was in operation, London Mining would pay between 16 billion and 18 billion kroner in taxes – an astronomical amount by Greenlandic standards. It did not take long for intelligence analysts and lawmakers in Copenhagen to figure out that if Chinese investors controlled the mine they would conceivably have considerable leverage in Nuuk.

For some, the worries seemed unfounded. China, they said, knew better than to act assertively in a country that the United States considers to be within its sphere of influence. But among politicians in Copenhagen, the fear of rising Chinese influence in Greenland dominated the discussion. Copenhagen lawmakers also started worrying about what Beijing's involvement in Kvanefjeld and Kringlerne – the two major mining projects in southern Greenland – would be.

Early in 2014, things got heated when GME announced that the ore it extracted at Kvanefjeld would in all likelihood be refined in China by a subsidiary of China Non-Ferrous Metals Mining Group. In Denmark, the newspaper *Berlingske* reported that the Chinese company might also fund operation of the mine. In an interview with *Weekendavisen*, Greenland's responsible minister, Jens-Erik Kirkegaard, maintained that no country would be excluded from mining in Greenland. 'We cannot decide whom people should be allowed to work with. Monopolies are never beneficial, but then it is up to European firms to start getting involved in Greenland.' Then, in late 2014, tension lowered for a while as London Mining, holder of the Isua iron ore licence in central Greenland, gave up. The company's sole other operation, a mine in Sierra Leone in West Africa, was badly hit by a violent outbreak of the Ebola disease, and the company no longer had the funds to pursue the project in Greenland. London Mining sold its licence in Greenland to the Hong Kong-based 'General Nice Group' for an undisclosed sum, and as the price of iron plummeted the prospect of a large iron ore mine in Greenland disappeared over the horizon.

On the whole, 2014 offered harsh headwinds and severe challenges to the entrenched optimism in Nuuk. The key challenge was a report titled 'To the Benefit of Greenland' that was warmly welcomed by the Danish political establishment but wildly divisive in Greenland.

The report traced its roots back to 2012 and a widely read op-ed in *Politiken*. Written by Minik Rosing, an internationally respected professor of geology born in Greenland, and Kuupik Kleist, then the Premier of Greenland, the op-ed suggested an entirely new approach to the relationship between Denmark and Greenland. 'Is it not time, after 300 years as partners, most of it perfectly amicable, that we now openly declare our love and mutual respect for each other? We are still not totally comfortable with each other, and at times we find ourselves stepping on each other's toes, while we consequently neglect to make important decisions that will be of mutual benefit for all parties to the Kingdom of Denmark. Let us agree that mistakes have been made – as they often are – but let us also agree that the mistakes of the past will not prevent us from living happily together as two equal partners. It is said that those who are ignorant of the past are condemned to repeat it. Let us agree on a Greenlandic version that says if we are ignorant of the successes of our past, we risk not being able to repeat them.'

This was news. The message was a direct challenge by Greenland's political leader and one of its leading intellectuals to remain close to Denmark, even though Greenland had recently been granted self-rule and the right to declare its independence. Commentators, including Uffe Ellemann-Jensen, a former Danish foreign minister, and Torben Ørting Jørgensen, a former Danish rear admiral and now an executive with Maersk, Denmark's most influential private company, welcomed the new attitude. They found it visionary, friendly towards Denmark and a refreshing alternative to Greenland's rush towards China and other foreign powers.

When Aleqa Hammond took over the Premier's Office just four months later, the ideas expressed in the op-ed were already being turned into action. Minik Rosing and Kuupik Kleist in their op-ed had proposed that Danish and Greenlandic university experts should explore what the most beneficial way of using Greenland's mineral resources would be.

Helle Thorning-Schmidt, the Danish Prime Minister, threw her full support behind the idea.

A year later, by January 2014, a full scientific report on the prospects for oil, gas and minerals in Greenland was done: A 50-page easily digestible summary, 450 pages of academic documentation and wave upon wave of op-eds, newspaper articles, and TV reports, most featuring Minik Rosing as the carrier of the hugely controversial message that most of the optimism surrounding oil, gas and minerals in Greenland was unfounded.

By this time, though, the situation on the ground in Greenland had changed dramatically. Kleist was out of office, while Aleqa Hammond and her entourage were comfortably in power.

Minik Rosing and Kuupik Kleist had pledged their allegiance to the Kingdom. They argued that focus should be on what Greenland and Denmark could do together – for the benefit of Greenland. This was the underlying philosophy of the report that was presented to the public in January 2014, and which Aleqa Hammond – no doubt much to her chagrin – would now need to take under consideration. Thirteen experts from Greenland, Denmark, Sweden, and Iceland had worked for a year and the fruit of their labour was peppered with pictures, graphics, and charts that made it easily available to the public.

Aleqa Hammond was invited to Minik Rosing's Copenhagen home, where she was briefed on the report over dinner. Greenlandic officials and certain members of Inatsisartut were given the report well ahead of time, and its release in Nuuk was arranged so that Jens-Erik Kirkegaard, the responsible member of Naalakkersuisut, would be able to attend.

At the event where the release took place Minik Rosing was nervous. The presentation was to take place at his alma mater, the University of Greenland, where he was now head of the board, but even here he was unable to suppress his discomfort. By this point in his career, Rosing had long since made his name as one of Greenland's most accomplished sons.

Now a professor of geology at the University of Copenhagen, he entered the international academic limelight in the 1990s, when his studies of Greenland's geology turned up evidence that photosynthesis had taken place in Greenland as early as 3.7 billion years ago. His findings turned back the scientific clock on life's emergence on Earth by as much as 200 million years and added new dimensions to the way we understand the climate. Legions of honours were bestowed upon him, including a post as a visiting researcher at Stanford University in the United States. He is friendly with the heir apparent to the Danish throne. As a scientist, he was frequently asked to hold public lectures, and his ability as a speaker won him one of the country's highest awards for oration. He was also highly esteemed in Greenland. The third youngest of four siblings born to a Danish mother and a Greenlandic father, he had lived most of his life in Denmark, and he had described his own ability to speak Greenlandic as 'heart-breakingly poor', but he often underscored his close connection to Greenland, and his concern for his country was unquestioned.

But now he was nervous. The day before, Jens-Erik Kirkegaard, Aleqa Hammond's colleague, had published an op-ed of his own, this one in *Sermitsiaq*, Greenland's main newspaper. Writing on behalf of the entire Greenlandic government, he reiterated the main points of the draft mineral resources strategy: A handful of mines in operation within five years, 1,500 people hired to work in mines, 30 billion in tax revenue over a 15-year period and two active oil fields.

At Minik Rosing's presentation in Nuuk, Kirkegaard sat in the front row, waiting. Also on hand were Vittus Qujaukitsoq, Aleqa Hammond's finance minister, and, at the back of the auditorium, Kim Kielsen, the environment minister.

Minik Rosing warmed up the audience with a joke. 'Two thousand years ago, Jesus called a press conference on the banks of the Sea of Galilee. *This will show them*, he thought. But the next day, the headlines only read "Jesus can't swim".'

The joke was the icebreaker Rosing needed and he now dived into the hard facts: Most of Greenland is covered by an ice cap, but the ice-free areas along the coast still cover an area larger than Norway. There had to be minerals buried there somewhere. As far back as the nineteenth century, there had been efforts to mine graphite. At that time, the pencil was a high-tech communication tool, and the British were making a fortune by exploiting their monopoly on graphite. Greenland had significant graphite deposits, but by the time a mine was developed, the pencil's heyday had passed. The lesson to be learned here, Rosing said, was that on average, 50 years passes between when a mineral resource is identified in the Greenlandic underground and production begins. 'Graphite is a good example of how we tend to build mirages and vastly overestimate the potential of something that, in reality, is very, very, fragile.'

He talked of mirages. Many in the audience now understood where he was headed. Minik Rosing was about to burst the most popular bubble in Greenland! Everyone had been blinded by the potential of oil and minerals, he said. He was witty and made sure to use simple terms, but the hard message was clearly understood.

Minik Rosing believed in the minerals – but not in the same way as Aleqa Hammond's staff in Nuuk. With the aid of an oversized map, he walked the audience through the geological studies of Greenland that scientists, mostly Danish, had already carried out. Their findings indicated the presence of molybdenum, iron, zinc, rare earths, platinum, nickel, copper, gold, uranium and several other minerals. Rosing made it clear that he too believed that minerals were going to be important for Greenland. It was just that his faith was of another character than Aleqa Hammond's. What she would do fast, he would do slowly. What she saw as a way to independence, he saw as an option only available through enhanced co-operation with Denmark.

Then he punctured the oil and gas bubble. His educated opinion was that Greenland would not be earning money on natural gas at any point in the near future. No one in the Arctic would. The world price was just too low for it to be profitable. 'The type of investment you need to make in order to be able to exploit gas reserves and transport them to market is unrealistically large.'

When it came to oil, he brought up the 2008 American study suggesting that as much as 15 per cent of the world's untapped oil reserves are in the Arctic and explained how such prognoses are often misread. He did not bring up Nuuk's draft mineral resources strategy directly, but he explained that in general, people's expectations for Greenland's oil reserves were vastly overestimated. 'On this particular point, a high degree of unpredictability and cockiness has gone hand in hand', he quipped. On top of that, he added, experts expect that sea ice will remain a significant challenge to oil producers in Greenland for many years to come – despite global warming. 'Yes, the Arctic ice cap is receding, but that is irrelevant for the area where they want to drill. It will still be covered in ice during the winter.' Oil production would not come online for at least 25 years, maybe even 50 – if at all, he explained.

The gauntlet had now been thrown down in a high-stakes game. The government's mineral resources strategy was based on demanding and costly studies, some of them carried out using costly aerial surveys. Government officials had spent thousands of hours working on the strategy. They had travelled the globe to meet with representatives from oil firms, invited them to briefings and compiled packages of expensive seismic data showing how easily accessible Greenland's off-shore was. Now, Rosing and his team of experts were about to put the kibosh on their work. He described the discussion that had taken place up to this point as 'nebulous', and made it clear that the authors of the government's draft strategy failed to delineate between fact and fantasy. A cameraman at the front of the auditorium caught Kirkegaard as he looked on, stone-faced, while Rosing moved on to the next topic: How Greenland could best earn money on its minerals.

The audience included a significant number of Greenland's elite: Cabinet members, business people, lobbyists, Danish military brass, Kuupik Kleist, the former premier, and Asii Chemnitz, the mayor of Nuuk.

Minik Rosing was rolling. 'It is extremely difficult to say anything specific about what we can expect.' In order to deal with this uncertainty, however, his group of scientists had formulated a theoretical mining venture to average the five mining projects that were closest to becoming a reality. The average productive lifespan of these mines was estimated to be ten years. For each mine that started production, Nuuk could expect to collect about 300 million kroner in taxes from the mine itself plus 400 million kroner in income tax and tax on the profits earned by contractors. From these 700 million kroner, however, Nuuk would need to deduct 262 million kroner to Denmark as a result of the Self-Rule Act. Roughly speaking, the agreement entitled the Danes to half of the income from Greenland's underground for as long as Copenhagen was still paying the annual block grant to Greenland.

Some of those in the audience already knew where this was heading. The previous day *Politiken* had summed it all up in a single headline: '13 experts shoot down Greenland's independence dream'. The newspaper underscored how Rosing's report contradicted Hammond's independence plans. 'If Greenland is to wean itself off the 3.6 billion kroner annual block grant from Denmark, it will take the income from 24 large-scale mines in order to fund social welfare programmes at the current levels. That is the equivalent of one new mine every second year. Right now, only two are on the drawing board.'

In Nuuk, Rosing's initial jitters were far gone as he chalked up five scenarios for Greenland's future. The first showed what would happen if Greenland pursued all current plans for mining projects, and if they all got up and running in a short period of time, while others were developed to come online once the first batch were no longer active. Even if all this was to happen, a block grant of 2.8 billion kroner would still be needed, the scientist said. 'The grant will still make up a significant portion of Greenland's economy. Even if there are five large-scale projects going on at any one time, and with a new one starting every other year', Rosing said.

The other four scenarios did not improve the situation. No matter how they approached it, Greenland, the experts concluded, was going to be dependent on Denmark for a long, long time to come.

Minik Rosing appeared to favour the scenario he called 'the harp approach', in which Greenland sought to develop several different types of economic activity. This scenario also called for five mining projects at a time, but they would only be started when the timing was right for Greenland, and mining would not take place inside certain protected areas.

'The projects would be located outside the zones of special natural and cultural value, and all revenue from the natural resources industry would be placed in a natural resource wealth fund. Introducing special zones would also mean that Greenland would more easily be able to capitalize on its status as a pure land of vast wilderness areas and thus attract other types of businesses and organizations that could provide the country with revenue.'

In the fifth and final scenario, the report explained how hastily opening as many mines as possible would lead to a dependency on foreign labour and capital. 'Extracting sufficient mineral resources for Greenland's independence within 20–30 years would require such extensive foreign investment and massive inflow of foreign labour that there is a real risk that the current Greenlandic population would become a minority in Greenland.' Were this to happen, enormous social problems would emerge, the experts forecasted. There is 'a high risk that the current population will be kept in their current typically lower-paid jobs while a new class of better-paid foreign workers is established. This could lead to increased impoverishment of the present Greenlandic population. Similarly, mining of this magnitude would radically change the entire structure of Greenlandic society, contributing to impaired access to major areas of wilderness and thus hindering the development of other industries. In certain areas, the basis for cultural activities deemed to be Greenland's core domestic values, such as hunting, fishing, berry picking and general outdoor activities, would also be impaired'.

Rosing summed up: 'If we want to be independent, we must ask ourselves whether we are truly independent if someone else owns the country, and if most of the people living here are foreigners?'

Lawmakers in Copenhagen were uncommonly enthused by Rosing's and his associates' report. Claus Hjort Frederiksen, a leading member of the opposition in the Danish parliament, was quick to the point. 'I am always taken aback when I hear Aleqa Hammond speak. You would think she was basing her policies on dreams she has had and it is unhealthy for a country's lawmakers to base their work on something illusory or unreal. This report and the description of Greenland's options it contains are going to be invaluable.' Søren Espersen, of the populist Danish People's Party, was more frank. 'The report makes it clear; they are best off staying in the Kingdom. This ought to convince them to let go of their fantasies about independence. Greenland tells us, "We might be married, but as soon as we get rich we are going to divorce you". I find that grotesque.'

Flemming Møller Mortensen, a Social Democrat, had to walk a finer line. Aleqa Hammond's party, Siumut, is officially linked to the Social Democrats in Denmark as a sister party, but his disdain was clear. 'I think they ought to listen to what the report has to say, just as they would listen to the findings of any other report. I would like to help that process, but it needs to be as an equal, not as some kind of older brother.' A number of the Danish political parties asked Rosing to present his report directly to them behind closed doors.

The Danish press applauded the scientists' report as if paid by Rosing's budget. *Berlingske Tidende* carried an editorial titled 'Greenland's dependence', calling the scientists' report 'a gift to Greenland'. It argued that the scientists had given Greenland a true picture of its prospects. 'Their answer is as clear as the air on a frosty Nuuk morning. Greenland can base its economy on neither mining nor oil for at least the next 20 to 50 years. Maybe never.'

Martin Lidegaard, the newly appointed Foreign Minister in Copenhagen, called for Copenhagen and Nuuk to work even closer together. 'All the members of the Kingdom need to think beyond the here and now. I would like to reach out to the Self-Rule Government and say: Can we consider reforms and ways of working together as equals under the current set-up in order to identify our common interests? What can we do that we are not already doing?'

In Nuuk, however, the report received an entirely different reaction. The Greenlandic government felt that the experts had misunderstood Greenland's realities, underestimated the potential for finding oil, misread oil companies' ability to operate in Greenland, and miscalculated the potential economic impact of mining. As one official said, 'This report will change nothing'.

Hammond and her cabinet tried to strangle the report in a strategic embrace. Kirkegaard, in an interview with *Sermitsiaq*, claimed he could not identify a single phrase in the report to disagree with. 'All input is welcome. It is good to look at things from a different angle. Time will tell what we can use the report for.'

The true depth of the government's irritation came only a week later. Vittus Qujaukitsoq, who was responsible for Greenland's financial policies, at the time, appeared unaware of the official line when he described the report to a journalist from KNR as 'political': 'I think it way, way underestimates the outlook for what mining can contribute to the economy.'

Rosing understood quickly that Nuuk was working to push the report out of the spotlight and at the University of Copenhagen he lashed out at his critics for their continued faith in the overly optimistic figures. 'It is quite convenient for them. They do not need to do anything about the problems facing them because before you know it we will be pumping money out of the ground. As scientists we have been accused of being part of a political effort to stop the independence movement, but they are wrong. Everyone we have spoken with in the private sector says the report is highly optimistic.'

Rosing repeated his call for lawmakers to identify what their political goals for the country were. 'We need to come

to terms with whether the whole point of all this is really to
help Greenland cut its ties with Denmark for good. If that is
the case, then, seen from Denmark's perspective, there is no
longer a point in working together. Politically, there would be
no motivation for Denmark to take any sort of big financial risk
if the end goal is to bury the relationship.'

Sermitsiaq printed 'To the Benefit of Greenland' as a
supplement and several of the report's proposals were co-opted
by the opposition. Hammond, too, admitted that she found
it important to develop all parts of the economy. Shortly
afterwards, however, the government's own draft mineral
resources strategy was formally adopted by her cabinet.

12

DENMARK AND GREENLAND CLAIM THE NORTH POLE – AND MORE

In 2014, in a move bound to conflict with Russia and other states, Denmark and Greenland jointly claim the rights to an astonishing 895,000 square kilometres of ocean floor in the Arctic Ocean, including the North Pole. This follows a series of other moves by Greenland to widen its international reach. In 1985, long before Brexit and following three years of arduous negotiations with Brussels, the people of Greenland became the first to exit the European Community. Since then, Greenland has been still more active on the international scene and still more often not in concert with Copenhagen. On many issues, Denmark and Greenland still act in bold unison, but the world is also increasingly meeting Greenland in its own right as the island takes on still more independent aspirations.

* * *

In 1982, Jonathan Motzfeldt became the first elected official from the Kingdom of Denmark to visit the Pope in Rome since the Reformation, in the sixteenth century. Their meeting was about fish.

In 1982, Motzfeldt was head of the Home Rule government in Nuuk, and the meeting with Il Papa happened during Greenland's secession from the European Community. Not long after Greenland was granted home rule, in 1979, a majority of Greenlanders voted against staying in the European Community; they wanted to maintain control of Greenland's rich fishing grounds. Copenhagen did not stand in the way, and in 1985 Greenland became the first territory ever to secede from the EC.

Now, many years later, it is easy to summarize the sequence of events in a single, short paragraph, but it took three years of difficult negotiations to do it. Just as Great Britain is now battling to find the proper way out of the European Union, so was Greenland. Motzfeldt and other Greenland officials butted heads with Brussels and hordes of diplomats from EC member countries time and again so that Greenland would still be able to sell its fish to Europe duty free, to reap the benefits of European fishing in Greenland's waters and to tap into the EC's myriad training programmes, research funding and other programmes even if Greenland was no longer a member of the European Community.

This was the first time Greenland took responsibility for its own foreign policy at such a momentous level. The goal for the negotiators was to situate Greenland as well as possible by trading in its membership for binding agreements on collaboration with the EC. Motzfeldt and other Greenlanders were seeking to avoid isolation in a backwater at the top of the world, but the Europeans were proving a tough sell. Germany and Italy dug their heels in especially deep. The Europeans would not let the Greenlanders have it both ways: They could not secede and also remain an insider. No country or territory had ever left the EC before, and the Italians feared that if Greenland got to have it both ways, it would give Sicily the idea that it too could start asking for its own special arrangements. Rome refused to recognize the narrow victory for the secession at the Greenland referendum.

Josef Motzfeldt agreed with Uffe Ellemann-Jensen, the Danish Foreign Minister, that he would go to Rome to lobby for Greenland's secession. The Danish ambassador to Rome set up a meeting with Mario Fioret, Italy's minister for EC relations, and Pope John Paul II. Well known as a humorist, Josef Motzfeldt later described the meetings in Rome:

> The meeting with Fioret got off on a cool note. Fioret was clearly against Greenland seceding, and Italy was willing to go to lengths to get us to return to the negotiating table. He did not feel that the narrow outcome of our referendum was enough. I have to admit that I was getting impatient. Continuing the discussion seemed pointless, and in order to find a way to bring the meeting to an end, I told him that I had lived in Rome for a few months while I was studying, and that while I was studying at Qassimiut University a certain Professor Andersen taught me that Italy, in 1946, had held a referendum about whether the country should be a monarchy or a republic. The result was an even narrower majority than ours in favour of the republic. Then I excused myself, saying I had an audience with the Pope. The effect was magical. Fioret clearly did not want to show that he had never heard of Qassimiut University or the professor, even though there was no reason why he should, but he knew who the Pope was. He promised that the government would re-consider their position and then asked me to send his greetings to Il Papa. A few days later, Italy announced they would recognize the result of our referendum.
>
> (Jonathan Motzfeldt in *Grønland i Verdenssamfundet*
> (Greenland: Atuagkat Ilisimatusarfik, 2006))

Josef Motzfeldt, who passed away in 2010, had made up Qassimiut University and Professor Andersen on the spur of the moment. Qassimiut is the settlement in southern Greenland where Motzfeldt was born – and there is certainly no university, only a very modest elementary school. Motzfeldt, himself a vicar, had once again showed his legendary skills as a diplomat and, perhaps equally important, laid the groundwork for what was to become a long-term relationship that would prove lucrative for both Greenland and the EC.

Motzfeldt and his negotiators hammered out the myriad of details on the secession and the so-called 'Greenland Treaty' took form. The agreement with the EC ensured that Greenland retained duty-free access to the European market, and in exchange European fishermen were permitted to continue fishing in Greenlandic waters. Greenland was also granted status as an overseas territory. The complicated agreement, which is renegotiated regularly, secures an important source of income for Greenland, and the process marked the start of a flurry of activity in Greenland's foreign relations, which continues to this day.

Thirty years later, in 2014, during the Greenlandic Premier's annual New Year's reception in Copenhagen, Aleqa Hammond explained to me that she was considering opening a Greenlandic representative office in Beijing. Poised and elegantly dressed in a salmon-coloured anorak-style dress, trimmed with polar hare fur, Hammond, carefully balancing a plate of appetizers and a glass of wine, greeted diplomats and others with ties to Greenland. The previous evening, she had addressed members of the Danish Greenlandic Society and explained that the work of a Greenlandic diplomat in Beijing would be to develop the rich contacts Greenland had already built up in China, Japan and South Korea. Nuuk had concluded that its interests in Asia's tiger economies were now so great that it made sense to station an envoy there permanently.

Hammond made it sound as if it was a simple matter of hiring the right person. In reality, it was anything but. In Copenhagen, officials in the Prime Minister's Office, the Foreign Ministry and the Defence Ministry, as well as leading lawmakers, were already concerned that Nuuk was not capable of managing the complexity of its foreign relations. Hammond, however, did not let Danish scepticism hold her back. She was on her way to Brussels, where she was going to hold another large reception for more diplomats. In the crowd in Copenhagen was Inuuteq Holm Olsen, the former top civil servant in Greenland's Foreign Affairs Ministry, and now on his way to Washington, where he would serve as the country's first diplomat in the United States.

To many observers in Denmark, Greenland's mushrooming diplomatic ties with the rest of the world are hard to grasp. Greenland is still a part of the Kingdom of Denmark, and the constitution of Denmark places responsibility for Danish foreign policy squarely in the hands of Copenhagen. The Kingdom's envoys, like that of other countries, must maintain a stringent course and look out for the country's key commercial interests as well as its fundamental values. Consequently, to prevent any confusion or lack of clarity the constitution makes international relations the sole responsibility of the king, or more recently, of the government in Copenhagen. Neither Nuuk nor Tórshavn in the Faroe Islands have the power to formulate foreign policies; according to the constitution this is the prerogative of the government of the Kingdom of Denmark, based in Copenhagen.

In practice, however, the constitution has proven to be flexible and subject to changing interpretations. Constant pressure by Nuuk and Tórshavn has eroded the might of Copenhagen, and the foreign relations of Greenland and the Faroe Islands are subject to frequent skirmishes with the Danish capital.

One episode, in November 2013, showed how carefully Greenland's foreign affairs were now being watched from Copenhagen. Søren Espersen, of the Danish People's Party, had been irked by a piece of news in *Jyllands-Posten* discussing Greenland's decision to send an envoy to Washington. A long-time employee at Greenland's representative office in Copenhagen explained to the newspaper that there were a number of foreign policy issues where Greenland's interests differed from Copenhagen's. 'Opening a representative office in the USA is a sign that Greenland is now placing more importance on foreign affairs than before', he said. Lars Hovbakke Sørensen, a University of Copenhagen historian, concluded that 'it is clearly an aggressive policy move that is targeted at Copenhagen. They are flirting with an open, independent foreign policy, and that is no doubt a source of consternation for some Danish lawmakers'.

Søren Espersen, as a member of parliament, felt things had gone too far. The way he understood it, Greenland was preparing to follow its own diplomatic course in Washington.

'If that is the case, then they should not be allowed. The Self-Rule Act states that Nuuk has no right to initiate foreign or security policy discussions with foreign powers.' Espersen demanded Prime Minister Thorning-Schmidt explain to the Greenland sub-committee of the Danish parliament what exact status Greenland's representative would have in Washington.

Meanwhile, there was also trouble over uranium and rare earth elements, over who was responsible for cleaning up oil spills, foreign workers in Greenland, the status of Greenland and the Faroe Islands in the Arctic Council, Greenland's access to Danish intelligence, the response to the EU's sealskin ban, possible American espionage against Greenland, the US presence at Thule Air Base, and US responsibility for cleaning up nuclear reactors built under the ice cap.

Many in Greenland also found themselves questioning why Copenhagen had twice appointed a Dane to serve as Arctic ambassador. Why not someone from Greenland? Canada, in contrast, named Mary May Simon, an Inuit from Kangiqsualujjuaq, Quebec, as its Arctic ambassador as far back as 1994.

Søren Espersen could also have asked who was looking out for the Kingdom's foreign and security policy interests when Nuuk was now negotiating with major oil firms on contracts worth billions of dollars or when Greenlandic cabinet members met with representatives from China to discuss mining rights. Who was looking out for the Kingdom's interests when Greenland reached agreements with South Korean officials about satellite mapping in Greenland, or when Greenland negotiated with the European Commission on how Greenland's minerals would reach the market? Where were the Kingdom's core interests when lawmakers in Nuuk voted to permit uranium mining, while Copenhagen was deeply involved in global nuclear non-proliferation efforts? Could Copenhagen really be said to be in charge of the foreign affairs of the Danish Kingdom, when Hammond appeared in Reykjavik, Halifax, Brussels, London and on foreign TV stations telling the world that Greenland would soon be independent?

Flexible interpretation of the constitution gained sway in earnest in 2005, when the Danish parliament passed a proposal put forth by Anders Fogh Rasmussen, then Danish Prime Minister. A new arrangement gave both Greenland and the Faroe Islands the right to enter into bi-lateral agreements with other governments, provided the agreements related to administrative powers that had been devolved to them by the government in Copenhagen. Later, this arrangement was included in Greenland's 2009 Self-Rule Act, which states:

> Naalakkersuisut may, on behalf of the Realm, negotiate and conclude agreements under international law with foreign states and international organizations, including administrative agreements which exclusively concern Greenland and entirely relate to fields of responsibility taken over.

This paragraph would seem clear enough, but the wording immediately before clouded the matter:

> The Government and Naalakkersuisut shall co-operate in international affairs as laid down in this Chapter with a view to safeguarding the interests of Greenland as well as the general interests of the Kingdom of Denmark. The powers granted to Naalakkersuisut in this Chapter shall not limit the Danish authorities' constitutional responsibility and powers in international affairs, as foreign and security policy matters are affairs of the Realm.

Søren Espersen was not the only one to eye a potential conflict in the two statements, and Danish diplomats are often hard-pressed to convince others than themselves that Copenhagen and Nuuk are in lock-step in their dealings with other countries and international organizations.

A fine example of Nuuk's foreign policy assertiveness involved the Arctic Council. Despite its former status as a diplomatic backwater, the Arctic Council has taken on increasing importance for Copenhagen and the rest of the Arctic world. The Arctic Council is where Denmark expands its contacts with the world's major powers through Arctic collaboration.

In early 2013, Aleqa Hammond and Danish Foreign Minister Villy Søvndal were making final preparations to attend a crucial Arctic Council summit in Kiruna, Sweden. They were to meet and negotiate important deals with John Kerry, the US Secretary of State, and Sergei Lavrov, his Russian counterpart, and foreign ministers and ambassadors, diplomats and other envoys from a host of other countries. The line-up underscored the crucial role the Arctic Council had come to play in international affairs, and now the Arctic Council was to make one of the most important decisions in its history: Should China, Japan, India, South Korea and the EU be admitted as observers? They had been pushing for admission as permanent observers for years. Now was the moment of truth, and China, South Korea and Japan would be sending high-level representatives.

It was then that Aleqa Hammond made her surprise move. As the final travel preparations were being made, the Danish foreign minister received a call from Nuuk: Greenland was considering a boycott of the Arctic Council. Greenland was going to stay home, and in doing so would be sending a message to the entire gathering at the Arctic Council Summit that the Kingdom of Denmark was split, at odds and coming unwound. The Danes were badly dismayed. Greenland was not just skipping the summit; it was pulling out of all of the Arctic Council's scientific committees and task forces.

In the days leading up to the summit, the Danes did what they could to reverse the decision by Nuuk, but Hammond had her mind set. The boycott was a reality and Denmark, once again, had to accept that there were deep fissures in the Kingdom's foreign affairs. Hammond felt that Greenland's influence within the Arctic Council was being watered down. By staying away, she indicated strongly that Denmark was doing too little to sort out the matter.

Her reasoning resulted from a new practice within the Council. Since the Arctic Council was established in 1996, the Kingdom of Denmark had often had more than one seat at the negotiating tables. At some – although not all – meetings,

Greenlandic and Faroese representatives had been permitted to have their own flags on the table next to the Danish flag. In contrast, the seven other Arctic Council member states had only ever had one seat and one flag each. Hammond and her officials were upset because the Swedish chairmanship was not going to give the Danish Kingdom the extra seats at the Kiruna summit. This practice seemed a new norm rather than the exception. Aleqa Hammond felt that Sweden was acting at the behest of other council members who wanted to minimize the influence of Greenland and the Faroe Islands while Denmark, in her mind, was not fighting sufficiently for Greenland's continued influence.

Hammond's critics were tense and outspoken. She was over-reacting, they said, and making a fool of herself. Yet she was not the only one who felt something was amiss. From its founding, the Arctic Council set itself apart from other international organizations by giving permanent participant status to indigenous Arctic groups – the Sami, Native Americans, Greenlandic and Canadian Inuit and the many Russian indigenous groups. The indigenous groups had their own secretariat located in Copenhagen and funded by the Danish government. Aleqa Hammond and others with her sensed that by 2013, this unique position was being threatened, in particular since China, Japan, and other major powers were now to be included as permanent observers. Writing in *Polar Record* after the Kiruna summit, Philip Steinberg and Klaus Dodds, both geographers and both among the world's leading experts when it comes to Arctic affairs, agreed that the Arctic Council was on its way to becoming a forum in which governments could conduct the hard business of state and that, as a consequence, the indigenous groups were gradually seeing their influence diminished.

It was not until well after the Kiruna ministerial that Greenland once again made peace with Denmark and the Arctic Council. Assuming the chairmanship from Sweden, Canada sent a high-level diplomat to Nuuk and Copenhagen to negotiate a compromise. A compromise – mainly that

Greenland and the Faroe Islands would keep their seats, but not their flags at the table – was accepted, but as a temporary measure.

Hammond declared the compromise a victory on the Self-Rule Government's website: 'Greenland has spoken up for itself by making a significant demand that secured our interests in the Arctic Council. It was a tough fight, but it was worth it.' Her opponents in Nuuk and Copenhagen said she had misunderstood what had happened. They saw the boycott as a troubling lack of diplomatic finesse and found the outcome to be anything but a victory for Greenland.

The development of Denmark's and Greenland's joint claim to the ocean floor at the North Pole further illustrated just how complex power sharing between the two is and just how large the international implications are.

The claim was negotiated in deep secrecy. The claim entails the largest geographical expansion of the Danish Kingdom in several hundred years, but for years only a small handful of key politicans were informed of the proceedings and the potential conflicts with Russia and others they entailed.

Once again, there were traces of Jonathan Motzfeldt. During the previously described three-way summit in 2001, the old Greenlandic premier, Denmark's Prime Minister at the time, Poul Nyrup Rasmussen, and the Faroese Prime Minister, Anfinn Kallsberg, agreed that they would fight for the right to hundreds of thousands of square kilometres of ocean floor in the North Atlantic and the Arctic Ocean.

It was a gigantic project. The three political leaders sensed potential oil discoveries and to Poul Nyrup Rasmussen, the plan offered a unique chance to demonstrate to the Faroese and Greenlanders that their relations with Denmark had real value to them.

The UN's Convention on the Law of the Sea from 1982 gave all coastal states the right to claim the ocean floor far beyond established maritime borders. This provided the three parties to the Danish Kingdom a host of opportunities. A team of officials, diplomats, and scientific experts started preparing claims to the UN concerning two grand areas of ocean floor off the coast of the Faroe Islands and three areas east, west and north of Greenland. Everything was done with utmost discretion. The project would bring Denmark on a collision course with Iceland and Great Britain off the coast of the Faroe Islands and with Canada and Russia in the Arctic Ocean by the North Pole. The Danish parliament was not informed, no press releases were published, but an extensive and methodical gathering of ocean floor data was initialized. The LOMROG III expedition, already described in a previous chapter, was merely one out of three icebreaker expeditions in the waters off the coasts of Greenland.

Overall, the co-operation between Denmark, the Faroe Islands, and Greenland went well, but North Pole complications arose in the high Arctic.

In 2010, during Greenlandic Premier Kuupik Kleist's time in office, the Greenlandic administration worried that Denmark would not stand its ground against Russia and defend Greenland's interests. They feared that the Danish negotiators would let Russia have its way at the North Pole in return for other concessions to Denmark.

Denmark and Greenland were both preparing for many years of negotiations with the Russians. In December 2014, Denmark and Greenland's formal claims and scientific ocean floor data were to be sent to the UN's Commission on the Limits of the Continental Shelf (CLCS), which would then decide whether the scientific data supported Denmark's claims. But, as previously described, this was only phase one. The UN committee will not settle the dispute if Denmark and Russia's legitimate claims to the ocean floor by the North Pole overlap. Such a dispute is to be settled by the states.

In spring 2014, the deadline for any claims by Denmark and Greenland was approaching and Denmark and Greenland were at odds on which course to take. News from Ottawa and Moscow had created uncertainty about not only Russia's but also Canada's intentions in the Arctic Ocean, and there was no longer full agreement on which strategy to follow between

Denmark and Greenland. From Moscow, the message was that the Russians aimed to submit their claims to the UN only in summer 2015, and in Nuuk tensions were rising. Aleqa Hammond's people feared that the Russians were holding back their claim because Denmark was in the process of tying itself down with a far too limited claim to the Arctic Ocean floor.

In Nuuk, the prevailing thought was that Russia would claim everything in their power and thus establish the best possible position of strength prior to negotiations with the Danish Kingdom and Canada. From a Greenlandic point of view, the Danish officials were in the process of formulating the smallest imaginable claim to the UN, meaning that Greenland and Denmark would corner themselves and lose crucial negotiation power.

Nuuk was pressuring the Danish government to prepare a more aggressive claim. Initially, this idea was not well received in Copenhagen. The Danish data on the ocean floor, which had been meticulously gathered by Christian Marcussen and his crew in the Arctic Ocean, only documented the ocean floor up to and including the North Pole, as well as a small area onwards towards Siberia. Greenland was now arguing for a far greater area.

The course of events from this point on illustrates just how strong Greenland's position in the Danish Realm has become. The expeditions into the ocean north of Greenland had cost the taxpayers approximately 150 million kroner and Greenland had not contributed one cent. The Danish diplomacy was in for years of difficult negotiations with the UN's expert committee and then the Russian government – while Greenland was the one to benefit from any rights to the ocean floor won in the process.

Video conferences across the Atlantic were set up and the Danish Foreign Minister, Martin Lidegaard, and his officials were paying constant attention to Nuuk's priorities. It was in this final phase of the process that the Danish government, led by the foreign minister, decided to maximize the

Kingdom's claim in the Arctic Ocean – a decision that led to the unexpectedly huge claim of 895,000 square kilometres of seabed all the way to Russian waters.

Originally, Denmark's intentions were entirely different. Prior to the LOMROG III expedition in 2012, the Danish scientists and officials had worked on a desktop model of the Danish–Greenlandic claim that amounted to 150,000 square kilometres. This plan was carefully coordinated with Canada. Denmark wished to maintain a standing agreement with Canada, which meant that the western edge of Denmark's and Greenland's joint claim was to follow a line equally far from Greenland and Canada all the way to the North Pole. The agreement was that Canada would adhere to the same line when its claim was submitted to the UN.

But then Canada jumped. Without warning, in December 2013, the deal between Denmark and Canada was shoved off the table by Canadian Prime Minister Stephen Harper. After many years' work gathering data in the Arctic Ocean, the Canadian scientists were ready to submit Canada's claim to the ocean floor to the UN, but when Stephen Harper, mere days before the deadline, realized that the claim did not include the North Pole itself, he discarded the entire draft. Harper would not submit a claim to the UN that did not encompass the North Pole.

In Copenhagen and Nuuk this caused great commotion – even if the public was still kept in the dark. The Canadian move had dissolved an essential part of the Danish–Greenlandic plan. It was now necessary to develop a new strategy at a time when the deadline was fast approaching.

This time, the technical experts in Copenhagen drafted three possible solutions: (1) Denmark and Greenland could submit a relatively modest claim to the UN in accordance with the original plan; (2) they could submit a somewhat larger claim; or (3) submit a very large claim based on maximum utilization of the options allowed by the UN's Convention on the Law of the Sea.

During a series of still secret negotiations between Denmark and Greenland, a swift decision was made: Denmark and

Greenland chose the full-scale solution. The Danish scientists had gathered data in the Arctic Ocean only to support a modest claim of approximately 150,000 square kilometres, but now the two governments decided to reformulate their submission to the UN into the much larger claim. In the final months of drafting, the Danish experts used publicly available data, in particular from American databases. They added this to Denmark's own data and finally presented a draft claim of 895,000 square kilometres of ocean floor beneath the Arctic Ocean to the politicians in Nuuk and Copenhagen.

It was now clear that Denmark's and Greenland's submission to the UN would stretch all the way across the Arctic Ocean to the Russian 200 nautical mile economic zone. Denmark and Greenland were in the process of claiming ocean floor which overlapped with Russia's expected claims by more than 500,000 square kilometres, and which would probably also overlap Canada's claims.

Nuuk was very satisfied.

The claim was ambitious, some would say overly so, but it also followed a pattern. In two instances around the Faroe Islands, Denmark and the Faroe Islands had already submitted claims to the UN which exploited all options in the Convention on the Law of the Sea.

Denmark's assessment of Russia's expected reaction also played a part. Danish diplomats had had ongoing contact with their Russian colleagues. In Nuuk and Copenhagen, the belief was that Russia would find it quite natural that Denmark and Greenland utilized all options laid out by the UN Convention on the Law of the Sea. To some degree this was also what the five Arctic coastal states had agreed to in Ilulissat back in 2008. It was obvious that nationalistic Russian forces would possibly try to ignite a row over the North Pole, but in 2014, Russian Arctic policies were still in the hands of the more liberal foreign minister, Sergej Lavrov, who, since Ilulissat, had assured the world that Russia would follow the rules of the UN in the Arctic. Also, in 2010, Lavrov was part of a surprisingly smooth solution to a border dispute in the Barents Sea that

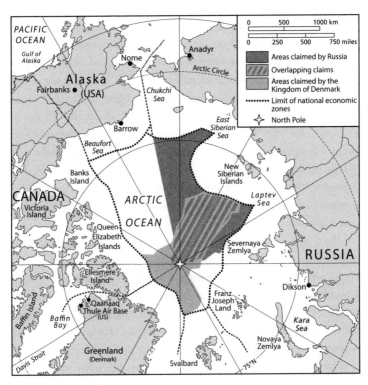

In 2014, Denmark and Greenland submitted to the UN a claim for 895,000 square kilometres of seabed in the Arctic Ocean. The claim was unexpectedly ambitious: It reaches across the North Pole all the way to Russian waters. Russia filed its final claim in 2015, and the two claims now overlap by more than 500,000 square kilometres close to the North Pole. Canada is expected to file its claim in 2018 or 2019, one that will most likely overlap both of the two previous claims in the central part of the ocean. A UN commission will evaluate scientific data submitted by the three governments as proof of right. If the commission approves overlapping claims, a final settlement will be reached only through direct negotiations between the nations involved.

Norway and Russia had tried to solve for more than 40 years. This supported Denmark and Greenland's beliefs that Russia would understand their claim to the North Pole.

Denmark and Greenland submitted their claim to the UN on 15 December 2014. The technical data were handed in at the UN's headquarters in New York in three large cardboard boxes and in Copenhagen the public was informed accordingly. There was a media briefing at the Ministry of Foreign Affairs in Copenhagen, and Foreign Minister Martin Lidegaard issued a press release: 'Our submission of the claim to the continental shelf north of Greenland is a historic and important milestone for the Kingdom of Denmark. The aim of this enormous project is to determine the outer boundaries of our continental shelf and thus, in the end, for the Kingdom. In this process, we have enjoyed great co-operation within the Realm as well as with our Arctic neighbours.' After a few days, the Russian Ministry of Foreign Affairs issued a short message confirming that Russia considered the Danish–Greenlandic claim to be thoroughly uncontroversial.

Then came a period in which Nuuk and Copenhagen tensely awaited Russia's claim. A number of observers expected Russia to size up the enormous Danish–Greenlandic claim along with Canada's new aggressive strategy and then present a huge claim to the UN. Many speculated that Russia would stretch its claim all the way past the North Pole and all the way to Greenlandic waters. But this did not happen.

On 3 August 2015, Russia submitted its claim to the UN as experts like Canadian lawyer and Arctic specialist Michael Byers praised Russia for its pragmatism and modesty. The Russian claim illustrated two points: Firstly, the new Russian claim to the ocean floor showed an overlap with Greenland and Denmark's claim of more than 500,000 square kilometres. Secondly, Russia now signalled a wish to win the right to the ocean floor all the way around the North Pole itself. In its first claim from 2001, Russia claimed only a triangular pizza-slice of ocean floor pointing to the North Pole, which would allow other nations to do the same. The claim in 2015 covered all of the North Pole, stretched all the way past the North Pole and approximately 100 kilometres farther south towards Greenland. Russia seemed to be not only interested in the potential raw materials below the ocean floor, but also in the North Pole's symbolic value.

There was no official reaction from Denmark or Greenland. Former Danish Foreign Minister Uffe Ellemann-Jensen argued that Denmark would have to strengthen its military in Greenland if they wanted any respect for their claim north of Greenland, but officially Denmark and Greenland remained silent. It was a clear signal: 'Everything is in order; Russia's claim is, just like Denmark's and Greenland's, a natural part of a peaceful negotiation process, so no comments from us are necessary.' A few press reports highlighted the huge overlap between the two claims, but then a relative calm took over. Most of those directly involved prepared themselves for several decades of negotiations. The Canadian claim was expected sometime in 2018 and 2019 – and then years of waiting for the UN.

13

DENMARK PREPARES FOR INCREASED ARCTIC ACTION

In 2015, strong voices in Denmark question if Greenland will be able to run its own affairs and defend its own sovereignty as an independent state in any foreseeable future. The defence of Greenland's sovereignty is still shouldered by the Danish defence forces, as it has been for centuries. Danish analysts claim that Greenland will face grave difficulties and new challenges from foreign powers without steadfast support from Denmark's military. But Greenland looks towards neighbouring Iceland, a former part of the Danish Kingdom, which is now a successful democracy with no military, yet a cherished member of NATO and a close friend of the United States. If Iceland can exist without a military, relying on modern Western alliances, why then look at Greenland as forever dependent on Denmark's defence forces? In Nuuk, I talk about independence with Kim Kielsen, who was about to become Greenland's premier. He is eager to lower tension with Denmark and to focus on the economy: A devastating deficit looms on the horizon.

* * *

After a year and half as the commanding officer of Denmark's Arctic Command in Nuuk, Major General Stig Østergaard Nielsen is no longer convinced that a majority of those living in Greenland are in favour of independence. 'I have heard repeatedly that most people support the vision of an independent Greenland, but I doubt it. I have not seen any polls to suggest this is the case. People here do not travel around much because it costs so much. They live from hand to mouth, and when they find out that Greenland would need to find another country to help them out should they secede from Denmark, do you not think most people would just decide to stay with Denmark anyway?'

From his second-storey office in 2014, Nielsen can just see the containers stacked up at Nuuk's port facility. Outside the air is thick with the smell of fish emanating from the processing plant next door. The three flags of the Danish Kingdom – the Faroese, the Greenlandic and the Danish – hang limp on their poles in the frigid air. This is the nerve centre of Denmark's military activities in the North Atlantic. Officially opened by Queen Margrethe in 2012, the new headquarters placed Nielsen, a former fighter pilot, and his staff close to Greenland's political leadership.

The Joint Arctic Command was the latest addition to Denmark's 300-year military timeline in Greenland. Just like the *Blaa Heyren* and its mission to display Danish might to seventeenth-century Dutch whalers, the naval vessels, aeroplanes, helicopters and dog sleds stationed in Greenland today have the capacity to defend the Kingdom's frontiers in Greenland 24 hours a day, 365 days a year. Were anyone to actually attack Greenland, it would be American forces – on behalf of NATO – that came to its defence, but in times of peace Nielsen and his staff are still responsible for keeping watch and for patrolling Greenland's borders in order to enforce Danish sovereignty. Their area of operation stretches 3,000 kilometres from Greenland's northern territorial waters to the southern edge of the Faroese exclusive economic zone. Thule Air Base remains under American control, but on a day-to-day basis the Danes defend Greenland's sovereignty.

In the operations room one storey below Nielsen's office an electronic map constantly updates the positions of ships sailing in Greenlandic waters. Naval vessels patrol the sea and in eastern Greenland the soldiers of the Sirius Patrol monitor the coast on dog sleds all winter. Nielsen is worried, though. 'I understand if people in Greenland are frustrated that the Danes are making all the decisions. A lot of the top positions here are held by Danes. We would be upset if Germans administered Denmark, but I do not think people here are ready for the next step towards independence. I remember a taxi driver complaining to me once about Danish labourers and a Danish firm being hired to repair a road here in Greenland. But there is a big difference between complaining and wanting independence.'

Nielsen is not alone in his concern about Greenland's course towards independence. Like many other Danish observers, he wonders what would become, for instance, of the thousands of Greenlanders living in Denmark if Greenland should secede from Denmark. But what worries him more is how Greenland would defend itself. The sceptics claim that without warships or aircrafts or experienced personnel, Greenland would be incapable of performing even the most basic task of protecting its borders. If Danish warships, purchased at a cost of millions and manned by well-trained Danish seamen, no longer patrol Greenland's coasts, keep their weapons ready and constantly train to fire them, who will? Who will then administer the complicated enforcement tasks that the Danish military carries out, like fisheries inspection to protect Greenland's fish stocks from being illegally overfished; or environmental protection, crucial to head off any oil spill; or search and rescue in Greenland's vast territorial waters, crucial to Greenland's own fishermen and all international traffic? Nielsen feels the goal of independence is untenable. 'The Danish state spends half a billion kroner a year on the Joint Arctic Command. And that is just the operational costs. It does not take into account investment in new ships or aircraft. An independent Greenland is unthinkable.'

Few members of the Danish military are as outspoken as Nielsen, but his point of view is shared by many in both the military and among Danish political decision makers. Bertel Haarder, Denmark's Minister of Culture and former head of the Danish delegation to the Nordic Council, put forward a variation of the same thinking in a January 2014 op-ed published in *Jyllands-Posten,* a daily. 'Greenland is enormously important for Denmark and the entire Nordic region at a time when people are paying increasing attention to the North Atlantic and the Arctic. I love Greenland. I love the Kingdom of Denmark. I fully support the idea of self-rule, and I look forward to the day that Greenland can stand on its own two feet economically.'

He felt it was unrealistic that Greenland could go it alone. 'Mineral resources, new Arctic sailing routes, maritime search and rescue, environmental protection and all the exciting new research opportunities ought to be argument enough in favour of a much closer relationship between Denmark and Greenland. But on top of that comes the required aerial surveillance that will be necessary to ensure peace and stability in a vast and strategically important area, and which will be necessary for preventing the emergence of a military void that someone else could be tempted to fill out.'

Nils Wang, a rear admiral in the Danish navy, former head of the entire navy, commandant of the Defence College, and one of Denmark's leading experts on Arctic security, in 2014 published a critique of the ongoing quest for independence in Greenland. With his co-author Damien Degeorges, a French Greenland expert, Nils Wang concluded, 'Could Greenland become an independent country? Our answer is that it in likelihood will remain an unattainable goal for the next 30 to 40 years, or even longer, if Greenland hopes to avoid being considered a vulnerable state. For a variety of reasons, the Kingdom of Denmark and the Self-Rule Act are Greenland's best bet if it hopes to continue on its path to becoming a modern, economically independent and nearly independent state.'

Nils Wang, like other Greenland experts, sees the strong continued focus on secession as a serious security challenge to the entire Danish Kingdom. In his opinion, Denmark's

clout internationally was put at risk by the continued focus
on Greenland's potential secession. In a 2013 interview Wang
pointed out to me that still more observers in the United
States, Europe and NATO believed that Greenland was in
fact disassociating itself from Denmark. For foreign analysts
and other observers, it had become prudent to ask whether
Denmark and Greenland would still remain close partners,
capable of pursuing common goals and defending common
interests. One illustrative example came in 2013 when the
Council on Foreign Relations, an influential American think-
tank, weighed in on the matter. Paula Briscoe, one of the
Council's experts, wrote, 'China could at some point in the
future use its economic might and the lure of more money
flowing into Greenland's economy to persuade Greenland
to allow Beijing to base permanent military and intelligence
capabilities in Greenland'.

Others have speculated that the Kingdom of Denmark is
unlikely to survive for more than a few years. In a 2011 volume
on sovereignty in the Arctic, Shelagh D. Grant, one of Canada's
leading Arctic scholars, cited Hans Enoksen, Greenland's
premier between 2002 and 2009, who said that Greenland
should declare its independence in 2021, on the 300th
anniversary of the arrival of Hans Egede. Grant saw Greenland
as a 'potential wild card' in the Arctic.

Nils Wang was frustrated; he worried that this still more
widespread assumption was weakening Denmark's overall
strength in the world community. 'Danes need to remember
that Greenland gives us clout. Without Greenland, Denmark
would be reduced to an average little European country that was
occasionally granted an audience with the United States, Russia,
or China', he said, adding a word of caution for Nuuk. 'Greenland
should be careful not to let its pursuit of independence
unintentionally, but irreparably, damage the partnership it has
built up with Denmark over the past 300 years.'

Until an agreement on uranium between Greenland
and Denmark was reached, Nils Wang was also among the
toughest critics of Nuuk's insistence that Copenhagen should

not interfere with Greenland's plans for uranium and rare earth minerals. He found that this rendered it unclear who controlled the Kingdom's foreign policy. 'It is not helpful for any country to have an unclear foreign policy. When Nuuk denies that uranium has anything to do with national security you really have to ask whether they can be considered to be mature foreign policy makers. Everyone is petrified about what could happen to the uranium. The disagreement between Copenhagen and Nuuk about it adds to the perception that the Kingdom is falling apart.'

Uffe Ellemann-Jensen, a former Danish foreign minister, shared this line of thinking. In 2014, Ellemann-Jensen said he was 'deeply concerned and deeply amazed' that Hammond and those close to her were unable to see that Greenland will need Denmark just as much in the future as it does today. 'It is the first rule of foreign policy: A power vacuum will get filled. Let us be frank: This is a military issue; naval vessels, troops, and warplanes are all necessary to enforce sovereignty in Greenland. If Denmark does not do it, then someone else will.' Ellemann-Jensen was speaking of Russia. Slowly but surely, Russia would, in Ellemann-Jensen's opinion, move in if Denmark were no longer preserving its sovereignty over Greenland. 'You may label me as an old cold warrior for saying this, and that is what I am, but I find it naïve that we are not paying more attention to Russia's military build-up in the form of new Arctic brigades and more aircraft in the Arctic. We saw in Crimea that Russia was willing to set aside international law when Russia's key interests are threatened.'

In Sisimiut in Greenland, Ove Rosing Olsen, a former member of the government in Nuuk and a former head of health services in central Greenland, was also concerned. 'We should not be talking about independence if we are not going to discuss what independence means. Not talking about its consequences worries people here, it worries people abroad, and it worries the markets. We need to state clearly what our intentions are. That we want the Kingdom to remain as a state, but that we want to change the way the union is put together.

If we do not we are just going to create a lot of uncertainty
and give the impression that we will be a banana republic.
We have got no army and no civil defence, so we would need
to fall under someone's defence umbrella, and in my opinion
we would be better off as part of a Danish–Faroese–Greenlandic
state than we would be partnering with the USA or Canada.'

Ellemann-Jensen recalled taking a picture of the *Thor*,
Iceland's newest coast guard vessel, launched in 2011. The
impressive vessel was docked in the capital Reykjavik's
waterfront. Ellemann-Jensen wanted to document the contrast
between the *Thor* and the *Ejnar Mikkelsen*, a Danish naval vessel
that happened to be calling on Reykjavik at the same time. The
Ejnar Mikkelsen, launched just three years previously, is the
pride of the Danish fleet, and a valued element of Greenland's
naval defences. The *Thor*, however, was bigger, wider and
heavier. It measured 94 metres from stem to stern, and cost the
equivalent of three billion Danish kroner. For Ellemann-Jensen,
the *Thor* offered a lesson. 'The idea that Greenland could ever
find the means to provide for its own maritime defence is
utterly absurd.'

Interestingly, Greenland's politicians have often looked to
Iceland for inspiration. After declaring its full independence
from Denmark in 1944, Iceland successfully built a Nordic
welfare state and decided not to establish a military. With its
322,000 residents Iceland is thus the only northern European
country without an army, air force, or navy. After World
War II, the strong US military presence at Keflavik Air Base
brought the island under the umbrella of NATO and the US
defence forces. In 2006, Washington closed the American base,
but Reykjavik stuck with its unique non-military position.
Shortly after, Russian fighters began flying close, after which
NATO assumed responsibility for patrolling Iceland's airspace.
Fighters from NATO member states now patrol Iceland's skies
while the country's robust coast guard, led by the *Thor*, focuses
on maritime civil tasks. It is a model that Nuuk has expressed
a keen interest in as a seemingly obvious way to follow for a
future independent Greenland.

Nils Wang, Stig Nielsen and others in the Danish military give this idea little credence, and their position was, once again, supported by Ellemann-Jensen, the former foreign minister of Denmark. 'The two situations are entirely different. Look how big Greenland is – and compare with Iceland! It is not a matter of population or their ability to train crews; the problem is that Greenland will never be able to afford to patrol a territory that big. They need to accept that they will only be able to do it as part of the Kingdom. What would they do if the Kingdom did not exist? I cannot grasp why there are not more people in Greenland who understand this. In reality, the question is not whether Greenland can do it alone, but whether Denmark and Greenland will have the combined strength and capacity to take care of the growing number of responsibilities.'

Ellemann-Jensen and the other concerned voices had a growing audience in Copenhagen, but not everyone shared the scope of their worry. Mogens Lykketoft, also a former Danish foreign minister, told me he did not find that Greenland's moves towards increased self-reliance undermined Denmark's international position at all. 'Who sees it that way? NATO? The EU? The UN?', he asks. 'The reality is that the Kingdom will remain intact well into the future. Denmark is responsible for enforcing sovereignty in Greenland. I am certain that foreign intelligence agencies and the governments they report to will be under no illusion that this will change anytime soon. What people are talking about is whether Greenland will remain part of NATO, but there should be no question about that. The USA has a large base at Thule, and Greenland is a sovereign part of Denmark.'

The politicians in Nuuk have been loath to openly discuss these issues. No detailed Greenlandic strategies for the replacement of the Danish defence forces have been formulated. In 2014, there were several reasons for this absence of answers from Greenland. First of all, no one in Nuuk actually knew of any credible, concrete alternative to Denmark's military contribution, nor was anybody eager to develop one. Some politicians were eager to explain how they hoped for co-operation with Denmark even if Greenland formally declared its independence. Others expected that any proposal for alternative models at this early stage of Greenland's process towards independence would be perceived as a challenge to Denmark's authority – thus provoking unnecessary conflict.

Many of the key decision makers in Nuuk, however, rejected the idea that Greenland's dependence on Denmark's armed forces should prevent further autonomy or even full independence. As Aleqa Hammond explained when she was still head of the government in Nuuk:

> In a globalized world, issues like sovereignty, security, and defence are seen differently. Regions have taken the place of countries, and regional associations have taken on new importance in the past decade. The way countries organize themselves is changing, and that will have an impact. Iceland is a state, but they have no military. They have an arrangement with NATO that meets their needs and their obligations as a state. Iceland is our nearest neighbour and they have gone through the same process that Greenland is going through today. Iceland has shown us that it is possible to address these issues by approaching them in a different way than Denmark has. Denmark might, but does not necessarily have to, cover this need.

Like her predecessors, she underscored how she wished for the continuity of the Danish–Greenlandic relationship. 'Our common history is very important. We have been partners for 300 years. We have built up a successful relationship and that is not something Greenland will ever develop with any other country, whether that is Iceland or Canada. Denmark will still be our closest foreign relation after we become independent. Greenland wants a new political arrangement, but I am certain that we will continue to work together on all sorts of issues for many years to come. Anything else would be strange.'

In this fashion Greenland's and Denmark's politicians often aired very different thoughts about which security arrangements were more relevant for the future of the Danish Kingdom. They had different ideas about the relevance of the Islandic approach, they had different approaches to the security implications of Greenland's raw materials and they had different thoughts about Greenland's dependence on the Danish military.

In 2014, when talking with Kim Kielsen, who was later to become Greenland's premier, I learned how there were similarly large differences also in other fields and how certain aspects of life in Greenland inspired these differences.

Kim Kielsen, of course, had no way of knowing that he would soon replace Aleqa Hammond as head of Naalakkersuisut, the Greenland Self-Rule Government. In early 2014, he was still her Minister for Environment, and when we had talked for an hour or so in his office he got up and headed down the corridor past the other cabinet members' offices. There, where one would expect a copy machine or a coat rack, stood the minister's private chest freezer. Greenland's government has spacious offices in a high-rise with views that would have satisfied a law firm in Manhattan, but now Kielsen was proudly showing off the contents of his freezer: cuts of muskoxen and seal, whole waterfowl, enormous chunks of whale meat from minke whales Kielsen and his friends shot from boats. There were bags of black crowberries, mattak, dried cod. More cuts of meat, reindeer, which Kielsen hunted and carried home on his back for butchering. The freezer ensured that Kielsen could always have Greenlandic food if he could not make it home for dinner. On his computer screen, he showed pictures of three dead muskoxen. 'I shot them the day after I got home from a trip to New York', he said. Other pictures showed him posing with two polar bears recently killed near his hometown of Paamiut or hunting reindeer with his daughter. In another, four porpoises with large entry wounds in their skulls lay dead on a rocky shoreline. 'I do not shoot them to hurt them', he said. 'I shoot to kill.'

During the interview, Kielsen, a tall, muscular former policeman, explained to me that he would rather be hunting than in his office in Nuuk. 'Being inside eats away at me.'

He avoided saying it – just as most lawmakers in Nuuk would – but his message was clear: Kielsen felt that his connection to the great Greenlandic outdoors provided a guarantee that when it came to protecting Greenland's environment, the decisions he made would be prudent and strong. This is an attitude that one often meets in Greenland. The ever-present ocean, the hunting, the seals, the food, the frequent trips into the mountains, the dogs, the boats and the fishing, the crowberries, the mattak, the seal blubber, the rifles, the trout, the salmon and the coldness out on the ice all blend into a constantly experienced symbiosis with nature. For many in Greenland, this call to nature is an essential part of one's identity, clearly acknowledged, and for Kielsen it had become political.

On the surface, Greenland's nature is well-suited to charming tourists, but there is far more to it. For Kielsen and many others in Greenland, their close connection to their natural surroundings is a deep and deeply treasured quality in and of itself that in their own perception separates them from others. They will often explain that without a clear sense of this dimension, outsiders will have difficulties grasping the context in which difficult political decisions in Greenland must be made. During our talk, Kielsen claimed that no mining or oil firm will ever be granted permission to drill anything or anywhere in Greenland unless they can convince him and the other members of the cabinet that they will display the utmost respect for Greenland's nature. He did not substantiate this claim; instead he implied that his close and life-long personal connection with Greenland's impressive wealth of unspoiled nature is a form of proof in and of itself. The best experts and the most in-depth studies would always be referred to in order to prevent unintended environmental damage, he said. Companies will be required to live up to 'best available practices' and the toughest rules available. The best assurance that those regulations will be enforced, Kielsen said, is the intimate and personal connection he and his countrymen have to the land.

This meeting with Kielsen and his freezer encapsulated much of the essence of the many journeys through Greenland that served as the foundation for this book. Kielsen's conviction that his ties to Greenland's fjords, mountains, ice and waters would guide his political decision making was a fine example of the growing importance Greenlandic lawmakers and decision-makers place on their roots.

Greenland is making a still stronger case on the world stage. Its relationship with Denmark is likely to undergo changes in the years to come and Kim Kielsen's appetite for dried fish and reindeer meat is a part of that process. Whenever she travelled abroad as head of the Nuuk government, Aleqa Hammond described Greenland as an independent entity that makes its own decisions about its own future. The close ties to Denmark were either downplayed or ignored entirely. Greenlandic culture, its past as a hunting society, its language and its deep ties to nature received a vaunted placement as the nation's foundation. Ulrik Pram Gad, a political scientist familiar with Nuuk's political circles, has written eloquently about the way many Greenlanders link key cultural traits to the development of their country, and Kim Kielsen is certainly no stranger to this line of thinking. To him and his allies, independence, democracy, and social welfare in Greenland must be improved to allow for the healthy development of Greenlandic culture, language and traditional way of life. In their outlook, uranium, iron, and oil are not goals in and of themselves but a means to building a strong Greenland that can wrest itself free of Danish dominance and allow the people of Greenland to finally live in harmony with great wonders of the natural world of Greenland and their own cultural identity.

In both Copenhagen and Nuuk, the story of the Kingdom of Denmark can still be told, as if the two parties work together to move Greenland towards even greater degrees of modernity, social welfare, and education. The 2009 Self-Rule Act drew together, in the best democratic tradition, Danes and the Greenlanders in a solid compromise, but deep disagreements about the future lurk below the surface. Professor Rosing's and his colleagues' report about Greenland's minerals argued that economic and political independence would remain elusive for the foreseeable future, and it was soon obvious that the majority of Danish politicians and Danish citizens were more than happy to accept this as the truth. The cold welcome the report received in Nuuk underscored how Hammond and her political allies had an entirely different approach and many in Greenland shared their preferences. An independent Greenland was not just a vision that Aleqa Hammond pulled from her hat to enchant local fishermen. The prospect of a politically and economically independent Greenland remained an important element of many of her voters' self-perceptions. As Ulrik Pram Gad, the scholar, explained it, the vision of independence and especially the quest for it had become part of many Greenlanders' core identity.

For decision makers in Copenhagen, the challenges were piling up. In 2015, the dire economic outlooks in Greenland were particularly worrying to Denmark. As Mogens Lykketoft, the former Danish foreign minister, explained, Denmark's current relation with Greenland is built on a firm understanding that the standard of living in Greenland cannot be allowed to lag more than slightly behind that in Denmark. The Self-Rule Act may have changed the relationship by giving the Greenlanders the right to secede when they want, but they are still Danish citizens. Denmark will never sit idly by, Lykketoft explained, if the social ills in Greenland grow to a point where children in Greenland go to bed hungry and cold. This understanding is not stipulated by law, nor engraved in stone, but it has informed Danish political thinking ever since 1930, when Prime Minister Thorvald Stauning, a social democrat, visited Greenland and his successor, Hans Hedtoft, worked to make Greenlanders Danish citizens in 1953.

As a consequence, Copenhagen now faces a historic challenge far beyond the skirmishes over uranium and foreign policy. As the politicians and the general public in Greenland and Denmark quarrel over reconciliation, natural resources and the future of the Kingdom, the economists suggest that by 2020 Greenland will be running a serious annual budget deficit. By 2030, the figure will grow to a billion kroner, or roughly

145 million US dollars, unless new sources of income are found and painful reforms enforced. If the fishing industry does not start to bring in more, if mines do not start producing, and if the politicians in Nuuk will not cut expenses, the finances to maintain the Greenlandic welfare state will not be there any more, and Denmark will have to sum up once again its responsibilities for the people of Greenland, forged over the past three centuries.

In Nuuk, the Self-Rule Government have taken note, of course, of the seriousness of the matter. The level of future debt Greenland is facing will be poison to any dreams of independence, and quite possibly to Greenland's relationship with Copenhagen. If Greenland has to ask for more money from Denmark, its dependence on the old colonizing power, already a source of deep frustration, will grow, bringing with it still more broken pride, upheaval, and shattered dreams. It is in this light one must evaluate events as they unfold. During Aleqa Hammond's tenure, Naalakkersuisut issued new licences to foreign mining companies and new offshore exploration licences, and Greenland's envoys met with diplomats from Japan, South Korea, China and many other countries, trying to expand relationships with anyone that will land them new investments.

14

THE TWO STILL TANGO – BUT WILL IT LAST?

After years of hesitation, Denmark is eager to gradually present, equip and project the Danish Kingdom as a major player in the Arctic, responsible and ready to co-operate with others, but also in hot pursuit of its own interests. The strategy will only work if Denmark's Arctic tango with Greenland continues. Meanwhile, in Greenland, the quest for independence continues unabated. Hopes of oil and gas are dwindling, mining is slow, uranium remains a distant option, but the majority of those living in Greenland continue to long for the day when Greenland emerges as an independent state. They want Greenland to remain a democratic welfare state, a member of NATO and of the Western world, but independent from Denmark. Nuuk and Copenhagen continue to officially work as a team, but at times with visible difficulties. A complaint from Greenland to the UN lodged in early 2017 as the first ever of its kind illustrates the fragility.

* * *

In 2016, recognition of the significance of Greenland for Denmark reached a new peak in Copenhagen. For the first time ever the union between Denmark, Greenland and the Faroe Islands was described as 'an Arctic superpower'. Then, in June 2016, after three years of preparation, a bulky analysis about the future work of the Danish defence in the Arctic was published by the Ministry of Defence. In addition, most Danes sensed a new focus on 21 June, Greenland's national day, when the Greenlandic flag was flown for the first time ever from all of the 530 state flagpoles in Denmark and from all Danish embassies abroad. The idea came directly from Prime Minister Lars Løkke Rasmussen as yet another way to glue Greenland and Denmark more firmly together.

In Greenland, the flag is a symbol of Greenland's increasing ability and will to be independent. The Greenlandic flag was only invented in 1985 and for many symbolizes how Greenland follows its own ambitions still more efficiently. But in Denmark, the government now used flag-flying day to underline the coherence between Denmark and Greenland.

Lars Løkke Rasmussen was the first Prime Minister ever to give a speech at the Greenlandic House in the centre of Copenhagen. He explained that the flag-flying day was a mark of respect for Greenland and of the close connection between the two nations. 'It is the first time in history that Dannebrog – the oldest national flag in the world, and a symbol of one of the oldest kingdoms in the world – retreats and makes room for another flag on Denmark's state buildings. We hoist the Greenlandic flag because we acknowledge Greenland. And because we wish to mark our union in the Realm', he said. 'We have a special place in each other's hearts. So what could be more appropriate than quoting a person whom I know cares especially much for Greenland: Her Majesty the Queen. On multiple occasions, she has stated that in a successful marriage there are three parties: You, me and us. Those are wise words. And I think they apply to the relationship between Denmark and Greenland. In many other places, differences are a source of conflict. It is not like that between us. We do not always agree, but we solve our differences in an orderly fashion.'

A less advertised but even stronger indication of Denmark's new prioritizing of the Arctic came a few weeks prior to the flag-flying day. On 3 May 2016, after a request from the government, one of Denmark's top diplomats, Ambassador Peter Taksøe-Jensen, published a series of recommendations for Denmark's future foreign and security policy. One of his key messages was that Denmark should do much more about its commitment in the Arctic. In his recommendations to the government, he argued, 'The Kingdom of Denmark is an Arctic superpower [...] The Kingdom should give higher priority to efforts in the Arctic to promote a peaceful, economically and environmentally sustainable development to the benefit of the region, the Kingdom and the people of Greenland and the Faroe Islands. It requires a reinforced effort and co-operation internally in the Kingdom, but also internationally, in order to take advantage of the influential possibilities of the Kingdom as an Arctic superpower'.

It was historic. For more than 200 years, the Danes had viewed Denmark as a very small state. The Danish Kingdom lost Norway in 1814, subsequently the German parts of the Realm in a great war with Germany in 1864 and, most recently Iceland, which detached itself in a process from 1904 to 1944. During all these years, the Danes learned to talk about Denmark as a pocket state and the foreign policy of the nation was one long adjustment to stronger powers. With the new recommendations, this worldview was turned upside down. Ambassador Taksøe-Jensen emphasized that the Kingdom encompassing Denmark, the Faroe Islands, and Greenland is the twelfth largest country in the world and the third largest in NATO. The colossal geographic extent of Greenland was suddenly turned into a decisive factor in the comprehension of the Danish state.

Peter Taksøe-Jensen was a product of his many years in Danish diplomacy and quite the expert in Arctic relations. In 2007 and 2008, he was the chief aide of Foreign Minister Per Stig Møller and one of the principal architects behind the Ilulissat Declaration introduced in a previous chapter. In 2016, when Peter Taksøe-Jensen designed his recommendations to the Danish government, he had just completed five years as

Denmark's ambassador to Washington and was well versed in the interests of the United States in Greenland.

Shortly after he published his recommendations, he explained the central points of his views to me: 'We *are* a regional superpower in the Arctic. A relatively small number of people live in the Arctic and with Greenland we take up a lot of room and attention. It is not something we think much about in everyday life, but it gives us a bigger responsibility for the development of the entire region and bigger opportunities for affecting the situation than we have in many other places – in the Baltic Sea, for instance.'

Size commits, he said, and for this reason also it is important to underline how large Greenland looms in the Arctic: 'It illustrates how big a task Defence Command Denmark has in the Arctic. There is a significant gap between what we want in the Arctic and what the Defence Command is capable of at the moment.' In his report he recommended that the Danish navy should have more manpower for operations in the Arctic and that the Arctic Command in Nuuk should gear up to collect more satellite data from space in order to form a much clearer image of what happens in Greenland's airspace, at sea and on land. This would assist in his view in keeping the Realm together, it would illustrate the responsible ways of the Danish and it would assist in forging bonds with the Kingdom's Arctic neighbours – Canada, Iceland, Norway, Russia and the United States. Also, ultimately, it would strengthen the overall capacity of Denmark and Greenland to meet any emerging future challenge.

'I am not making an argument that we should militarize the Arctic. There are no serious signs that the Russians are threatening our sovereignty', he said but the message was mixed. In his report he added that 'it cannot be excluded that Russia will be willing to pursue tight national goals in the Arctic'. His final assessment was that peace could most likely be kept in the Arctic. The Defence Command must increase its preparedness and situation awareness, but especially its capacity to solve its civilian problems better: fisheries control, search and rescue, environmental control, ice breaking for Greenland's cargo ships and others.

According to Peter Taksøe-Jensen, the preservation of the Realm with Greenland is absolutely critical for Denmark: 'The biggest threat towards Danish interests in the Arctic is not the Russians, but the prospect of a weakened cohesion in the Realm. We must continue down the path where we say that if someone wishes to be independent, they should be free to do so. However, I believe that it will be very damaging for Denmark as well as for Greenland if that should happen. If you read between the lines in my report, you will see how much I care about ensuring the positive effects we can create for Greenland by a stronger commitment in the Arctic.' In his report, he explained how new access to satellites for Defence Command Denmark would ensure civilian broadband connection for the Greenlandic settlements, and how a stronger Danish diplomatic effort in the Arctic would benefit Greenlandic fishermen. For instance, Denmark could help argue against those who would rather see nature reserves than economic development in the Arctic.

Peter Taksøe-Jensen recommended that co-operation between Denmark and Greenland should happen 'on an equal basis', but he also maintained that Greenland should only be involved in the formation of the foreign policy of the Kingdom when Greenlandic interests were at stake: 'I remember one time when our Foreign Minister was to meet with Hillary Clinton and Nuuk demanded to be a part of the meeting because there was a small Arctic matter on the agenda. In such instances, it is going too far.'

'We must talk to each other more, have more meetings. We must know each other better. A lot of progress has been made during the past years, but we are still not good enough at coordinating with Greenland. Today the Ministry of Foreign Affairs only has five people handling all Arctic matters – but 50 people on the Middle East', he said. 'We have an obvious interest in supporting Greenland in finding their own identity, but also in doing it in a way so that Denmark remains a crucial partner for Greenland.'

Peter Taksøe-Jensen's report and the hoisting of the Greenlandic flag illustrated how Danish foreign policy was taking a clear northerly direction. This came as a surprise to many Danes. Denmark's political leaders had downplayed the importance of Greenland for decades, partly because they administered policies which they thought would not benefit at all from public scrutiny. The decision to secretly allow the US to arm its Thule Air Base with nuclear weapons in the 1950s and many years on was just one policy that was not designed for public consumption. From 2012, however, politicians were becoming more eager to talk openly of Greenland's importance. In 2012, when I asked the Danish Foreign Minister Martin Lidegaard what importance Denmark's ties to Greenland carries for Denmark, he was quite blunt: 'The influence we have on the Arctic carries great value geopolitically. It means that we can better pursue Denmark's overall foreign political interests and goals. We can work towards safe conditions for Denmark and ensure that the people of Denmark can live safely; we can pursue strong multilateral frameworks which allow for smaller countries' influence; we can work for peaceful conflict resolution, a healthy environment and socially balanced global development. We can pursue all these vital interests because we are linked with Greenland. Without Greenland we would not be able to take on the same type of rhetoric and that also applies outside the Arctic – just in a more figurative sense.'

In 2016, Danish Prime Minister Lars Løkke Rasmussen expressed the same opinion at a press conference with the political leaders of Greenland and the Faroe Islands: 'It results in a significantly larger role in the international community than Denmark, Greenland and the Faroe Islands could achieve on their own.'

Denmark's interests in the Arctic were broadly defined in the Kingdom's Arctic strategy of 2011: Denmark should first and foremost contribute to upholding the Arctic as a peaceful region where the extraction of natural resources is pursued in balance with the climate and the Arctic environment and to the continued benefit of the Arctic peoples. At no point in history has a previously inaccessible ocean suddenly become accessible to human activity. Globalization and climate change made the Arctic increasingly more important to the international community, and in 2016 the Danish politicians began to genuinely understand how all the other Arctic states worked hard to increase their influence on the new Arctic trade routes; the new opportunities for military mobility in the Arctic; the access to minerals, oil and gas as well as the Arctic fishing grounds and other marine resources.

Denmark also began to fully acknowledge what others had acknowledged for some time: For everything to turn out well and for the peace to be kept, co-operation in the Arctic demands huge efforts. The governments in Nuuk and Copenhagen agree that the real Arctic superpower is Russia, while strong players outside the region – China, the EU, Japan, South Korea and India – argue that they have legitimate rights in the Arctic. The new Arctic freight routes, the natural resources and climate change in the region all have global implications.

For the Danish government in 2016, the main objective was to seek continuous influence in this dynamic. In this respect, the preservation of the unity of the Danish Realm with Greenland and the Faroe Islands had become vital. Without the island communities in the North Atlantic, Denmark would potentially lose any access to the Arctic and the cultural and social riches which Greenland and the Faroe Islands bring to the Realm. Still more of the central actors in Copenhagen began to realize that the ties to Greenland and the Faroe Islands are not only important for the politics, security and finances of Denmark but also for its historical composition and national identity. Denmark has been, through its Norwegian, Icelandic, Faroese and Greenlandic extensions, a North Atlantic power since the Vikings. Should Denmark lose Greenland, the Faroe Islands or both, it could cause havoc to the identity of many Danes, or at least that was the new understanding. These were matters far beyond the legalistic language of the Kingdom's formal Arctic strategy, but still more prevalent in political discussions.

In June 2016, a comprehensive analysis of Denmark's defence needs in the Arctic was published by the government in Copenhagen. Denmark's Arctic plans were becoming clearer still: A defence in the region that lacked fundamental equipment would no longer suffice. In particular, it is important for Denmark that the United States remains confident that Denmark will handle its responsibilities in Greenland in a trustworthy manner, and the task is mounting. Military analysts not only speculate about Russia's military capacity in the Arctic, but also about China's. In the future, the Chinese nuclear-armed submarines may, like the Russians, position themselves under the ice in the Arctic Ocean close to the United States and thus further increase Greenland's strategic importance.

The Danish government's new plans for Denmark's defence forces were an attempt to navigate between at least three challenges: Firstly, Denmark must appear as a capable guardian over the sovereignty of the Faroe Islands and Greenland. Danish naval vessels and planes must patrol the outermost borders and maintain capacity to react to transgressions. They must possess credible situation awareness and deliver a solid maritime rescue service, airspace overview, up-to-date nautical charts and the capacity to adapt rapidly to new challenges. Secondly, defence build-up must not have an aggressive character that would give Russia the opportunity to blame Denmark, the United States and NATO for unnecessary militarization in the Arctic. Peace must be preserved at all costs. Thirdly, the Defence Command Denmark in Nuuk must shoulder its civilian tasks in Greenland so that the partnership with Greenland is strengthened – including fisheries inspections, environmental monitoring and rescue services. The Defence Command in Nuuk is regarded as a central part and connecting link in the Danish Realm.

The government's analysis contained almost 300 recommendations on how to modernize the work of defence forces in the Arctic and shortly after its publication the relevant parliamentary committee approved all 300 and promised to finance the entire operation. The head of the investigating team behind the analysis had already been made chief of command in Nuuk.

In 2017, the Arctic connection allowed the Danish government, ministers, politicians, business people, military officers and researchers substantial influence in the Arctic. Danish decision makers had access to important circles of power and collaboration across the Arctic, and they often reminded themselves how Greenland is actually part of North America. Since the early nineteenth century, Greenland has been part of what the United States defines as its strategic area of defence and since World War II Greenland has played an essential, practical role in the safety of the United States. Thule Air Base remains important for American defence against long-range missiles – also against the arsenal of North Korea. Meanwhile, Denmark and Greenland enjoy a close relationship with the United States. Denmark has also gained influence in a long list of international forums pertaining to the Arctic, especially as one of only eight member states in the Arctic Council. Here, Danish ministers and officials meet decision makers from the United States, Russia, Canada, Norway and a host of other states in a manner that is difficult to imagine in other contexts. When the Danish foreign minister, Kristian Jensen, visited Alaska in 2015 for an American conference on the Arctic, he met with Secretary of State John Kerry several times and I reported how he was able to personally invite President Obama to visit Greenland. This resulted in John Kerry's, the foreign minister's, aforementioned visit to Greenland in 2016.

In early 2017 Denmark's new foreign minister, Anders Samuelsen, travelled to Arkhangelsk in north eastern Russia to attend a Russian conference on the Arctic. He had a three-hour dinner with Russia's foreign minister Sergei Lavrov, the only other attendees of which were the foreign ministers of Norway and Iceland. I met Anders Samuelsen at his hotel just afterwards and noticed his elation; such deep and intimate diplomatic encounters with the top echelons of the international community cannot be taken for granted when one represents a nation as tiny as Denmark. Denmark's nature as an Arctic nation had once again proven phenomenal as a platform for Danish interests and views.

The Arctic Council has admitted the large Asian economies – China, Japan and South Korea – as permanent observers, which allowed Denmark's Arctic connections to spread in still new directions. Danish scientists are centrally involved in long-term Arctic projects regarding everything from climate to communication; they have access to important research results and they influence the conclusions. Denmark's influence in the international community grows as the Arctic region becomes more important and this trend develops in still new leaps. Shortly after Great Britain opted to leave the EU in June 2016, the President of Iceland, Ólafur Ragnar Grímsson, argued that Great Britain's possible exit from the European Union would lend new meaning to political collaboration in the North Atlantic region, as Britain would soon be looking for new alliances. In these developments, however, Denmark will only remain truly relevant as long as Denmark, Greenland and the Faroe Islands form a united community. Without Greenland, Denmark would lose 98 per cent of its territory and potentially any weight in the Arctic.

Danish diplomats often stress how co-operation between Denmark and Greenland on most days works excellently. Even difficult conflicts of interest are solved peacefully and Greenland's and the Faroe Islands' role in the Kingdom constantly evolve according to the wishes of Nuuk and Tórshavn. The challenge, still unresolved, is how to somehow connect this well-oiled machinery of day-to-day collaboration with the persistent wish of many people in Greenland that in time the Danish Realm should be dissolved, or perhaps replaced by a more voluntary co-operative arrangement between Greenland and Denmark. (A constitutional committee set up in 2017 is to provide a road map for such possible future co-operation between an independent Greenland and Denmark. In Greenland a model known as 'free association' is often mentioned. Free association already ties a number of island states in the Pacific to New Zealand and the United States.)

The complexity of the state of affairs between Denmark and Greenland will often defy easy interpretation of events.

Greenland's reception of the new plans for the Danish defence forces in Greenland has been positive and co-operative. Paradoxically, the popular wish for independence does not translate into any dislike of the Danish defence forces in Greenland. Vittus Qujaukitsoq, at the time responsible for Greenland's foreign policy, stood next to the Danish Minister for Defence as the comprehensive 2016 analysis was published. Qujaukitsoq was 'very positive' and explained how the extra resources for sea rescue capacity were particularly vital to Greenland's economy. He was also excited that the report suggested a new civilian corps, 'Greenland Guards', which would sound the alarm in case of oil spills. Qujaukitsoq thanked Denmark for the way in which Greenland's Self-Rule Government had been closely consulted during the three years of analytical work.

Co-operation between Denmark and Greenland often works well, but this does not mean that Copenhagen and Nuuk have identical interests. In 2017 the Greenlandic urge for independence and the Danish government's wish to play a key role in Arctic geopolitics was still not moulded into a joint, cohesive strategy. The Danish government envisaged how Greenland and Denmark could meet their full common potential by acting dynamically and forward-looking in flawless allegiance. In this vision, Greenland and Denmark were tightly connected by a common history, democratic ideals and Christianity. Nuuk and Copenhagen in this vision strove for the same political goals and maintained common views on fishing and climate, environmental protection, oil and minerals and the rights of indigenous peoples. In this vision of the future the two nations consulted each other as equals and agreed that they would both gain from the partnership.

In Greenland, this representation of the future of the Kingdom was met by many with scepticism, especially by those who did not believe that Greenland's interests could be pursued in earnest as long as Greenland was not independent. As an example, the previous Self-Rule Premier, Aleqa Hammond, was so upset about Denmark's lack of investments in maritime rescue services that she predicted dissolution of the Kingdom. 'The Realm is at a crossroad. If Denmark is unable to live up to its responsibility towards Greenland there are other countries that will', she wrote in an op-ed published in both Denmark and abroad. Later, Vittus Qujaukitsoq, who served as the foreign affairs representative of the Self-Rule Government until 2017, recommended that 'Danish politicians and diplomats ought to gain better insight and fundamental competences concerning the Realm's structure and division of responsibility'. In a Danish foreign policy journal, *Udenrigs*, Vittus Qujaukitsoq argued that Danish politicians regularly misinterpret Denmark's modern relation with Greenland: 'If Denmark and Greenland are to obtain a stronger position in the Arctic it is vital that the co-operation between the two countries is not seen as a competition between two parties that both have a need to assert themselves. If Denmark's ambitions of being taken seriously as an "Arctic power" are to be realized it is a necessity that Denmark recognizes Greenland as the Arctic partner that Greenland is, with its own interests, resources, competences and historical knowledge.'

In late 2016, Premier Kim Kielsen formed a new coalition government. In the very first sentence in its declaration of intent, the coalition stipulated that 'Greenland is irrevocably on the path towards independence'. For the first time in Greenland's history, the cabinet included an independence portfolio. Three weeks later, a large majority in Inatsisartut, the parliament, mandated the new coalition government to establish a committee to draft Greenland's first constitution. Also, the coalition was mandated to push for a renegotiation of the 1951 defence agreement between the Kingdom of Denmark and the United States in order to secure more substantial benefits for Greenland from Thule Air Base.

Vittus Qujaukitsoq, as responsible for Greenland's foreign affairs, was also convinced that Denmark did too little to ensure clean-up at abandoned US military installations, including Camp Century, some 130 kilometres east of Thule Air Base. Here, in 1958, the US armed forces dug tunnels for a sub-ice experimental military camp powered by a portable nuclear reactor. Camp Century was vacated in 1963, but its remains, including radioactive waste materials, were now, according to new scientific discoveries, likely to re-emerge from the ice within only decades as a result of climate change. In early 2017, discussions escalated when Vittus Qujaukitsoq met with the General Secretary of NATO, Jens Stoltenberg. According to press reports, Vittus Qujaukitsoq explained to Stoltenberg how Greenland was now pondering renegotiation of the defence agreement of 1951 with the United States. This was remarkable. Vittus Qujaukitsoq was discussing matters with clear security implications for the entire Danish Kingdom directly with the head of the world's most important military alliance, even if security matters pertaining to the Kingdom of Denmark were still regarded by Copenhagen as a strictly Danish prerogative. A few days later, Vittus Qujaukitsoq gave an unusually blunt interview to a Danish daily. He reiterated that the Greenlandic parliament was behind him and that his quest was inspired by '75 years of frustration and helplessness'. In Nuuk, members of his own party suggested to the premier, Kim Kielsen, that he be fired for his outburst, but his statements were widely interpreted in foreign embassies in Copenhagen. Vittus Qujaukitsoq did not apologize for or detract from his 'verbal grenade', as the interview was designated by one foreign diplomat. Kim Kielsen, who favours a less confrontational tone, issued a reconciliatory statement, but only in April 2017 did he try to discipline his foreign minister. He told Vittus Qujaukitsoq that he was no longer to be Greenland's foreign minister, but that he was welcome to remain minister of trade and industry. Vittus Qujaukitsoq immediately resigned and announced that he would attempt to take over Kim Kielsen's position as head of the governing party and Premier of Greenland. A deep rift had developed in the ruling circles in Nuuk. Kim Kielsen and his allies favoured a more tempered process towards independence; Vittus Qujaukitsoq and his associates wanted a more pro-active, faster road to secession.

A few weeks after Vittus Qujaukitsoq had left office the public learned just how assertive he had been in his job. On behalf of Greenland's Self-Rule Government, in April 2017, he forwarded formal complaints to the United Nations over what he saw as Denmark's failure to firmly establish who was responsible for the clean-up at abandoned US military facilities in Greenland. No less than three of the UN's special rapporteurs on human rights were asked to look into the problem. No matter how this was resolved, Denmark would no longer be able to avoid the discomfort of an international inquiry. Vittus Qujaukitsoq was out of office, and Kim Kielsen's government tried to annul the complaint but it was not easily retracted. As I write these lines one of the UN special rapporteurs is readying to go to Greenland. Once again, the world is witnessing the intricacies of Denmark's and Greenland's new Arctic ways.

FURTHER READING

Breum, M., *The Greenland Dilemma: The Quest for Independence, the Underground Riches and the Troubled Relations with Denmark* [free e-book] (2014), http://www.fak.dk/publikationer/Pages/TheGreenland-Dilemma.aspx

Breum, M. and Gottschau, J., *The History of the Danish Realm* 1–6, [TV documentaries, Danish only] (2016), available on YouTube

Colgan, W., Machguth, H., MacFerrin., M., Colgan, J.D., As, D.A. and MacGregor, J.A., 'The Abandoned Ice Sheet Base at Camp Century, Greenland, in a Warming Climate', *Geophysical Research Letters*, 43 (15) (2016), 8091–6

Danish Ministry of Foreign Affairs, *The Ilulissat Declaration*, 28 May 2008, http://www.oceanlaw.org/downloads/arctic/Ilulissat_Declaration.pdf (last accessed 11 December 2017)

Dragsdahl, J., 'A Few Dilemmas Bypassed in Denmark and Greenland' (August 2005), Peace Research Institute, Frankfurt, http://www.dragsdahl.dk/A20050814.htm (last accessed December 2017)

Gad, U.P., 'Greenland: A Post-Danish Sovereign Nation State in the Making', *Cooperation and Conflict* 49 (1) (2014), 98–118

———, *National Identity Politics and Postcolonial Sovereignty Games - Greenland, Denmark, and the European Union* (København: Museum Tusculanum Press, 2017)

Gee, A., 'The Young Queer Writer Who Became Greenland's Unlikely Literary Star', *New Yorker*, 31 January 2017, https://www.newyorker.com/books/page-turner/the-young-queer-writer-who-became-greenlands-unlikely-literary-star (last accessed 29 November 2017)

Grant, S.D., *Polar Imperative: A History of Arctic Sovereignty in North America* (Vancouver: Douglas & Mcintyre, 2011)

Jacobsen, M., 'The Power of Collective Identity Narration: Greenland's Way to a More Autonomous Foreign Policy', *Arctic Yearbook 2015*

(2015), https://arcticyearbook.com/scholarly-papers-2015/42-local-and-sub-national-governance/192-the-power-of-collective-identity-narration-greenland-s-way-to-a-more-autonomous-foreign-policy (last accessed 4 December 2017)

Jacobsen, M. and Herrmann, V., 'Arctic International Relations in a Widened Security Perspective', *Politik*, 20 (3) (2017), 1–165

Jakobson, L. and Peng, J., 'China's Arctic Aspirations', *Sipri* (34) (2012), 1–26

Keitner, C.I. and Reisman, W.M., 'Free Association: The United States Experience', *Texas International Law Journal* 39 (1) (2003), 1–63

Kristensen, C. and Rahbek-Clemmensen, J., *Greenland and the International Politics of the Changing Arctic* (Abingdon: Routledge, 2017)

Leine, K., *The Prophets of the Eternal Fjord* (New York: W.W. Norton & Company, 2016)

McGhee, R., *The Last Imaginary Place: A Human History of the Arctic World* (Chicago: University of Chicago Press, 2005)

Ministry of Defence, *Danish Defence: Tasks in the Arctic and North Atlantic* (2016), http://www.fmn.dk/eng/allabout/Pages/TasksintheArcticandtheNorthernAtlantic.aspx (last accessed 12 December 2017)

Østergaard, M.U., *The Greenlandic Wish for Independence: An Investigation of the Possibilities within Free Association* (Denmark: University of Aalborg, 2017)

Raghavan, M., DeGiorgio, M., Albrectsen, A., Moltke, I., Skoglund, P., Korneliussen, T.S., Grønnov, B., Appelt, M. and Willerslev, E., 'The Genetic Prehistory of the New World Arctic', *Science* 345 (6200) (2014), 1020–30

Skaale, S. (ed.), *The Right to National Self-Determination: The Faroe Islands and Greenland* (Leiden: Martinus Nijhoff Publishers, 2004)

Steinberg, P.E., Tasch, J. and Gerhardt, H., *Contesting the Arctic: Politics and Imaginaries in the Circumpolar North* (London: I.B.Tauris, 2015)

Wang, N. and Degeorges, D., *Greenland and the New Arctic: Political and Security Implications of a Statebuilding Project* (København: RDDC Publishing House, 2014)

INDEX